ROME'S
GR
DEFEAT

ROME'S GREATEST DEFEAT

MASSACRE IN THE TEUTOBURG FOREST

ADRIAN MURDOCH

The History Press

First published in 2006 by Sutton Publishing
This edition published by The History Press 2008

Reprinted in 2009, 2010, 2012

The History Press,
The Mill, Brimscombe Port,
Stroud, Gloucestershire, GL5 2QG
www.thehistorypress.co.uk

British Library Cataloguing in Publication Data.
A catalogue record for this book is available from the British Library.

ISBN 978 0 7509 4016 0

Typesetting and origination by The History Press Ltd
Printed in Great Britain

For Susy

Contents

List of Illustrations

Maps

Varus' Germany.

Varus' Asia Minor.

Family Trees

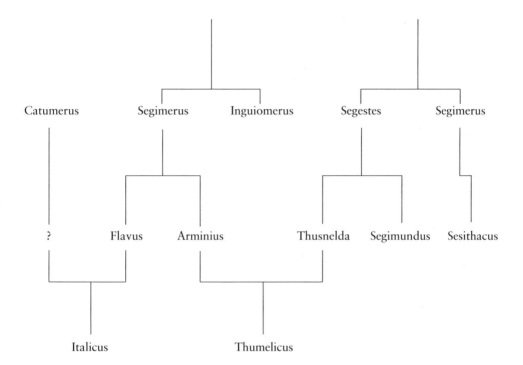

Family tree of Arminius.

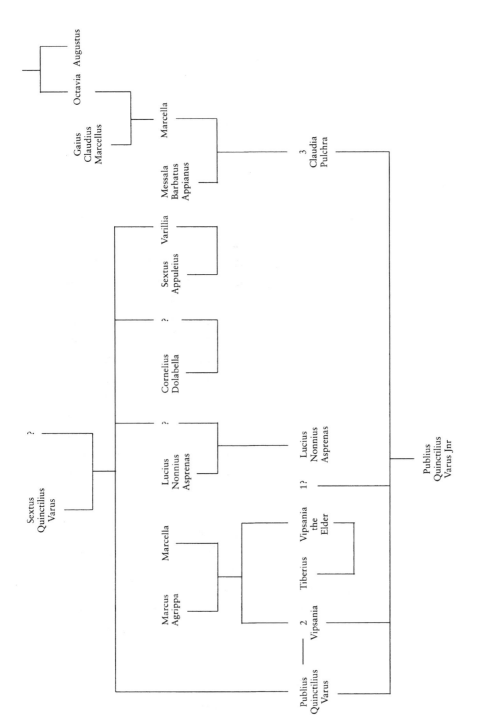

Simplified family tree of Publius Quinctilius Varus.

INTRODUCTION

This Savage Forest

Bones were all he could see. Although the German soil had reclaimed most of the traces, he was standing in the remains of what had been a marching camp. The ditches had slowly silted up and weeds had grown back over the boundaries and the fort's streets. Not even the charred traces of campfires had survived. Six years previously three legions, three cavalry battalions and six auxiliary units had died around here. Some 14,000 men had been wiped out in a matter of days.

It was dangerous, an indulgence almost, to come here. It had been a brutal and gruelling year. He and his legions had been on campaign since the spring. He had first seen off the Chatti, a tribe that lived in what would become the state of Hesse, razing their capital and destroying their farmland. Then he had savaged the area around Münster in a combined cavalry, infantry and marine assault that had paralysed the enemy.

And now, in the early autumn of AD 15, he was here. In his mind's eye he could see how the surviving cavalry and infantry had formed up in the cutting rain under the barbarian onslaught, as their colleagues built some protection. He could hear the trumpets of the heralds blasting out orders and centurions shouting at legionaries as they constructed a marching fort; tough veterans trying to rally shaken groups of soldiers with that same mixture of humour and contempt common to every army, doing anything to keep their minds off what could happen. It was the might of the Roman army working like clockwork, manoeuvres that every soldier present would have practised many, many times before.

He only had four legions with him today. His deputy, Aulus Caecina Severus, was currently patrolling the surrounding area with another four legions as planned. With any luck they should have been reconnoitring for ambushes, checking the passes and making the swamps and waterways safe with bridges and causeways.

He rode on. Ahead the second redoubt – the word 'camp' was too generous – spoke of dying men and of desperate and hurried construction. All that remained was a partially collapsed rampart and a shallow ditch. This could not contain three legions; it was space for hundreds, not thousands of men. This was the place for a last stand. The field was strewn with the remains of men. Some skeletons lay on their own, some in clusters, their bones now whitened and impersonal. Yet even after five German summers it was still obvious that the legionaries lay where they had fallen, some making a last stand, others caught trying to escape.

It was the perfect spot for an ambush, this unforgiving German landscape, along the main west–east road from the mid-Weser to the safety of the Roman camps and nascent towns on the lower Rhine. Near the remains of the camp he could see the 6km-long narrow pass, the *via dolorosa* along which Legions XVII, XVIII and XIX had marched to their deaths. The army had been funnelled along an uneven and difficult path, clogged with drifting sand and only 200m wide in places, with the oak- and beech-lined Kalkriese Mountain to one side, the waterlogged Great Moor on the other.

Some of the survivors of the disaster showed their commander around. They pointed out the stained and scorched altars. It was here that the Germans, under the command of the turncoat Arminius, had burned the tribunes and first-rank centurions alive. They reported, blow by blow, how the three eagles, Rome's military standards, had been captured. They pointed out where senior officers had been killed. This is where Numonius Vala was cut down from his horse while trying to make a break for the river; that is where Ceionius surrendered once he realised that there was no chance for survival; over here is where Lucius Eggius was killed. And then they re-enacted Publius Quinctilius Varus' final moments. This is where the architect of this disaster, the governor of Germany had first been wounded, where he had taken his own life, and finally where his adjutants had buried him.

It was his successor, Germanicus, who now stood deep within German territory. The governor of Upper and Lower Germany, commander of eight legions, adopted son of the Emperor Tiberius and heir to the Roman Empire had come on a pilgrimage, to try and lay to rest the shame of Rome, to exorcise some ghosts and to pay his last respects. The greatest emperor that Rome would never have, had to see it. His soldiers had to see it.

This expedition to the battlefield of the Varian disaster would earn Germanicus an official imperial reprimand. Romans, unlike Christians, did not sanctify death. His very presence at a mass grave, at a German sanctuary, was inappropriate and inauspicious for one of Rome's most senior priests. More seriously, the remains of the makeshift gibbets from which Roman soldiers had been hanged, the pits into which still-living infantry men had been thrown, the skulls nailed to nearby trees were not an appropriate sight for Roman legionaries. It could be too much of a blow for morale and make them slow to fight. The visit was opening up old wounds that were, at any rate, barely healed.

To Germanicus and his men, the battlefield looked like the one-sided slaughter that it had been. He could see no trace of German corpses nor any of their weapons. Like the ancient Spartans, Germans came back with their shields or on them. The Germans who had fallen in battle were long since buried at home. If he had spotted it, an iron spur with a small, spiked wheel that lay on the battlefield was certainly of native design, but had the German auxiliary cavalry soldier who had lost it fought for Romans or had he fought for Arminius?

He could see only Roman arms, too broken for even the Germans to scavenge. A spearhead could not speak, could not tell Germanicus whether it had been thrown in anger or in defence. Some of those shattered and bent pieces had been used by the traitors, former auxiliaries for the Emperor Augustus who had then fought the Romans with their own weaponry. Anything usable had long been salvaged and handed out by the tribal chieftains as gifts and honours. Since the battle, whenever the Germans had met the Romans in warfare, they would use the spoils of Kalkriese against the legionaries. They were even, eventually, to use them against each other.

Germanicus did not care about any of this now. As the legionaries began to collect all the bones they could find, not knowing whether they were burying a friend, a relative or a stranger, he laid the first turf on the funeral mound himself. For his legionaries it was a sign of respect and honour from their commanding officer, seeing him share their sorrow for friends and colleagues they had known and fought alongside. It was a communal expiation of loss and guilt.

Germanicus' tumulus was not to survive the year. At some point in the next few months it would be torn apart by Germans furious that the Romans had defiled what had been preserved by them as a cult site. But not all bones had been collected together. There were simply too many for a single barrow. During excavations in the mid-1990s, archaeologists found collections of bones which had been gathered together and buried in five pits. A muddle of human and animal remains, they were confirmed by scientific analysis to have been lying above the ground for some years. The human remains were all male and of military age (between 20 and 40), and a glance at the human teeth that were found, both singly and in sets, suggested that the individuals had been in good health. Trauma to the skulls from swords and blunt instruments pointed to the reasons for death. One – grave number five – speaks of the pains that some of the soldiers went to over the remains of their fallen comrades. Were they somehow recognisable? Rather than heaped into the pit, the bones look as though they were laid in there with care.[1]

Germanicus' almost voyeuristic gamble paid off. The bones on the battlefield had made his men more angry and more anxious for a battle and for revenge, not slow to fight or afraid of the Germans. But however many triumphal marches through Rome were awarded to commanders who fought in Germany and however many jingoistic coins were issued that proclaimed victory in Germany, the defeat of Varus and his men in the autumn of AD 9 was a blow from which the Romans were never to recover fully.

Contemporaries visibly struggle to find an analogy large enough for the defeat. Even by the standards of a mechanised modern society, the losses give pause for thought, comparable as they are to total US losses during the campaign for the Philippines in the Second World War, and marginally smaller than British losses on the first day of the Battle of the Somme in July 1916. Little surprise, then, that one Roman historian, an old Germany hand, called it 'the heaviest defeat the Romans had suffered on foreign soil since the disaster of Crassus', a reference to the loss of 22,000 soldiers two generations previously at the hands of the Parthians, Rome's great imperial rival to the east. Another compared it to Cannae, the Roman Republic's greatest defeat, when some 55,000 men were wiped out by the Carthaginian general Hannibal in 218 BC after he had crossed the Alps.[2] But those stains were eventually washed off the military record; they only delayed the inevitable for those who dared oppose Rome. Parthia was levelled and Hannibal was defeated. After the Battle of Teutoburg Forest there was never another attempt to impose Roman life east of the Rhine. This truly was Rome's greatest defeat.

'I found a city of brick and I left it one of marble', was Augustus' proud boast of Rome.[3] Glory, expansion and conquest dominate the emperor's rule. By the end of his reign the empire had the use of twenty-five legions, some 140,000 men and as many auxiliaries. In the eastern empire the emperor's legions had pushed south into the Sudan and across into the Persian Gulf, and had consolidated his hold in Armenia. In the southern empire he had taken on the African tribes. And in the west, the Alps, northern Spain and southern Germany all fell to the Romans. It was a legacy that none of Augustus' predecessors could rival and few of his successors were to equal. The nature of Augustus' imperialism still causes debate and divides scholars. Was it relentless expansion versus cautious growth, or imperialist aggression versus defensive evolution? In one sense the question is irrelevant. All that matters is that the Roman Empire was growing.

Roman citizens did not care whether it was pragmatism rather than policy that shaped the boundaries of Augustus' empire. Jupiter had promised Aeneas' descendants an empire without boundaries. Augustus' power would be limited only by the ocean and the skies. In the 1960s, US president John F. Kennedy challenged Americans to ask what they could do for their country and they in turn raced to put a man on the moon. The same sense of optimism and enterprise pervades the writings of most of Augustus' contemporaries. It was a world and many decades away from the catty asides of Martial and languid cynicism of Juvenal. Not only was Augustus 'the son of a god who would bring back the age of gold', but this new generation would 'inherit the earth'. The poet Horace felt he could encourage the emperor to hurry up and mobilise against 'the Britons, farthest of the world'. It was not that the poet particularly wanted to see Britain conquered, but that it was the furthest land he could think of.⁴ The divine impetus that drove on the British Empire in the nineteenth century and the self-belief that has been evident in US foreign policy since the Second World War would have been remarkably familiar to the Romans.

An empire built as much on mythology and self-aggrandisement as on action, however, had neither the language nor the emotional maturity to cope with defeat. As much as anything, Augustus needed foreign expansion as a distraction from the domestic. After generations of civil wars, foreign enemies that could be defeated were necessary. Arminius' victory therefore had to be buried and ignored. The fact that Roman attempts to colonise Germany had been a total shambles were mentioned only indirectly. The only admission of failure is the historian Tacitus' rueful and slightly oblique aside almost a century later that 'in the course of the past 210 years much punishment has been given and taken by us in Germany'.⁵ Within a generation, Varus had become a scapegoat and the few survivors of the encounter in the Teutoburg Forest were quietly moved to other legions or banned from ever setting foot in Italy. And as for Germany, the Rhine became the border, the barrier between civilisation and barbarism, one only unwillingly crossed throughout the rest of the Roman Empire.

There are few defining battles in history that have stopped an empire in its tracks. The Battle of Britain, which halted Hitler's western ambitions during the Second World War, or the Battle of Poitiers in 732, when Charles Martel saved Europe from the threat of Islam, are two that come to mind. It is fair to say that the reputation of the Battle of Teutoburg Forest in modern times has to some extent rested on this. Edward Shepherd Creasy, in his 1852 classic, listed it as one of the *Fifteen Decisive Battles of the World*, putting the Varian disaster on a par with the US victory over General John Burgoyne at Saratoga and the defeat of Napoleon at Waterloo. The brilliant German historian and Nobel prize winner Theodor Mommsen went even further, regarding it as the turning point in Germany's national destiny.

The battle also reinforced another effect, one less tangible, but one that has had a profound psychological and social impact on Europe and is still being felt today. It confirmed the fault-line between north and south. History could now be used to back up long-held prejudices. This divide has been most archly articulated by the British journalist and writer A.A. Gill: 'The slaughter in the Teutoburg Forest divided Europe into the warm south, who forever saw forests as dreadful places to be avoided and cleared, homes to dragons and trolls, antitheses of the civilised city, and the north, who understood them to be healing, protecting, mystical, spiritual places. How you feel about a silent birch forest at twilight says more about your blood and your kin than your passport.'[6]

For northern Europeans, forests are both spiritual spaces and a place of safety. One of the central themes of Norse mythology is that of Yggdrasil, the evergreen ash, beneath whose branches stands the well of wisdom. Similarly, when Nietzsche's Zarathustra comes down from the mountains, the first person he meets is a holy man in the forest. Even in – some – British myths, the forest is a place of honour and refuge. Robin Hood preserves the memory of Richard the Lionheart and battles King John from the sanctuary of Sherwood Forest.

In southern European and Middle Eastern tradition, forests are places of fear and loathing. That they are to be avoided has been ingrained from time immemorial. The world's first hero, the Mesopotamian warrior Gilgamesh, has to go into the Cedar Forest and defeat its guardian to prove that he has a right to rule. The book of Deuteronomy explicitly equates forests with pagan rites. 'Ye shall overthrow their altars, and break their pillars, and burn their groves with fire,' it says.[7] It is telling that one solution to suppress paganism, posited by Martin of Tours, patron saint of France and the first great leader of Western monasticism, was to chop down trees. The archetype and most moving articulation of this position is the opening few lines of *The Divine Comedy*, where Dante wanders in a 'wilderness of sin and bestiality', before his descent into the Underworld:

> How hard a thing it is to say
> What was this forest savage, rough, and stern,
> Which in the very thought renews the fear.
> Speak will I of the other things I saw there.

Not for nothing are forests the backdrop to, and scene of, the resolution of virtually every one of the folk tales that the Grimm brothers collected. Yet the fairy story that immediately springs to mind where the forest remains a source of fear and evil throughout is *Little Red Riding Hood*, written by the Parisian Charles Perrault. That same tradition is alive and well today. The one part of the school grounds that is out of bounds for the pupils at Hogwarts in J.K. Rowling's Harry Potter novels is the appositely named Forbidden Forest. Whenever the narrative takes the young wizard there, it is invariably unsettling or dangerous.[8]

But forests are not just dangerous for the individual, they threaten the very fabric of society. In Euripides' *Bacchae*, surely the most terrifying of all classical plays, when the Thebans reject Dionysus' divinity, the god drives the king out of the city and into the countryside, where his mother and the women of Thebes in a bacchanalian frenzy tear him to pieces; when Birnam Wood comes to Dunsinane, the Scottish king Macbeth is unseated. Forests are so dangerous they can even cost kings their thrones.

For all of these reasons, an account of the Battle of Teutoburg Forest is long overdue, or, more accurately, an account of the disaster in English is long overdue. The bimillenary celebrations of the battle, which will round off recent anniversary festivities for a number of German towns (Bonn, Cologne and Trier, to name just three) are only a few years off. But although Arminius and Varus are, naturally enough, part of Germany's national consciousness, their names often warrant barely a flicker of recognition in the English-speaking world. It is fair to say that Roman Germany as a whole, specifically the country's early history under the first emperors, has been conspicuously ignored outside Germany. Even in the academic field, only a handful of critical book-length studies have appeared in the last thirty years. The sheer volume and variety of discoveries in the last decade alone – archaeological, historical, epigraphic – make this nothing short of a scandal.[9]

The intention of the first five chapters of *Rome's Greatest Defeat* is to reconstruct what happened and to put the events of AD 9 into some kind of context. Space is of course given to Augustan foreign policy and its implications, but the primary aim is to look at the personalities and events that led to the disaster. Too much of what we know is understood in the same way as the Battle of the Alamo or the defeat of the Spanish Armada. Myth has glossed reality and, all too often, Varus and Arminius are rendered as stereotypes. The former becomes an arrogant lawyer, incompetent and out of his depth, the latter a freedom fighter, throwing off the shackles of imperial Rome. Of course neither view is strictly fair. Above all, Varus and Arminius deserve to be looked at on their own terms.

Until fifteen years ago any historian attempting to look at the Battle of Teutoburg Forest would have been reliant on a handful of literary sources. It is worth taking a few moments to look at them, to understand their perspectives and, above all, to grasp the different intentions between history in the classical world and now. As the German historian Dieter Timpe warns, when reading Tacitus (though his observation holds for all classical writers), 'a paraphrase of the text does not give a view of the war as a modern reader would understand it'.[10]

The earliest surviving accounts of the battle are arguably the most valuable. One such was published around twenty years after the event by a retired cavalry officer from Campania called Velleius

Paterculus, and dedicated to a friend from his home town who had just become consul. His work is commonly called *Roman History*, though it was not given that title until the early sixteenth century. The word that he uses for his work is *transcursus*, a sketch, and that is certainly a more accurate description for this romp through world history.

Velleius' name is rarely mentioned in the same breath as great historians like Livy or Tacitus. One translator goes so far as to suggest that Velleius 'does not rank among the great Olympians of classical literature either as stylist or as historian', concluding rather backhandedly that 'there is much in this comparatively neglected author that is worth reading once, at least in translation'.[11] Even if his sympathetic treatment of Tiberius has made many suspicious of his judgements, it is an unfair précis and it is Velleius' partiality that makes him such a joy to read. Rarely do historians wear their bias so clearly on their sleeves.

Velleius' significance lies not only in that he almost certainly knew Varus, but that he had unparalleled experience of Germany. When he writes that the Germans are so fierce and so treacherous that 'it is scarcely credible to one who has had no experience with them', it is clearly a comment that is written from the heart. His father had been stationed there, and both he and his brother had risen to become senior staff members under Tiberius during the German campaigns. Velleius was in his late twenties when Teutoburg occurred and, at the behest of Augustus himself, left a nascent political career in Rome to take part in retaliatory campaigns. His views of the Germans, therefore, are not tinged by any kind of idealism. 'Humans only in shape and speech' he calls them. From his soldier's perspective, his view that the disaster was caused by bad leadership and Varus' naivety – 'the commander's lack of judgement', as he puts it – carries weight.[12]

Our second literary source is Publius (or Gaius – the matter is still debated) Cornelius Tacitus, arguably Rome's greatest historian. Born almost half a century after the events discussed here, in the late 50s AD, Tacitus combined a stellar career in politics and oratory with writing. Although he was not of senatorial birth, his father had both the money and connections to set his son up on an upwardly mobile career path.

His father's faith paid off. By the time he was 20, Tacitus had married the daughter of Gnaeus Julius Agricola, consul, governor of Britain and the first well-known invader of Scotland. Within a few years more, Tacitus was able to tick off the stages that indicated a serious political career: treasury official, member of the priesthood, a stint in the provinces. By AD 97 he had reached the pinnacle when he held the consulship in the latter part of the year.

It was around now that Tacitus embarked on a second career as a writer, the one on which his reputation would be based. After the death of his father-in-law, he published his first book, *Agricola*, a curious mixture of biography and political spin. This was followed soon after by *Germania*, a monograph on the customs and character of the people, again wrapped in political caul, inspired possibly by his own time as commander of a legion in Germany. These two books (as well as a third monograph on oratory and poetry) proved both popular and influential. Pliny the Younger wrote him a fan letter: 'I was still a young man when you were already winning fame and fortune and I aspired to follow in your footsteps.'[13] Tacitus' final two greatest works, *Histories* and *Annals*, straddled his last political posting, as proconsul of Asia. Of the former, a twenty-seven-year history of Rome from AD 69, sadly only a third survives, while around half of his *Annals* of the reigns of Augustus to Nero have come down to us.

Tacitus was an incomparable prose stylist. In literary terms, few historians have managed so perfectly to keep the human element and the larger geopolitical themes in sharp focus at the same time. But he also had a clear political agenda and this must be borne in mind when looking at his allusions to the events of AD 9. He saw the role of the historian as that of a doctor, trying to find a prognosis for Rome's ills. He found it in the nature and effects of power. Although he alludes to it frequently and covers the subsequent retaliatory campaigns, Tacitus does not write about Varus' fated campaign directly. Nonetheless, like any Roman, especially one pondering his own generation's failure to conquer Germany, he was profoundly influenced by where the previous generations had gone wrong.

It is important also to appreciate the extent to which Tacitus' writings have affected the way that the battle has been perceived; indeed he gave the battle the name by which it is known today. As one historian commented, Tacitus 'let a genie out of a bottle that could never again be controlled'.[14] With the rediscovery of the manuscript in the fifteenth century, and the publication of the *Annals* in the early sixteenth century, the German people began to appreciate that they had a past; that their predecessors were brave and warlike and that they were nothing like the Romans. It was not just that modern Germans had a history of their own, their hero had a name: Arminius.

The third author is Cassius Dio, born in the early 160s in the prosperous provincial city of Nicaea (now Iznik in north-western Turkey) and writing in the first quarter of the third century. His *Roman History* is an account of the empire from Aeneas' landing in Italy to the accession of Septimius Severus in AD 193, of which a third survives. It is sometimes forgotten that, like Tacitus, Dio was an exceptional career politician as much as a historian. He was consul twice, and municipal governor of Pergamon and Smyrna on Turkey's western coast. Like Varus, he served as governor of Africa; and he also oversaw the provinces of Dalmatia and Pannonia Superior. His achievements are the more remarkable, given the fact that it was rare to find a Greek in that position.

The raciest and one of the longest accounts of the battle – it takes up a significant part of Book 56 – Dio is generally more sympathetic towards Varus than either Velleius or Tacitus. Dio emphasises the frontier nature of Germany and, where he does criticise Varus, it is for his failure to recognise in what a fragile and unstable environment he found himself. Varus, he suggests, was trying to administer as if Germany were already a province. As if that were not enough, he was certainly overconfident in his security.

But what emerges most strongly of all in his history is Dio's dislike of barbarians. He writes scathingly of their 'ancestral habits' and sneers that they 'did not understand siege craft'. This is less inherent racism than cultural snobbery. In the ancient world, no one could hold a candle to the Graecophones for sheer social distain. Elsewhere in his *Roman History* he tells the story of an actor who 'bombed' in Rome, but was a theatrical triumph in Lyons. If that's the level of sophistication you could expect from the provinces, then it is no wonder that they would stoop to trickery.[15]

Finally there is the brief *Epitome of Roman History* by Lucius Annaeus Florus, a stylish outline of Roman history, which was written at some point in the middle of the second century. We know little about the author; indeed even his name is suspect. He was born, so we are told, in Africa but came to Rome as a young boy. Disliking the cliques that dominated Rome's literati, he travelled for a time before settling in Spain. At some later point, probably during the reign of the Emperor Hadrian, he returned to Rome.

Although the *Epitome* was hugely popular throughout Europe as a school text in the seventeenth century, the reputation of Florus has suffered in recent times because of his notorious errors, inconsistencies and exaggeration. Nevertheless, he should not be dismissed out of hand. His account does furnish some details which have the ring of truth about them. He passes some of the strategic blame for the debacle on to Augustus – 'Germany's loss was a disgrace which far outweighed the glory of its acquisition'[16] – but like his historian colleagues, he gives the non-military nature of Varus' rule as reason that he so easily had the wool pulled over his eyes by Arminius.

Even though historians bemoan the fact that the classic Roman history of the region during this period, Pliny the Elder's *German Wars*, has been lost, under normal circumstances only the most churlish would complain about the richness of this vein of history. There are many events throughout the classical age that rely on far fewer sources.

Germanicus and his men had been the last people to see the battlefield of Teutoburg Forest in person. This did not stop both amateurs and professionals looking for it. From the country's first real flickerings of national consciousness in the early nineteenth century, fanned by what was the first recorded event in German history, debate about where the Battle of Teutoburg Forest had taken place became a national pastime. Some 700 different locations were proposed and debated in print.

Then in 1989 and armed only with a metal detector, Tony Clunn, at the time an officer with the Armoured Field Ambulance in Germany, found the site at Kalkriese, north of the modern town of Osnabrück. This discovery, an account of which makes up the final chapter of *Rome's Greatest Defeat*, is on a par with Heinrich Schliemann's excavation of Troy. Now archaeologists could corroborate – or not – the classical accounts of the battle from a part of the battlefield itself. It is difficult to stress quite how much of a significant find this was for the history of the west. As the leading German ancient historian Reinhard Wolters writes, 'the possibility of an interdisciplinary overview like this is a rare piece of luck'.[17]

It is important here to emphasise that Kalkriese is not the battle-field itself. What rapidly became apparent as the archaeologists started their surveys is that, strictly speaking, the Battle of Teuto-burg Forest is a complete misnomer: the conflict between Arminius and Varus took place over several days within a large area, esti-mated at some 50sq km. If you look at the remains plotted on a map, as one modern historian has written with painful poignancy, they bring to mind more modern conflict: 'A German colleague told me that it reminded him of the scatter of arms and personal possessions along the line of flight which he had seen as a child when the German army was in full retreat after the Allies crossed the Rhine in 1945.'[18] Instead what we have here is one of the – possibly decisive – climaxes of a battle.

More disconcerting still, not only was there no battlefield, there was comparatively little forest. The image that many have had in their minds, of a conflict similar to the opening moments of the Ridley Scott film *Gladiator* from 2000, of Romans and Germans fighting in heavy woodland, was proved false. Much of the surrounding area was farmland. Tacitus' phrase, *Teutoburgiensi saltu*,[19] which gave its name to the battle and to the range of mountains in Lower Saxony and North Rhein-Westfalia, where the battle was thought to have taken place, appears to have been misinterpreted. While it may indeed be rendered as 'Teutoburg Forest', it may also be translated as

'Teutoburg Pass'. This seemed to be a much more plausible version as archaeologists examined the terrain.

If that seems slightly deflating, it must be emphasised that it is rare to have sight of a battle at all. Unlike other classical conflicts that can be precisely dated and that have been excavated – for example the site of Alesia, where Julius Caesar laid siege to the Gallic chieftain Vercingetorix in 52 BC, or Masada, where the Jews made their last stand in AD 73/4 – here there is no connection with a camp or a settlement. The Roman army was on the march. It is an incredible archaeological discovery that adds a valuable dimension to our understanding both of the battle itself and Roman warfare in general.

On its own, this would be a rich enough treasure to prompt consideration of a re-evaluation of the period. But numerous other finds make a new account essential. Most noteworthy of all has been the discovery of an early Roman settlement, east of Koblenz, deep in the heart of Germany. Excavations which have continued at Waldgirmes in the Lahn valley since 1993, together with those at Gaukönigshofen and Marktbreit in Bavaria since the 1980s, have shed an entirely new light on our understanding of what it was that the Romans were attempting in the years before Varus' governorship.

This newly acquired wealth of information aside, a caveat is still in order. When looking at the Roman protagonists of the period, few would argue that there is enough of a depth of knowledge about even members of the imperial royal family for a plausible biography in the modern, full-psychological sense of the word. That is not even the case with some of the other characters in this book. At best the historian is faced with a handful of comments scattered throughout the classical canon, together, if he is very fortunate, with a couple of inscriptions. At worst, he must extrapolate a life from the sparse lines on a gravestone.

If that appears a perilous task for the Romans, it is much more so for the Germans. Inevitably, given their non-literate culture, Arminius and his Cheruscan comrades start off as much more shadowy characters than their Roman counterparts. Conclusions may be drawn only from Roman sources (hostile or fictional in pretty much equal measure) and from archaeology. It is easy to slip into the trap of seeing the Germans as noble savages, roaming around their Elysium.

An additional and country-specific twist is the almost total lack of modern research that has been carried out on the various barbarian tribes. Despite the vast amount of work that has been done on Roman Germany in the last decades, German academics have, perhaps understandably, been unwilling to engage in discussions that touch on ethnicity since the end of the Second World War. The crisis of confidence in postwar archaeology in Germany resulted in the precedence of methodology over analysis, and of description over interpretation. The point is that hard facts are often few and far between. Almost more than for any other period, two historians are rarely going to agree on an interpretation of early Roman Germany. The path I have nonetheless tried to follow is one of consensus. Where I have strayed, my arguments for having done so can be followed in the endnotes.

While a deliberately tight focus on the events themselves is paramount, it is also important for the historian to see beyond this, to see the wood beyond the trees. *Rome's Greatest Defeat* has the secondary aim of highlighting the ways in which the battle has been transmitted through history.

The last fifty years alone are littered with examples of forces finding ways to neutralise their technologically superior aggressors. A dinner party voguishness has crept over the whole branch of military science devoted to what has been dubbed 'asymmetric warfare'. This technique of nullifying an opponent's technological and numerical superiority to make him fight stupidly is very much a feature of modern warfare, with practitioners from the Viet Cong in Vietnam to rebels in Somalia; from groups like al-Qa'eda to insurgents in Iraq. The strategic and tactical decisions taken by Arminius have forceful parallels with the contemporary military landscape. It is telling that the US military has considered it worth analysing the Varian disaster, for the light it can shed on modern conflicts.[20]

While that is a significant form of transmission, I shall be focusing, later in the book, on the political lessons that have been drawn from the battle, rather than the military ones. All too often since the nineteenth century, Arminius' uprising has been used as an excuse for war rather than a warning from history; a *casus belli* rather than an *exemplum belli* if you will. The ideologies that have co-opted Arminius himself range from the merely bellicose to the utterly abhorrent.

Despite the (comparative) modernity of the concept of nationalism, paradoxically it is history that suffers its indignities. In the past our nation was glorious, pure and unified, so the argument of nationalists goes. Now we are living in a present that has been degraded by some agency or trauma, be it the invasion of Napoleon or the perceived unfairness of the Treaty of Versailles. Only through collective action can we reverse this. While the two examples just mentioned, together with Arminius, had a specific resonance for Germany, the argument is as valid for France's promotion of Charlemagne or Giuseppe Mazzini's harking back to the glory of Rome during the Italian independence movement.

It would be wrong, though, to dismiss this as a nineteenth- or even twentieth-century phenomenon. It remains wholly apparent today. Some modern examples are obvious, such as the Serbian citing of the battle fought on the Field of the Blackbirds in 1389 as justification for taking Kosovo in the 1990s, or the relentless bickering between Macedonia and Greece over who owns Alexander the Great. But this kind of manipulation can also be more subtle. 'Everything (well, almost everything) you know about American history is wrong,' states the back cover of *The Politically Incorrect Guide to American History*, 'because most textbooks and popular history books are written by left-wing academic historians who treat their biases as fact.' In Thomas Wood's agitprop, which spent a good part of early 2005 in the *New York Times* bestseller list, we see history being politicised, a reflection of the popular political climate in a country.

As one of the earliest battles in history to have been misused in this way (especially given the extreme depths to which this practice sank under the Nazi regime in Germany from 1933 to 1945), this transmission of the Battle of Teutoburg Forest is examined in chapter six.

A few concluding notes are in order. The potential pitfalls that face those who try to find a uniform contemporary style for the classical names of cities of the ancient world is well known. It is impossible to do so when, for example, Köln, Ara Ubiorum and Colonia Agrippinensis all refer to the city of Cologne at one time or another in its history. Although, generally speaking, modern names are used here, familiarity and common usage have prevailed over consistency.

As *Rome's Greatest Defeat* has been written with a non-specialist audience in mind, all Latin and Greek texts have been translated mostly by the author and technical terms have been explained, except where context or linguistic similarities make that unnecessary. (For that matter, so too have comments in German.) For those who wish to follow up the translations in the original, all of the references to ancient authors are available in the Loeb Classical Library, and correspond with the chapter and section numbering in that series. In the small number of cases where I have been guided by another translation, this is mentioned in the footnotes.

I hope that purists will forgive the fact that I have followed the English convention with names. Thus Publius Quinctilius Varus is referred to as Varus throughout, Marcus Tullius Cicero is Cicero, and in the index they are to be found under 'V' and 'C' respectively rather than the more strictly accurate, yet more confusing, 'Q' and 'T'. In much the same manner, I have simplified the names of the imperial royal family where it would cause confusion not to do so. Just as the Emperor Augustus was called Octavian until he took the throne, so too in some older translations, and even some secondary literature, the Emperor Tiberius is referred to as Nero. Here he is referred to as Tiberius throughout.

A brief explanation is also needed about the terms 'Celts', 'Gauls' and 'Germans'. These were terms foisted fairly arbitrarily by the Romans upon people who lived in what modern geography calls Germany, Switzerland, the Netherlands, Belgium and France. They themselves had no national ethnicity as we would understand it today and their loyalty and cultural identity was predominantly tribal. The geographical area west of the Rhine that corresponds to the Roman province, I have referred to as Gaul, and the peoples, interchangeably, as Celts and Gauls. The Roman tradition has been passed down to modern history. For the sake of simplicity, the people east of the Rhine have been dubbed 'Germans' or are referred to by their tribal names. As for the etymology of '*Germani*', that remains shrouded in controversy and it seems unlikely that there will ever be any consensus on the name.

The final challenge to mention has been that of the bibliography. As mentioned above, much of the critical discussion and certainly the majority of the archaeological literature on the Battle of Teutoburg Forest are in German. For example, there is not a single piece of secondary literature solely devoted to Arminius or his tribe, the Cherusci, in English. Nonetheless it would be presumptuous in the extreme to take for granted that this would cause readers no difficulty. In the Select Bibliography at the end of the book, I have therefore purposely placed a greater emphasis on articles and books written in English. Where I have cited articles and books in German, it is in the hope that some will find them useful and because they are so critical to the discussion that to leave them out would be a disservice bordering on neglect.

The most enjoyable part of a project like this is to thank those who have been kind enough to help. First of all I would like to thank the Authors' Foundation of the Society of Authors for its kind and generous grant that enabled several trips to Roman sites in Germany. Special thanks to Anthony Barrett, David Kennedy, Lawrence Keppie, Jan Hirschmann, Jona Lendering and Mike Middleton, who have all been extremely generous with their advice. I have also benefited greatly from the help of Ilona Gymer, David Derrick and Vernon Baxter. Christopher Feeney and his colleagues at Sutton Publishing have been unfailingly helpful, as have the staff of Glasgow University Library. The manuscript was much improved in Alison Miles' hands. Finally, I must thank my father, Brian Murdoch, without whose constant counsel I could never have finished *Rome's Greatest Defeat*. All mistakes, of course, remain my own.

As ever, I would like to thank my wife Susy for her patience and support, and to her this book is dedicated, with love.

ONE

The Tangled Paths of War

Towards the end of the summer of 17 BC, three German tribes revolted. An alliance of Sugambri, Usipetes, and Tencteri, all of whose territory bordered the Rhine, arrested some Roman nationals as illegal immigrants and crucified them. This ragtag gang of tribes then rampaged across the river and started to raid into Gaul itself.

Under normal circumstances the incident would have been barely worthy of note. While not irrelevant, events like this were not uncommon at the very edges of civilisation. But what turned a frontier incursion into a diplomatic incident is that sometime in late summer, the marauders then ambushed a Roman cavalry unit. Giving chase, they surprised the legate Marcus Lollius, commander of the armies in Gaul, who was out on patrol. At that time in his early 40s, Lollius was the senior officer in charge of Gaul.

Lollius is one of the more controversial bit-players in the early empire and few have ever had good words to say about him. The Emperor Tiberius disliked him so much that he was still ranting about him almost forty years later. To a contemporary who knew him, Lollius was greedy, dishonest, vicious and a traitor, while a modern historian refers to him as 'egregiously incompetent and almost certainly corrupt'.[1] They are difficult conclusions with which to disagree.

Although Lollius was obviously talented enough to be considered for high office – he had been consul four years previously, in 21 BC – and had served the empire well, he was widely disliked. There was the stench of new money about him and the sense of a man on the make. He exemplified everything the old guard hated about the nouveaux riches: he was subservient with superiors and arrogant to those whom he perceived to be beneath him. His daughter, briefly married to the Emperor Caligula, inherited her father's vulgar sense of style; her conceits proved to be as large as her gems. The writer Pliny describes seeing her at a wedding 'covered with emeralds and pearls, which shone in alternate layers upon her head, in her hair, in her wreaths, in her ears, round her neck, in her bracelets and on her fingers', prepared, he continues wincingly, 'to show the receipts' to anyone who wanted to take a look.[2]

The most embarrassing aspect of the ambush was that the German bandits had captured the standard of Legion V. 'The Larks', as it was known, was a Gaulish brigade, indeed Rome's first legion to be recruited in the provinces and it had been founded less than forty years previously by Julius Caesar. The loss of the eagle was a humiliation, but as soon as Lollius started to mobilise in earnest, the Germans backed off. The tribes withdrew into their own territory, made peace overtures and gave hostages as good faith.[3]

It was too late for Germany though. This was the excuse that the Romans needed. No matter that Augustus had been mobilising for at least the last twelve months or that this was little more than a border skirmish. Few in Rome would question its actual affront to imperial dignity. What was soon dubbed the '*clades Lolliana*', 'Lolliusgate' in modern newspaper demotic, could prop up that great Roman lie, the imperial self-delusion that its foreign policy was always defensive. Augustus 'never invaded any country nor felt tempted to increase the empire's boundaries or enhance his military glory', was the Roman historian Suetonius' barefaced claim.[4]

In the same way that popular opinion saw the Jameson Raid in 1895 as the precursor to the Boer War, so too the Lollian disaster achieved a prominence out of all proportion to its actual importance. In the imperialist tub-thumping of the contemporary poet Crinagoras:

> The Roman warrior, by the Rhine's wide strands
> prostrated, from his wounds half-slain,
> saw his beloved Eagle in barbarian hands

and rose up, as if brought to life again,
and slew the man who'd held it in those lands,
and died, but earned himself undying fame.

Several generations later, by the time of the Roman historians Suetonius and Tacitus, Chinese whispers had made this a disaster as 'severe and ignominious' as that of Varus.[5]

Although it is with the Lollius incident that Rome set off on the path that would lead to the Battle of Teutoburg Forest, it is worth stepping back for a moment to look at Roman–German relations before then. Rome had been aware of the Celtic nations for centuries, certainly since the meanderings of the Greek traveller Pytheas in the fourth century BC, but it is really with Julius Caesar's campaigns against Gaul in the early 50s BC that the Germans enter recorded history. For him, in stark contrast to the effete Gauls, the tribes that lived east of the Rhine were a brave and martial race. 'Gradually accustomed to inferiority and defeated in many battles, the Gauls do not even pretend to compete with the Germans in bravery,' he writes.[6] He also believed that the Germans lived a more simple life than the Gauls and this is corroborated to some extent by the archaeological evidence of the settlements on the lower Rhine, which were comparatively small-scale.

In 58 BC Caesar was petitioned for help by a tribe called the Aedui, in what is now roughly Burgundy. They were voicing a genuine concern that within a few years they would be driven off their land and that 'all the Germans would cross the Rhine'. Three years later – the fateful year for British history when Roman soldiers also first landed on Deal Beach in Kent – Caesar crossed the Rhine. The exact spot is much debated. Traditionally it was held to be around Bonn; nowadays it is thought much more likely that Caesar crossed the river somewhere near Koblenz or Andernach. It had taken him ten days to build a bridge, and the two and a half weeks he spent in Germany were little more than reconnaissance. The same might be said about his second visit in 53 BC, but symbolically they resonated out of all proportion to their strategic importance. As one modern historian has it, his objectives were not dissimilar from

US president John F. Kennedy's in placing a man on the moon: 'Both achievements beamed a warning of technical supremacy eastwards and a signal of pride and reassurance westwards.'[7]

Strangely, after his murder on the steps of the senate house six years later, on 15 March 44 BC, Caesar became an object of reverence in Germany. His sword stood in the Shrine of Mars in Cologne, near where the town hall stands today.[8] Respect for his personal prowess, however, did not mean that the Germans were prepared to bow down to Roman might. After the defeat of Vercingetorix at Alesia, Gaul might have been bruised and punch-drunk, but the Germans were still fighting fit and not even the Roman propaganda machine claimed that Caesar's forays across the Rhine had been anything more than punitive raids. To be fair to him, he had never intended them otherwise. Caesar's attention rarely wandered from the object in hand, which for him was the conquest of Gaul.

But with the accession of Augustus, Julius Caesar's adopted son and Rome's first emperor, Germany began to emerge as a territory in its own right, worthy of its own policy and not just an adjunct to Gaul. Augustus' specific intentions towards the Rhine frontier remain a matter of intense scholarly debate. It would clearly be wrong to suggest that Augustus and his cabinet had conceived a northern boundary of the empire that ran across the Danube and up the Elbe from the mid-teens BC. That credits the emperor with divine foresight. But few would argue with the idea that the general strategy was hawkish expansion.

Broadly speaking, there are three distinct phases in the Roman relationship with Germany up to the time of the Varian disaster. The first period was characterised primarily by intimidation, the result of policies inherited from Julius Caesar. Roman intervention was generally limited to occasions when Germanic tribes threatened security considerations in Gaul. In the decade after, from 17 BC to the end of Tiberius' campaigns in 7 BC, attitudes hardened. Thus the second chapter became one of conquest. Roman armies, often large in number, trudged along rivers, through forests and against violent native opposition. From then on, for the twelve years before

Arminius' revolt, the policy of civilisation – misplaced as it turned out – was adopted.

If there is a constant in all of this, it is in the articulation of the inner conviction that Germany was Rome's for the taking. From as early as 29 BC, the great elegiac poet Propertius celebrated the 'slavery of the marsh-living Sugumbri' and the mood became gung-ho, if not complacent. Horace was able to ask, 'While Caesar lives unharmed, who would fear the Parthian, who the icy Scythian, who the hordes that rough Germany breed?'[9] There was never a question whether the Germans would be subjugated; it was merely a matter of when. And there was certainly no question that the Romans were the chosen people to do so.

Augustus confirmed his position as leader of the west at Brindisi in the spring of 40 BC. The consolidation and, crucially, the security of the western empire now became a priority. As under Julius Caesar, Gaul was the primary object of military attention and in 38 BC, Marcus Agrippa, the emperor's consigliere and the future victor of the Battle of Actium, was sent west as governor of Gaul. As well as coping with Gaulish uprising, Agrippa became 'the second Roman to cross the Rhine for war'.[10]

It is apparent that Roman policy during this period was to secure the Rhine as the border, to create a marked and physical zone of differentiation between 'us' and 'them'. Yet one of the more curious aspects of Augustan politics is the enthusiasm with which entire tribes were resettled in more diplomatically appropriate areas. The Ubii had long been supporters of Rome and in the late 30s BC Agrippa relocated them – a tribe from around the River Lahn, east of the Rhine – across the river in the sparsely populated low-lying area of the Cologne basin. This was not a punitive measure, it was at the request of the Ubii themselves. They had suffered numerous attacks from a neighbouring and much larger tribe called the Suebi for many years.

Their relocation was not a gesture born solely out of magnanimity on Agrippa's part. As allies, the Ubii could now act as a buffer zone – traces of small Ubian settlements have been found on the west bank of the Rhine from Bonn northwards – and shield Gaul from marauding Germanic tribes. They proved to be much more than that. Even in the times of Julius Caesar the tribe had been known for its commercial prowess. He called them 'more refined than the rest of the Germans' and 'comfortable with Gaulish ways of doing business'. By the turn of the first century AD this emigration had become more formalised with the construction of the urban and economic hub that was to become Cologne.[11]

The resettlement should not give the impression that the Romans were moving into the second, more developed, military phase just yet. Germany was still the wild and the untamed. In the four years between 31 BC and 28 BC, there were three significant Germanic uprisings that required action, on top of the many Gallic uprisings throughout the decade that were bolstered by German assistance.

By April 27 BC Gaul was deemed sufficiently stable for the Romans to risk taking a census. This was always the first step before the real nuts and bolts of Roman life were attached: taxes and laws. But it is likely that the move was more a gesture of optimism than a reflection of the political realities in the province. In an experience that was mirrored, much more fatally, a generation later when Varus was governor, the frontier remained fragile and unsecured. Two years later, tensions were still high enough for a Roman commander to have to cross the Rhine seeking revenge for the murder of a number of Roman traders.

It should not seem curious that the business community was so swift to rush into such an unstable region. Despite the physical dangers, Roman traders were frequently to be seen in the frontier regions throughout the empire. That's where the greatest profits were. For the Romans, the military and the economic generally evolved together; a model for development that is alive and well today. As the *New York Times* columnist Thomas Friedman acerbically notes in *The Lexus and the Olive Tree*, his book on globalisation, 'McDonalds cannot exist without McDonnell Douglas, the designer of the US Air Force F-15.' When the Rhine became formalised as a frontier, the ad hoc back and forth between tribes became restricted and Roman businessmen moved in to tap these virgin markets.

The commercial influence of Rome should not be underestimated, nor should it be thought of as a case of Roman merchants pushing their goods on to an unsuspecting and naive market. Traders were reacting to a demand for their wares. A useful analogy is the way that companies like Levi-Strauss and Coca-Cola, whose products were deemed to confer social status, were pulled into eastern Europe as the communist economies fell in the 1990s. Linguistic evidence can give some idea of how important this was. The Old High German word for 'trader' ('*choufo*' or '*koufa*'), indeed the modern German verb '*kaufen*' meaning 'to buy', derive from the Latin for 'wine merchant' ('*caupo*'). Both wine and wine-drinking sets were hugely popular and have been found as far afield as northern Poland and Denmark. It was not just a case of high-value items being traded though. More than 1,600 Roman bronze vessels dating to the first or second centuries AD have been recorded in northern Europe from burials and other sites. It goes without saying that business must have been profitable for the merchants. The gravestone of Quintus Atilius Primus, which dates to the first century, tells us that he began his career as a translator and, in all likelihood, commercial attaché on the Danube frontier. After he had completed his military service with the rank of centurion, he capitalised on his linguistic skills and became a merchant.[12]

It would be a misapprehension to think of this trade as confined to the river regions. Roman traders did not just sell to intermediaries who then acted as distributors for them. There is evidence of both long-distance and direct trade that went far beyond the immediate Rhine frontier. Pliny the Elder records a story of Julianus, the manager of the gladiatorial exhibitions for the Emperor Nero, who travelled north to trading markets around the Baltic Sea and acquired a vast amount of amber, including one lump that weighed 5.9kg.[13] It is inconceivable that Julianus' trip was unique. The discovery of large numbers of Roman coins close to the Sambian Peninsula in the oblast of Kaliningrad suggests that it was a trading centre. It requires little interpretation to guess that up until now the amber trade had been a German monopoly and that Nero's agent was reconnoitring the area to see if he could cut out the middle men.

Despite the fact that virtually every commander who had crossed the Rhine had been granted a military triumph in Rome, when Agrippa returned for his second stint as governor of Gaul in 19 BC, he found the region unchanged, in virtually the same state as it had been twenty years previously. The Rhine remained porous and both people and arms flowed back and forth as they always had.

The fundamental weakness of Roman policy at the time was that until the Lollian disaster, Rome's position towards Germany was reactive. Roman commanders mounted punitive sorties across the Rhine as and when they were needed. With Gaul the number one priority, the Germanic tribes understood that there was never any permanent intention behind these police actions. As there was no chance that the Romans might remain on their side of the Rhine, they could carry on their raids with impunity.

The end of the war in the mountainous and least accessible parts of north-western Spain allowed Augustus to turn his attention more fully to Germany and to implement a much more active policy. No doubt this was given a fillip as the emperor himself was on hand in the west and in Gaul by 16 BC. There was now a swift and deliberate mobilisation of the Rhine frontier. The Lollian affair had proved that it was no longer enough to contain the Germanic tribes across the Rhine; a more dramatic gesture was required. In anticipation of this, several legions had been transferred from Spain in around 19 BC. Legion V 'The Larks' and Legion I Germanica were moved to the Rhine to provide additional manpower to the three legions already in place, presumably Legions XVII, XVIII and XIX.

When Augustus appeared in person, Roman military construction was already under way. By the end of his reign, six major military camps had been established along the lower and middle Rhine; at Vechten (Fectio), Xanten (Vetera), Mainz (Mogontiacum), Neuss (Novaesium), Nijmegen (Noviomagus) and Cologne (Oppidum Ubiorum). It is impossible to date their foundations with any precision, but work is likely to have begun in 18/17 BC, with pressure increasing to finish after the Lollius event. The first three were the earliest, the lynchpins of Rome's ground assault into Germany proper, bolstered by smaller support camps at Bonn and Boeselagerhof. They leave no doubt that invasion was the Roman intention from the outset. All three stand at the heads of the main invasion routes into the heart of Germany, while Vechten also doubled as a naval base, being perfectly positioned to launch amphibious operations along the North Sea coast.

These Roman forts were the physical expression of Rome's dominance. Deliberately intimidating, they provided both accommodation and defence for the soldiers within. Camps all broadly conformed to the same design, regardless of whether they were temporary or permanent, or built in Syria or Scotland: playing-card shaped, rectangular with rounded ends and gates on each side. This remained the structural design from the first to the fourth centuries.

Few descriptions of forts have survived. The Roman writer Arrian, friend of the Emperor Hadrian and best known for his biography of Alexander the Great, describes his first impression of a smaller frontier fort that was beginning to put down more permanent roots: 'The fort itself . . . occupies a position which appeared to me at once very strong by nature and admirably calculated to secure the safety of those approaching the town by sea. Two ditches run round the rampart, both of them broad. The rampart used to be made of earth and the towers planted on it were of wood. Now both rampart and towers are made of brick. The former rests on a substantial foundation and has artillery mounted upon it. In a word, the preparations for defence are so complete that there is little likelihood of any of the natives coming to close quarters or of the garrison ever being called to stand a siege.'[14]

This is a description of Phasis, the Roman Empire's most eastern city on the Black Sea, now under Lake Paliostomi, on the central coast of the Republic of Georgia, and dates from the mid-second century. To all intents and purposes, however, it mirrors what we see in Germany. The differences that there would have been – ramparts of wood rather than of brick – have much to do with the ease of brick manufacture in a warm climate rather than damp, forested Germany. The consternation and fear that a fort's construction caused among the barbarians can only be imagined.

It is apparent from any aerial photograph or plan that camps followed a uniform pattern internally too. The commander's quarters, barracks, stables, stores and so on were all erected around two main roads that ended at the camp's headquarters, a building that could be solidly permanent, like the wonderfully preserved one at Lambaesis in North Africa, or simply a large tent when the army was on campaign. 'Conveniently, the camp is divided into streets and the commanders' tents are placed in the middle. If we think of the camp like a city that has sprung up overnight, much like a temple, the general's own tent is right in the centre, and the camp has its market, a place for manual workers and with seats for both high- and low-ranking officers, where, if any differences arise, their causes are heard and determined', is the Jewish historian Josephus' description of a camp in Judea.15 The *via principalis*, the main road, ran from the fort's two long sides. Halfway through the camp, in front of the HQ, it met the *via praetoria*, the commander's road, at right angles. Marching camps were always oriented so that the *via praetoria* then ran out of the main gate towards the enemy.

When he returned to Rome from the west in 13 BC, Augustus handed over command of the mobilisation and invasion to his 25-year-old stepson Drusus. This was a sign of favour that went well beyond nepotism – the emperor clearly regarded him as one of the empire's most talented generals. Though Drusus would not have been aware of it, it was a fateful moment. For the next few generations, this branch of the imperial family would make Germany its own. His brother, his son and those who were connected to him by marriage, like Varus, would, for better or worse, make their names and reputations here. As Augustus returned to Rome, Drusus began to organise the Roman invasion of Germany. It was the first of what would eventually be four campaigns.

Although young, Drusus Claudius Nero was one of the most decorated and popular commanders of the Roman army.16 His temperament was easy-going; his support came from the emperor and his politics were solidly republican. 'A young man with as much character as human nature is capable of receiving or hard work can develop', was his reputation with the army. Born in mid-April 38 BC, there were mutterings about Drusus' parentage. His father had been persuaded to divorce his pregnant wife Livia so that Augustus could marry her that January – and Drusus himself was born three months after the marriage. Whether he was Augustus' bastard or not no one knows, but Drusus and his brother, the future emperor Tiberius, were brought up in Augustus' house as his stepsons.

Imperial association allowed Drusus to fast-track many of the usual stages of Roman public service. In 17 BC he and his brother were sent against the Alpine tribes who had made forays into northern Italy and Gaul, events celebrated on the Alpine Memorial, the *Tropaeum Alpium*. Still standing, it was set up on the orders of the Senate at La Turbie, the old Roman boundary between Italy and Gaul, on the Grande Corniche road to Monaco, and finished at the end of June 6 BC. Although details of the campaign are hazy (in all probability Drusus moved over the Brenner Pass then up the Inn valley to upper Swabia, while Tiberius advanced east along the Rhine valley to Lake Constance before rendezvousing with his brother), Drusus and Tiberius not only pushed the tribes back across the mountains, they added the country to the empire. It was a military operation that captured the popular imagination and was to inspire Horace to heights of Kipling-esque poetry:

> What will not Claudian hands achieve?
> Jove's favour is their guiding star,
> And watchful potencies unweave
> For them the tangled paths of war.[17]

Drusus had arrived in Gaul in 13 BC with his wife Antonia the Younger and their 2-year-old son Germanicus. Antonia was as much of a popular idol as her husband. Two years younger than her spouse (she had been born in Rome at the end of January 36 BC), she was the younger daughter of Mark Antony and Augustus' sister Octavia. Famous, so wrote the historian Plutarch, for her 'beauty and self-control',[18] she had married Drusus when she was 17, early in 18 BC. There is a remarkable homogeneity in the representations of her that survive which allow speculation that they are a fair reflection;

a triangular face that softens in statues of her as an older woman, with a strong nose, the hint of a double chin and a distinct hairstyle – wavy hair with a centre parting, pulled back behind the ears. By modern standards they are strong rather than conventionally pretty features.

Antonia's importance had nothing to do with her looks. Like her mother-in-law, the Empress Livia, she was one of several women of this era who had the paradoxical position of considerable power with political influence that was recognised and honoured, yet with no constitutional status. Never to remarry after Drusus' death, she was to become the grande dame of Roman politics, a Lady Bracknell who, to all intents and purposes, ran Rome's eastern foreign policy from her salon throughout Tiberius' reign. She came from a line of matriarchs. While pregnant, her mother had brokered the – admittedly short-lived – peace deal between Antony and Augustus in the late spring of 37 BC. The family tradition of political meddling was to continue. It should be remembered that she was married to the heir to the throne; her first son, Germanicus was also to be heir; her second surviving son Claudius did achieve the throne; her grandson Caligula was also emperor; as was her great-grandson Nero. But this is to get ahead of the story.

The campaigning season of 12 BC was presented to the world as a glittering success. That first year, Drusus' attention was focused on planning and exploration. Headquartered probably at the large military base at Nijmegen, his marines reconnoitred along the North Sea coast early in the year. Certainly Augustus claimed it as a success. He himself boasted that his navy had 'sailed through the ocean from the mouth of the Rhine eastwards . . . where previously no Roman had gone by land or sea'. Pliny the Elder provides more detail, writing that his fleet had sailed round the Jutland peninsula, 'from where they either discovered or heard about it from reports, an immense sea which extends to the country of the Scythians and regions that are chilled by excessive moisture'.[19]

He also undertook the construction of a 24km canal that bore his name – The Drusus Ditch – which connected the Rhine with the Ijssel and is probably identical to the Upper Ijssel. This canal, together with its brother which connected Zuider Zee with the Wadden Sea, was much more important than it at first appears. From a strategic point of view it was crucial as it simplified access into Germany. Suddenly the River Ems, the Weser and the Elbe became accessible to Roman forces. A commander with access to this route could not only have the element of surpise on his side when he wanted to attack tribes far beyond the Rhine (not possible if an invasion was preceded by a visible and ungainly Rhine crossing), but the issue of logistics suddenly became considerably easier when supplies did not all have to be carried on the legionaries' backs. A protected channel that avoided the open sea was also of psychological importance to the army. The Romans were never comfortable sailors and the North Sea especially made them nervous. So much so, in fact, that the Emperor Claudius' invasion of Britain across the English Channel, two generations later, was almost halted by mutiny. The troops shouted down their commanders before they were to board ships, terrified at the thought of having to cross the sea.[20]

In the second year it is likely that Drusus based himself at Vetera. The visitor to the modern town of Xanten which now occupies the site, is most likely to see the reconstructed second-century town of Colonia Ulpia Traiana, one of the best-restored Roman sites in Germany. It was one of only two towns in Lower Germany allowed to call itself a *colonia* – a high civic honour and a reflection of its importance as a trading centre. Nothing like this was to be seen when Drusus founded the first military camp at the junction of the rivers Rhine and Lippe. It was a solid fort, capable of holding two legions, to the south-east of where the later Roman city grew up, high on the Fürstenberg. Little, however, has survived for archaeologists to work on. The site was much plundered, even in ancient times, a situation made worse when several dozen boxes of finds vanished in the course of the Second World War. The discovery of a collection of 2,400 arrows in the *principia*, however, is a pointed physical reminder not just of the Roman defensive imperatives, but also their intentions.

From here, Drusus crossed the River Lippe and erected a series of camps along its banks as far as the River Weser, though he did not cross it. Following the discovery of a supply fort at Beckinghausen, which was also a manufacturing and distribution centre for pottery, it is clear that the main camps were intended as stepping stones for a putative invasion along the Lippe. They stand 20km apart and each had the capacity to take two legions. Drusus' choice of the River Lippe was ideal and by far the easiest invasion route into the heart of Germany. Much smaller and slower flowing than the River Main, for example, it was a comparatively painless waterway for the Romans to negotiate.

Cassius Dio's account of the year reveals how hard the campaign was: 'Drusus set out again for the war. At the beginning of spring he crossed the River Rhine and subjugated the Usipetes. He bridged the River Lippe, invaded the territory of the Sugambri and advanced through it into Cherusci territory as far as the River Weser. He was able to do this because the Sugambri, angry with the Chatti, the only tribe among their neighbours that had refused to join their alliance, had campaigned against them with all their population. Seizing this opportunity, he passed through their land unnoticed. Drusus would have crossed the River Weser too, had he not run short of provisions and had not the winter set in.'

So far so good. The tribes who had humiliated Marcus Lollius were now themselves beaten. But the march back to winter camp was much less straightforward. In an overture to Varus' military finale, Drusus was tricked into an ambush. Cassius Dio continues: 'The enemy ambushed him frequently and once trapped him in a narrow pass and all but destroyed his army. The Germans would have wiped them out had they not underestimated the Romans, as if they were already captured and needed only the *coup de grâce*.'[21] Drusus may have rallied his troops and beaten off the overconfident Germans, but his forces were harried all the way back to winter camp.

It is generally accepted that Drusus' main base, indeed the Roman's first semi-permanent camp on the wrong side of the Rhine, was now Oberaden on the River Lippe. Although the site was identified as a Roman camp as long ago as 1873, only recently has dendrochronology helped date the timber rampart more precisely to trees cut down in the autumn of 11 BC. It was a large site of 56 hectares, had a perimeter of 2.7km, and could quite comfortably accommodate two legions and auxiliaries, some of the latter in all likelihood from Thrace and Asia Minor. This was a total of some 15,000 men. The camp was perfectly situated. On a hill, 1.5km south of the River Lippe, it dominates its surroundings on all sides. Certainly the camp's defences go beyond what one might expect. With towers every 25m, they speak of how exposed the Romans must have felt. The north-west of the site was particularly well fortified and strengthened by a barrier of sharp wooden stakes. Although Oberaden only had one ditch – some 3m wide – this is a sign, not of Roman laziness, but more an indication of the difficulty in digging the heavy, red clay.

The theory that Oberaden was used as a base is given additional weight by archaeologists' discovery of a store containing some forty huge wooden barrels. This suggests that it doubled as a supply centre. The convoys of boats travelling up and down the Lippe from Xanten and beyond, carrying these casks, each capable of holding 1,200 litres, must have been a sight and the finds give a faint sense of the logistic challenge that was feeding the army.[22] The camp may have felt remote from civilisation, but in some ways this perception is wrong. It is a credit to Roman logistics that an analysis of the latrines suggests that the soldiers' diet included Mediterranean vegetables and, most remarkably of all, pepper from India. Physically remote it might have been, but that did not mean that the legionaries stationed here had to forgo all of the luxuries they could expect in Rome.

However transitory the practical achievements of the last two years might have been – the feats of 11 BC were broadly reversed the following year – Augustus was impressed enough to grant Drusus a triumph, the right to ride through the city of Rome on horseback. It was an event still remembered half a century later. The Emperor Claudius, by then Drusus' only surviving son, had a gold coin struck in his father's memory. The commander sits triumphant on a trotting horse over a victory arch on which is inscribed 'Victory over the Germans'. So pacified was Germany perceived to be that the Senate voted that the shrine of Janus Quirinus be closed that winter. This was an event that was supposed to occur only when the empire was at total peace.[23]

The following year, back on the frontier, Drusus continued his attacks on the Sugambri and the Chatti. When he returned to Gaul's provincial capital in Lyons, he was joined that summer by Augustus, who had come to the city to monitor the German situation and to oversee an altar, the *Ara Lugdunensis*, which was set up in the city to honour both him and Rome. It was hoped that the imperial cult would be a foil to the constant military activity in the province, help break down tribal loyalties and tie the Gauls even closer to the greater Roman family. As Roman mythology was later to have it, Drusus' second son, the future emperor Claudius, was born on 1 August 10 BC, the day the altar was dedicated.

Although Drusus was named consul *in absentia* for 9 BC and was riding high yet again in imperial honours, Rome might have been forgiven for thinking that his fourth campaign must soon signal the end of barbarian Germany. The more astute, on the other hand, could see him trying to recapture yet again what had been lost the previous year, this time from a base in Mainz. His camp there was situated on a flattened hill, some 30m or so above the River Rhine, giving him an unparalleled view of the surrounding country. Drusus crossed the Rhine and headed north into the territory of the Cherusci via that of the Chatti – once more – and the Suebi. It was clearly a difficult campaign. Cassius Dio comments on the 'considerable bloodshed' and mentions that the Roman army conquered only with 'difficulty'.[24] Drusus then crossed the River Weser and finally reached the Elbe, destroying everything in his path.

Drusus failed in his attempt to cross the River Elbe and instead built an altar, a monument to the difficulty of the season's campaign and to the glory of Rome. The language of the contemporary historians deliberately recalls Alexander the Great, the conqueror chasing the end of the world, halted by a river – in the Macedonian's case the River Jhelum. Alexander also constructed a monument when he had travelled as far as he could.

But now, for the emperor's heir, disaster. Never shy of invoking the supernatural, Cassius Dio reports the appearance of a gigantic barbarian goddess, Germania personified, predicting doom. 'Where are you hurrying to, insatiable Drusus? You are not fated to look on all these lands. Leave! The end of your campaigns and of your life is already at hand.'[25]

The German historian Dieter Timpe convincingly argues that the real reason for the halt at the Elbe had less to do with apparitions and more to do with a threatened mutiny – the goddess a narrative device after the fact. Certainly military discontent after a 500km march into unknown, dangerous and terrifying territory is hardly beyond the realms of possibility.[26]

Whatever the reality of the putative mutiny or indeed Drusus' actual military intentions, the commander was not to get any further. A nasty tumble from a horse towards the end of the campaigning season resulted in a broken leg. Then – the sources are a little vague – either gangrene set into the leg itself or the fall had caused internal injuries and Drusus began to sicken.[27]

When it became apparent that he was failing, Tiberius rushed 1,000km to his brother's side. There was certainly a political element to Tiberius' concern. It was imperative that the fractious legions be calmed down, but genuine concern seems to have driven him on and the trip soon became a literary ideal of fraternal love. The writer Valerius Maximus, writing at the end of the 20s AD described it like this:

How swift and headlong his journey, snatched as it were in a single breath, as evident from the fact that after crossing the Alps and the River Rhine, travelling day and night and changing horses at intervals, Tiberius covered two hundred miles through a barbaric country recently conquered, with his guide Antabagius as his sole companion and without a break. But in this very time of stress and danger, left without moral attendance, the most holy power of Piety and the gods who favour pre-eminent virtues and Jupiter, most faithful guardian of the Roman empire, kept him company. Drusus, too, though closer to his own fate than to duty towards anyone, in the collapse of spiritual vigour and bodily strength, yet at the very moment that separates life from death ordered his legions with their standards to go and meet his brother, so that he be saluted as commander-in-chief. He bowed to his brother's majesty and out of his own life at the same time.²⁸

Drusus' body was brought back to Rome and his stepfather, the emperor, had his ashes interred in the mausoleum he had built for himself on the banks of the Tiber at the northern end of the Field of Mars. At 12m high and with a diameter of almost 90m, it was, and remains, the largest Roman tomb in the world. 'A mound of earth raised upon a high foundation of white marble, situated near the river, and covered to the top with evergreen shrubs' is how the geographer Strabo describes it.²⁹

Today it stands somewhat incongruous and remote in the Piazza Augusto Imperatore in Rome. In 1937, overenthusiastic archaeologists cleared the area of the structures that surrounded it and erected instead the unpleasant Fascist buildings that the visitor can see there now. Its isolation is mirrored by the dynastic loneliness that grew around Augustus from now on. By the time of the emperor's death, the mausoleum already housed a large number of his friends and family.³⁰

Drusus was given the posthumous honorific 'Germanicus', a title that passed on to his son. Some idea of the international sense of tragedy that afflicted the empire can be gleaned from the cenotaph that was also raised to his memory on the banks of the Rhine in Mainz. It was a memorial that was protected up to the end of the Roman Empire and can still be seen today. Now rather forlorn in the city's predominantly Baroque citadel, then the 30m-tall memorial stood alone on a ridge overlooking the town, along the road that led south-east from the main military fort to another camp slightly further down the Rhine at Mainz-Wiesenau. It is significant that the structure, locally referred to as the Eichelstein, was made of stone at a time when even the fledgling town's military buildings were made of wood.³¹

No matter that the accident could have happened anywhere, the Germans were to blame. A contemporary poem that commemorates Drusus' death encapsulates the depth of feeling:

There is no pardon for you, Germany,
but only death, the supreme penalty;
cold chains will bind the great kings of your race,
by neck and hand, with fear on every face.
The evil that rejoiced when Drusus fell
will meet its doom inside a gloomy cell,
and I shall see, at ease and with a smile,
the naked dead bestrew your byways vile.
Goddess of Dawn, Aurora, with your might,
hasten the day that brings so great a sight![32]

It is important not to be too distracted by imperial propaganda and to ask what it was that Drusus had actually achieved. An altar and a triumph was the stuff of assault not of invasion, the Germans were cowed not beaten, the country was mapped not conquered. And even if a couple of permanent bases like Oberaden had been established along the River Lippe, not too much weight should be placed on one Roman writer's claim that 'Drusus built more than fifty forts on the Rhine alone.'[33]

One should not forget that Drusus had twice led his army into serious danger. In his first campaign along the North Sea, a mis-reading of the tides meant that his fleet had to be saved by his allies. More pertinently, as mentioned above, in his second campaign, he was tricked in an ambush and trapped in a narrow pass. It is clear that from the outset the German tribes were aware that there was no point in trying to defeat Rome on the open battlefield. Guerrilla tactics and ambushes would always be at the heart of their arsenal and as such, the Battle of Teutoburg Forest should be seen less as a tactical innovation, rather the refinement and culmination of a long-term strategic development.

Command now passed on to Drusus' younger brother Tiberius and, with this, Rome's policy towards Germany moved up a gear. Aside from his more general imperial ambitions, Augustus realised that any sign of lassitude following Drusus' death would be exploited by the Germans. What was now clearly an intended province needed a show of force. It needed to be conquered.

Aged 34 when he headed the Rhine armies the following year, 8 BC, the future emperor Tiberius was one of Rome's most efficient commanders. History remembers him as an old man; it recalls the tabloid gossip of the aged roué cavorting with his catamites on the island of Capri, not the young and successful general he had been.

Large, tall and broad, with fair colouring, marred only by recurrent acne, Tiberius was never popular, despite his success. Certainly he was rather a dour man with a parched sense of humour. On one occasion he compared his provincial governors to gorged flies on a sore – better to leave them than to drive them off and invite new ones he said. On another he chastised a governor's punitive tax policy, saying that he expected his sheep shorn, not flayed.[34] It is overly simplistic to say that his character was shaped because he was left-handed, but he is certainly one of the few figures in the ancient world who were attested as such. Almost the only sign of human weakness we have is that as a young man he was a heavy drinker. A nickname given in his earliest army days stuck. In an admittedly not especially clever wordplay, his name Tiberius Claudius Nero became Biberius Caldius Mero or 'Neat Wine Drinker'.

As a commander, he was slow and deliberate in all that he did. His caution won plaudits from his men if not from historians. Velleius Paterculus' praise of him is sincere and stands in sharp contrast to Augustus, overheard after a cabinet meeting to say, 'Alas for the Roman people, to be ground by jaws that crunch so slowly!'[35] But personal dislike did not mean that the emperor did not recognise his qualities.

The details of Tiberius' campaigns that year are vague. It seems he spent most of the time stabilising Roman power in territory that his brother had conquered. Velleius Paterculus, as ever, is hyperbolic. 'Tiberius so subdued the country as to reduce it almost to the status of a tributary province,' he writes.[36] It appears that the commander had targeted the Sugambri on the lower Rhine and, if any credence can be given to Velleius' account, it can be seen in the fact that treaties were signed with some tribes. The campaigns were perceived as successful enough to honour Tiberius with a triumph. A silver cup, found in Boscoreale in Italy and now in the Louvre Museum in

Paris, shows Tiberius riding through the streets of Rome crowned with the victor's wreath.

From the time of Tiberius' command it is possible to detect the change in strategy on the ground as well. The site of Oberaden on the River Lippe was abandoned around now, and then burned. In and of itself this should not necessarily be thought of in terms of either failure or even of Germanic aggression; rather it is an indication that the first phase of Romanisation was over. A new general, naturally enough, decided that the military imperatives required a different disposition of troops. Oberaden had simply served its purpose. The burning that the archaeologists have uncovered was not the effect of attacks, just standard procedure. The Jewish historian Josephus explicitly writes that when Romans withdrew from a site, 'they set fire to their camp, because it is easy for them to erect another one and so that it may never be of use to their enemies'. It was a policy followed throughout the empire. When the fort of Inchtuthil, on the banks of the Tay in Perthshire, was abandoned in AD 87, following a systematic withdrawal from Scotland under the Emperor Domitian, the site was deliberately and carefully dismantled.[37] What can be seen in Germany is a formal and organised withdrawal, possibly, but not definitely, to the Roman camp at Haltern.

Frustratingly for the historian, a largely impenetrable veil descends on Germany for the ten years from 6 BC. Irritated and disillusioned at perpetually playing second fiddle, Tiberius withdrew from public life and settled himself on the other side of the empire – in semi-exile on Rhodes. The reasons are as debated now as they were at the time. Most plausibly it was a combination of exhaustion – imperial expectations had rested largely on his shoulders since the death of his brother – and a desire not to get involved in succession politics.[38] But as he did so, the attention of the historians shifted away from Germany. Indeed we know shockingly little about the empire as a whole during this period.

This is not to say that the western front was quiet. The familiar pattern of attack and counter-attack continued. Tiberius was replaced by Lucius Domitius Ahenobarbus, again a family promotion. Ahenobarbus was the emperor's nephew by marriage and since he had married the elder of Mark Antony's daughters, he was Drusus' brother-in-law.

Even though he had had a successful political career – Ahenobarbus had notched up a consulship in 16 BC and ran Africa four years later – by almost all accounts the grandfather of the Emperor Nero was a deeply unpleasant man. 'Haughty, extravagant and cruel' and so addicted to games that Augustus was forced to rebuke him on at least one occasion, writes one. The one note of sympathy, and again, it is possibly a reflection of his reputation with Rhine armies, comes from Velleius Paterculus, who praises his 'eminent and noble simplicity'.[39]

Ahenobarbus had become involved in the German theatre of war indirectly. As legate for the province of Illyria, he had led an expeditionary force which had crossed the River Elbe, penetrating further into Germany than any Roman before him, where he erected an altar to Augustus and concluded a non-aggression treaty with tribes beyond the river.[40] He received a triumph and was promoted to the German commission, though in this Ahenobarbus was much less successful, managing somehow to alienate the Cherusci.

He was succeeded by Marcus Vinicius, the grandfather of the man to whom Velleius Paterculus dedicated his volume of history. His tour of duty was dominated by an escalating tribal revolt that became a vast war (*'immensum bellum'* is the phrase that Velleius Paterculus uses)[41] which staggered on for three years. No further details have survived other than that he must have acquitted himself adequately as he too was awarded a triumph on his return to Rome.

In AD 4 the veil begins to lift. The emperor appointed a new man to Germany – Gaius Sentius Saturninus. In his late fifties when he took command there, Saturninus, like virtually all the others posted here, was part of the inner circle of commanders that included Marcus Lollius, Lucius Domitius Ahenobarbus and, of course, Varus. He was already in position, presumably from the spring if not the autumn before, when Tiberius arrived to command the Rhine armies once more. His return was greeted with relief by his armies. 'The tears of joy in the soldiers' eyes at the sight of him, their enthusiasm, their exuberant greetings, their longing to touch his hand, and their inability to restrain such cries as "Is it really you, commander?" "Are you safely back with us?" "I served with you, general, in Armenia!" "And I in Switzerland!" "I received my decoration from you in Vindelicia [the area from Switzerland to the Danube]!" "And I mine in Hungary!" "And I in Germany!"' writes Velleius Paterculus, who was there.[42]

This acclamation was the preface to two years' campaigning, most of which was focused on the northern reaches of Germany well beyond the River Rhine. It is likely that Tiberius was intermittently based at Anreppen on the upper Lippe, the most easterly base that has been found on the river, and perfectly positioned for action beyond the hills to the east and towards the River Weser.

At first sight, Anreppen, which was discovered by accident in 1967, is peculiarly sited. For self-evident reasons, Roman camps were conventionally situated on higher ground to give the legionaries the greatest protection. Here, however, there was a more obvious spot, only 3km away, that was not used. The reason lies in the river and its role in transportation. Although it is not the case any more, the River Lippe was navigable this far, up to the Middle Ages. The camp, south of the river and just east of the confluence with the Stemmeckebach, is long and thin, some 750m by 330m, to take advantage of the land that was above the river's flood zone. It has a re-entrant some 140m long and 90m deep, which has been convincingly identified as a harbour docking zone for loading and unloading. As the German archaeologist Siegmar von Schnurbein has explained, Tiberius 'deliberately sacrificed tactical advantages in favour of proximity to the river'.[43]

During that first year, which took him to the Weser, three tribes – the Canninefates, the Attuarii and the Bructeri – were defeated, while the ever-quarrelsome Cherusci were subjugated. His second campaign took Tiberius to the Elbe, possibly as far as the modern city of Dresden. Velleius exaggerates the seriousness of the resistance put up to Tiberius during these two campaigns. His commander was certainly not the first Roman general to cross the Elbe, nor was he the first to winter on the wrong side of the Rhine. Nonetheless, it is clear that Rome now believed that the bulk of the pacification in Germany had been completed. 'Nothing remained to be conquered in Germany', is Velleius' overly optimistic conclusion.[44]

At any rate by the spring of AD 6, Germany was deemed secure enough for a campaign to be considered against Maroboduus, king of a tribe called the Marcomanni in what is roughly the western half of the Czech Republic, what used to be called Bohemia. Tiberius rated him as one of Rome's most formidable enemies. Philip of Macedon had not been as dangerous to Athens, nor any of those who had stood against Rome in the days of the Republic, as Maroboduus was to Rome, he said.[45] In one sense he was right. Maroboduus was later to become a significant factor in the war against Arminius, though not remotely in any way that Tiberius could have expected.

Compared to the manner in which barbarian kings were normally written off, and certainly how Arminius was described, Maroboduus stands out as the exception. As such, his career bears closer examination. Even Velleius Paterculus accords him respect. 'It would be inexcusable to omit him for reasons of haste,' he writes as introduction to a most generous characterisation. It is so extraordinary that it is here cited in full: 'A noble man, strong in body and courageous in mind, a barbarian by birth but not in mind, he achieved among his countrymen no mere chief's position gained as the result of internal disorders or luck or liable to change and dependent upon the whims of his subjects, but, conceiving in his mind the idea of a definite empire and royal powers, he resolved to take his tribe far away from the Romans and to migrate to a place where, inasmuch as he had fled before the strength of more powerful arms, he might make his own people all-powerful.'[46]

Maroboduus had come to Rome as a young man and had caught Augustus' eye. He had been educated at the elite school of princes on the Palatine Hill in Rome, where the sons of kings were taught the tools of their craft alongside the emperor's own grandsons.[47] This education, the experience of international *Machtpolitik* and the exposure to the Roman military, made Maroboduus a powerful figure. It gave him authority at home and in Rome.

It is not known either how or when Maroboduus became the leader of the Marcomanni, but he had certainly been chief for almost twenty years, since Drusus had pushed through their homeland on the River Main. As Velleius mentioned, the king had reacted to Roman encroachment by emigrating. He moved his tribe to the Bohemian basin, an area naturally protected by impenetrable virgin forest – far from the long arm of Rome.

In his woodland stronghold, Maroboduus subjugated and welded local tribes together, to create what one modern historian rightly calls 'the first German empire known to history'.[48] By the time that Tiberius started to mobilise against him, it is likely that Maroboduus' empire stretched from the Danube up to the Elbe.

Although the official reason was that the king intended to attack the Danube frontier, the justification for war was quite simply the perennial Roman *casus belli*; that he existed. It was irrelevant that Maroboduus had given every indication of wanting to avoid direct conflict with the Romans. It did not matter that Roman traders enjoyed a healthy and presumably profitable relationship with his empire. Assimilation of his territory would not only have cleared a path from the Balkans to the North Sea, it would also have removed the danger of uprisings in supposedly conquered territory. It would even have addressed the nagging fear of Maroboduus' army. Rumours circulated that it now had an infantry of 70,000 men with 4,000 cavalry and, unlike other barbarian forces in Germany, this was a standing army. The king had learned Rome's lessons well.

Tiberius assembled a huge task force (Tacitus has the force numbering some twelve legions, although that seems a trifle large)[49] split into two, in preparation for what was clearly a pincer strategy. Saturninus controlled one part, heading out from Mainz from the west and into the Hercynian Forest, while Tiberius himself led the force from Carnuntum, near Hainburg in Lower Austria, then one of the main crossings of the Middle Danube.

It was not to be. Five days before campaigning was due to start, Dalmatia and Pannonia exploded in revolt. 'Glory was sacrificed to necessity,' writes Paterculus, and Tiberius was rapidly forced to sign a peace treaty with Maroboduus.[50] This reaffirmed friendship between the two states gave the king favoured-trading-nation status. From the way that Maroboduus behaved during Arminius' revolt, there must also have been a clause of non-interference in each other's domestic troubles. Tiberius then rushed back to manage one of the most dangerous revolts the Romans ever had to face. It was the first sign of the general move in imperial policy away from ebullient expansion to gritted retrenchment.

What had happened? With Illyria relieved of troops which were all mobilising in the north for the invasion of Bohemia, with even the legate of the province marching out with Tiberius, it was the worst time to realise that the province was not as pacified as the Romans thought. Quiet resentment became a rebellion when a draft was demanded of the Dalmatians. With no troops available to prevent it, the revolt soon spread. Roman citizens were overpowered, traders were massacred, and a largish detachment of veterans stationed in the region was exterminated to a man.

An uprising of this magnitude shocked Rome. Augustus, not normally given to panicked pronouncements, was heard to say that unless something was done quickly, the enemy would be at the gates of Rome within ten days, while Suetonius described it as 'the most serious of all foreign wars since those with Carthage'.[51]

This was not exaggeration. Much like the wars against Hannibal, the three-year rebellion stretched Rome to the limit. As many as fifteen legions were involved (two were summoned from the eastern theatre); not only was the draft reintroduced, but freemen found themselves in the army too. The cost was so large that the exchequer imposed a 2 per cent sales tax on slaves. At one point the provinces saw the greatest concentration of soldiers since the dark days of the civil wars a generation earlier.[52]

Although Tiberius and the attention of the bulk of the Roman army was focused on Illyria, Augustus could not afford to disregard the rest of the empire, specifically newer provinces, given that it was imperial neglect that had encouraged this one. At this time almost more than any other, the emperor needed a safe and solid pair of hands to the north in Germany. He needed both a commander and an administrator; one who could carry on the policy of pacification and civilisation, yet who could be relied upon to act with military decisiveness should the need arise; a bureaucrat with the experience of managing a geographically large and difficult terrain, and a soldier with experience in tribal unrest and guerrilla warfare; one who would not panic if any of the unrest from Illyria overflowed into his province. The man he picked was Publius Quinctilius Varus.

TWO

A Wolf or a Shepherd?

A lingering and widespread suspicion remains, even today, that Augustus chose a second-division governor in Varus. The view persists that he was not up to a posting like Germany and certainly not to be spoken of in the same breath as either Marcus Agrippa or Germanicus. One modern historian has subtitled his profile of Varus 'the picture of a loser', another highlights the governor's 'limited experience' of warfare, and a third simply calls him 'inexperienced'. Even the cartoon of Varus that is featured on one of the websites of the Lippe Tourist Board is a grotesquely rotund caricature perched on a little horse.[1]

It is a point of view that comes directly from Varus' contemporaries. Immoral, proud and cruel, writes Florus; imperious, naive and militarily incompetent, suggests Cassius Dio; careless, notes Suetonius. But for true, out-and-out invective, it is necessary to turn to Velleius Paterculus. Lazy, greedy and negligent with a faint whiff of cowardice about him, is his conclusion. 'Varus was a man of mild character and of a quiet disposition, somewhat slow in mind as he was in body – more accustomed to the leisure of the camp than to actual service in war.'[2]

Given that he knew Varus, an understandable weight has been placed on Velleius' views, but to accept them is to buy into the sour grapes of a retired cavalry officer. If that alone is too revisionist a starting point, one should ask from the outset whether it is at all plausible that Augustus would have entrusted the command of the Rhine armies to an incompetent at a time of uprising in the west.

In reality, Varus had a career that verged on, even if it did not quite touch, the glittering, and there were few more able and talented sons of the empire among his contemporaries. He had proved his worth both on the battlefield and to the exchequer: he could collect taxes with an iron glove. Until the Battle of Teutoburg Forest, he had barely put a foot wrong and had steadily climbed almost to the pinnacle of Roman political life.

An intriguing parallel is with the Victorian hero General Charles Gordon, who was killed in Khartoum defending the city against Sudanese rebels. Gordon had distinguished himself in the Crimean War and had been so successful in successive campaigns in Beijing and Shanghai in the early 1860s that an adulatory British public dubbed him 'Chinese' Gordon. Sent out to the Sudan as governor-general, Gordon was famously skewered on the steps of his residency at Khartoum, trying to defend the city from the Muslim mystic the Mahdi in January 1885.

While their careers do follow superficially similar trajectories, the crucial difference between Varus and Gordon can be seen in the way they were treated after their deaths. Almost immediately, Gordon was canonised as a secular British saint, a martyred warrior, while popular opinion rounded on the British government. The monumental painting of the event, by George William Joy, in Leeds City Art Gallery captures it all. The proud but fated Gordon, arrogantly facing down those sent to kill him. The Romans on the other hand rapidly distanced themselves from the governor of Germany. With no cult of heroic failure, the blame was thrown squarely on to Varus' shoulders. It is inconceivable to imagine any coins, statues or medals commemorating his life. Varus had become a national embarrassment.

It is valid to ask whether it is at all possible to build up any kind of a three-dimensional picture of Varus. A great part of the written material that survives relates to that final desperate adventure in Germany and it would certainly be unwise to form a character sketch based on those accounts alone. But though any modern characterisation of Varus' life can only ever be impressionistic rather than photographic in its detail, there are enough literary hints and allusions, and archaeological titbits, to flesh out the man and his life.

Publius Quinctilius Varus was born in the late 40s BC (the precise date does not survive) which makes him in his late fifties or early sixties at the time of the Battle of Teutoburg Forest. He came from a minor patrician family, not exactly first flight, but senior enough to be a known quantity within the group of around 600 aristocrats which made up the Senate, the self-perpetuating and executive arm of Roman government. What his family did have in its favour was longevity, prized above all else.

A Sextus Quinctilius Varus had been consul in 453 BC and we know of Publius Quintilius Varus, a praetor in 204 BC in the middle of the Second Carthaginian War, who commanded two legions and governed the province of Cisalpine Gaul. He narrowly won a set battle against Hannibal's brother, acquitting himself honourably with one wing of the army while his son Marcus commanded the cavalry.

But the family did not achieve continuous prominence – become a political dynasty if you will – until the first century BC. Varus' father, Sextus Quinctilius Varus, was in his late twenties when his son was born. Something of a liability, Sextus managed consistently to back the wrong political horses in the dying days of the Roman Republic. In 49 BC, during the civil war, Sextus was one of the senators who held the town of Corfinium for Pompey the Great against Julius Caesar, fruitlessly as it turned out. A magnanimous Caesar pardoned him, something Sextus repaid by immediately flitting across to Africa to fight against him once more. Again Sextus lost. Showing astute foresight of how much clemency he could expect from Caesar a second time, he vanished for the next few years. Even though he is not named, it is not implausible that he was one of the sixty conspirators including Brutus and Cassius who assassinated Julius Caesar on 15 March 44 BC. Certainly he was there in mind, if not in body. The next we know for certain is that he was on the battlefield of Philippi in northern Greece with his co-conspirators when they were defeated by the coalition of Augustus and Mark Antony in October the following year. Without asking for mercy, Sextus committed suicide soon after the defeat, or rather forced his freeman to kill him.[3]

We know nothing of Varus' personal life before his late twenties. It is conceivable that with his father dead he was brought up by his uncle. The evidence here is sketchy in the extreme and based on guesswork and folk tradition, but a Quintilius Varus, a plausible uncle, is found at around this time in Tivoli, an ancient Latin town that still stands on a high hill covered with olive groves and dominates the route to the east along the line of the ancient Via Valeria. A favourite resort of the patrician class, the 'gentle soil' of Tivoli would have been a pleasant place for Varus to have grown up.[4] There was something of the moneyed Bloomsbury about the town; it was certainly more elegant and closer to Rome than the vulgar Baian coast. Virgil's patron Maecenas had a villa here; Virgil himself was a visitor; and the poet Horace had a farm down the road, some 8km away.

The little that is known about Quintilius Varus must be gleaned from the poetry of Horace. He appears to have been a lawyer from Cremona in northern Italy, certainly a patron of the arts, a friend of Virgil, rich enough to have a house at Tivoli (though of the equestrian, not senatorial class) and well-known enough for Horace to dedicate at least one poem to him. The poet leaves an affectionate portrait of Quintilius as a critic:

> Read to Quintilius, and at every line:
> 'Correct this passage, friend, and that refine.'
> Tell him, you tried it twice or thrice in vain:
> 'Haste to an anvil with your ill-formed strain,
> Or blot it out.' But if you still defend
> The favourite folly, rather than amend,
> He'll say no more, nor idle toil employ:
> 'Yourself unrivalled, and your works enjoy.'[5]

Although there is no direct literary corroboration for a connection with our Quinctilius Varus, he has long been popularly tied to the town. The Via Quintilio Varo crosses the Via Valeria, and the church of S. Maria di Quintiliolo sits on the remains of what is popularly thought to have been his villa. It is at least plausible that Varus inherited the estate in Tivoli on Quintilius' death in 11 BC.[6]

Consideration of Varus' professional life is less speculative. It can be reconstructed, albeit sketchily, by virtue of the rigid nature of a Roman public life. The dubious track record of his father's political leanings does not appear to have hindered his climb either on to or up the *cursus honorum*, the greasy pole of Roman politics. It can be presumed that he had dipped his toes in politics at the age of 18 as one of Rome's minor magistrates, the testing ground for any young man who had political aspirations. Then in his early twenties he would have seen army life as aide-de-camp or military tribune to a senior commander in one of the provinces, before heading back to Rome.

The first we know for certain is that by 22 BC as quaestor, an official akin to a private secretary, he accompanied the 41-year-old Augustus on a three-year tour of the East. Only two quaestors were chosen personally by the emperor and to be selected was a huge sign of favour for Varus, now in his mid to late twenties. Acting as the emperor's adjutant brought him an enviable intimacy with power and an insight into how the empire worked. From Sicily to Greece, the imperial party then wintered in Samos. When the sea routes opened again in the spring, Varus accompanied the emperor on to Asia. There, Cassius Dio writes that the emperor 'instituted various reforms when they were needed, donated money to some cities and commanded others to pay a surcharge on their usual tribute'.[7] As financial affairs were part of his portfolio, Varus would have been busy meeting town councils and city officials. We know, for example, from an inscription dedicated to him in the city of Pergamon, now in Turkey, that he must have spent some time there.

He clearly acquitted himself well, because in 13 BC, after what must have been stints as chief magistrate and as a legionary commander, Varus reached what he could reasonably expect to be the peak of his power. Now in his late thirties, he shared the consulship with his brother-in-law, the future emperor Tiberius.

One of the keys to Varus' political success was marriage. Trying to untangle the various familial and factional bonds of the early empire can be maddening and brings to mind the comment on the Habsburg monarchy that they conducted marriage not war. But it is something that Varus clearly understood, as can be seen from the way he managed to ally himself to the most powerful men of the era.

His own standing was buttressed by the nuptials he had arranged for his three sisters. These connections, all contracted in the earliest phase of Varus' career, probably in the mid to late 20s BC, supported and accentuated the young man as a person to watch. A fair amount is known about them and Varus made such good and early matches for his sisters that four of his nephews were to serve as consuls.

His eldest sister married new money. Her husband, Lucius Nonius Asprenas Snr, was the son of a recent consul and a close friend of Augustus. He is infamous for having committed arguably the ultimate social faux-pas. He managed to poison 130 of his guests at a dinner party by accident. Asprenas was eventually acquitted of malicious intent and although, presumably as a result, he was never made consul, it appears not to have done his family too much harm in the long term.[8] Their first son, Lucius Nonius Asprenas, was to play a significant role in the events of AD 9.

His second sister's husband, Cornelius Dolabella, had been a close companion of Augustus during the war against Mark Antony. That he was trusted can be seen in that he was chosen by the emperor to lead his negotiations with the Egyptian queen, Cleopatra.[9] His third sister, Varilia, the only one whose name has survived, came the closest of all to the throne. Her husband was one of Augustus' nephews, a certain Sextus Appuleius. He had a remarkable international career. As governor of Spain he had the honour of celebrating the last triumph from the province, before stints as proconsul of Asia and then, finally, as governor of the province of Illyrium.

As for Varus himself, of his first wife we know nothing other than that she must have existed. It was unheard of for a senior politician to be unmarried. His second wife, conventionally referred to as Vipsania, was the daughter of Marcus Agrippa. Their marriage, concluded probably just before 13 BC, allowed Varus into the imperial inner circle. It also brought him close to Tiberius, who was married to Vipsania's sister. The following year Varus and Tiberius delivered the orations at Marcus Agrippa's funeral. The great general had died in March 12 BC. While at this distance of time it is difficult to get more than just an impression of the importance played by his relationship with the future emperor, it does appear as though Varus' star followed that of Tiberius as long as it was in the ascendant.[10]

Returning to politics and the consulship, in 13 BC the brothers-in-law served together as consuls. It was becoming clear that Varus shared none of his father's Republican leanings. His most high-profile achievement during his year in power was overseeing the dedication of the Altar of the Augustan Peace, the *Ara Pacis Augustae*. Decreed on 4 July 13 BC, what is arguably the most impressive Augustan monumental sculpture in Rome was built to celebrate Augustus' safe return from three years spent clearing up Gaul and Spain. The altar took three and a half years to finish before it was finally dedicated on 30 January 9 BC.

In an incredible feat of archaeological reconstruction, it was put back together again in 1938 from hundreds of fragments and, more recently, in 2006, rehoused in a controversial new museum designed by US architect Richard Meier, on the east bank of the Tiber river near the Ponte Cavour. Originally, it stood facing the Flaminian Way, the road that linked Rome to northern Italy, and the route by which the emperor re-entered the city. Indeed it is likely to be the spot where the Senate formally welcomed Augustus back from his travels.

The sacrificial altar was the centrepiece of the monument, enclosed by a structure decorated with images of gods or heroes of the Roman people. Representations of Romulus, Aeneas and the goddess Peace all supported Augustus' state-sponsored notion of the return of the Roman Golden Age.

The most intriguing part of the structure is the frieze on the southern wall: a procession or parade of men and women, three-quarter size, celebrating the emperor's safe return from the West. Fortunately the original heads have survived and several of the figures are tentatively identifiable. There is Marcus Agrippa, his head covered by the end of his toga in respect, and a typically determined-looking Livia. But at the front – between a damaged Augustus (only his head and half of his body survive) and the city's four leading priests, distinguished by their spiked leather caps – are two consular figures. The leading one, his body half-turned outwards, with his left hand touching the emperor's toga, is Tiberius. The second consular figure, with his back to the emperor, facing the rest of the procession and partly blocked by Tiberius and the first of the priests, has been plausibly identified as Varus, though the image is too indistinct to allow any trace of personality to be distinguished. That he stands next to Tiberius emphasises the close political and familial relationships between the two, while the placement of Varus in the background is hierarchically appropriate.[11]

After his stint as consul, it was time for Varus to take up the first of what would be three foreign postings. In 8–7 BC, now in his early forties, he became governor of Africa, headquartered in the new provincial capital of Roman Carthage. The only other representations of Varus known today date from this period of his life: a profile from coins minted in the towns of Achulla and Hadrumentum. Unfairly one modern historian sees in this a 'weak and smirking face' that 'reveals no hint of soldierly disposition'.[12] Objectively, we see quite a heavy-set man with a nose more reminiscent of Rembrandt than the traditional Roman aquiline proboscis. His hair is cut in the same loose, slightly shaggy manner of Augustus and his mouth is slightly turned down.

Although the province was still fledgling, a long way off from its imperial grandeur of later years and with an area not much larger than modern-day Tunisia, the appointment was an indication of confidence in Varus' capabilities. Any governor of Africa was the servant of two masters and Varus' appointment had unique political and economic ramifications.

Since Africa was an administrative anomaly, Varus had to walk a political tightrope. Most provincial governors were directly responsible to the emperor, a status quo from which Augustus never showed any sign of deviation. What the emperor gave, he could also take away. Africa, however, had become a public province twenty years previously and technically was administered by the Senate. An even greater peculiarity was that the governor of Africa also commanded a legion, Legion III 'The Emperor's Own', which from

30 BC onwards had been permanently stationed in Africa, either at Carthage or at Ammaedara, modern Haïdra in north-west Tunisia. After the conclusion of years of civil war only a generation previously, this was a remarkable amount of administrative and military latitude to allow a governor. Of course, in reality no governor would have been sent against Augustus' express wishes but Varus had to maintain imperial favour without alienating his peers in the Senate.

As one of the empire's great grain producers, Africa had a disproportionately large economic influence. According to the great Republican orator Cicero, it was one of the 'major granaries' of the Republic, supplying two-thirds of Rome's grain. It was so important that Julius Caesar pointedly boasted about acquiring a province that was 'large enough to furnish for the public treasury eight thousand tonnes of grain and one million litres of olive oil annually'. And Augustus claimed that the province saved Rome from starvation on several occasions.[13] A rebellious governor in Africa had the potential to cause major disruption.

Circuses were a matter for the emperor, but Varus was in charge of the bread. Varus' main brief, then, will have been to maintain the flow of grain on which the empire was already dependent and to make sure that there was no disruption from the Berber tribes to the south. Although the natives had been comprehensively humiliated a decade previously, guerrilla threats were a permanent, nagging danger. The troubles in the region that hit the province during Tiberius' reign caused rapid price-rises in Rome and it is some indication of Varus' competence that we know of no major disruption in Africa until at least AD 2.[14]

Africa appears to have been a dry run for something bigger, and Varus passed the test with flying colours. By September 6 BC, Varus, now in his mid-forties, was made governor of Syria. At first glance, this might have appeared a cushy posting. He was based in Antioch, the East's boom town, a military centre and headquarters of the provincial government and an international trading hub. It had benefited aesthetically and in employment terms from a major imperial building programme since the time of Julius Caesar. The city was de facto capital of the East. Only Alexandria, further south in Egypt, was larger.

But it was anything other than a soft billet. In some ways, this was an unenviable position and clearly not one to be given to a political ingénue. It was a job that required discretion and guile. Although the province was technically at peace, the governor supervised several vassal kingdoms which were ruled by princes, aptly described by one modern historian as 'arrogant, conceited or insidious'.[15] More pertinently from a military point of view, Syria faced the Parthian Empire. Varus will have been all too aware of the threat posed by this looming presence to the East. Crassus' defeat, only a generation previously, had been more than a blow to Rome's prestige and confidence. It had left the empire dangerously exposed.

It was a distinct sign of imperial favour that Augustus considered Varus a safe pair of hands. For simple geographical reasons, governors could not hide behind Augustus' apron strings in this posting. Dispatches could take several months to get to Rome, especially during the winter months when all sailing pretty much stopped. The governor was on his own. As well as the diplomatic responsibility that went with the job, few could have forgotten that the region had been Mark Antony's stamping ground. Even twenty-five years on, Augustus would not have entrusted the province to anyone other than a member of his inner circle. Indeed he never did. It is no coincidence that Augustan governors of Syria included Varus' father-in-law Marcus Agrippa and, a few years after Varus, the emperor's grandson Gaius.

If an indication were still needed that the position had its difficulties, the brigades that were based there underline the region's internal and external security considerations. Varus found himself in charge of four legions: Legion X 'Of the Sea Straits' permanently stationed as a guard against Parthian incursions at Cyrrhus, 100km to the north-east of Antioch; Legion III 'The Gauls' and Legion XII 'Lightning' at Antioch; and Legion VI 'Ironclad' at Raphanaea, between Antioch and Damascus.

Varus' time in Syria should have been spent managing the larger cities, keeping an eye on religious festivals and checking banditry. In fact his stint in the East was dominated by one man and one region: Herod I and Judaea. Almost as soon as he had disembarked at Antioch, Varus had to head down to Jerusalem. Because the region of Judaea dominated so much of his time, in many ways this is the most visible period of Varus' life. The historian is fortunate to have a witness for Varus' governorship of Syria. Flavius Josephus, priest, soldier, historian and traitor who sold out his Jewish compatriots, was born just forty or so years after the events discussed. The main theme of his *The Jewish War* is the revolt of AD 66, a campaign that ended with the sacking of Jerusalem by the Emperor Vespasian, but Josephus does write eloquently and at some length about the previous hundred years, including, of course, Varus' governorship.

Rather like Varus, Herod the Great is unfairly known primarily for one event, the Massacre of the Innocents, an event which occurred only in the fevered imagination of St Matthew. Although the last few years of his life were overshadowed by palace intrigue and Stalinist-style purges, Herod had dominated Judea for the past thirty-seven years, skilfully managing the region's tendency towards violent nationalism and religious extremism and at the same time building a modern state. His success is an achievement the more remarkable not just because he owed his status, position and authority entirely to Rome, but because he was not a Jew.

Now in his late sixties, Herod's obsession was the question of succession, an issue that was to plague his remaining years as much as his health. After uncovering a plausible assassination plot by the sons of his beloved second wife Mariamme, he had them executed. His eldest son by his first wife was now named heir. In his forties, Antipater was, inevitably, given the environment in which he had grown up, an experienced and callous politician; but not quite ruthless enough. With the climate of paranoia at the court, it was almost inevitable that Antipater himself would be accused of plotting against the king. This is precisely what happened on his return from a trip to Rome. As he seemed unsure what steps to take against his son, Herod called on Varus to mediate.

It cannot have been a comfortable case for Varus. New to the region, he did not wish to alienate Herod. The king had been a particularly close friend to Marcus Agrippa – a grandson and a great-grandson had been named in honour of the Roman general. It is clear that Augustus had appointed Agrippa's son-in-law to the region because his voice would carry some weight. At the same time, Varus must have known Antipater from Rome. Herod's son was certainly unpleasantly ambitious, but it is by no means certain that he was planning murder. In an echo of one of his successors, Pontius Pilate, Varus washed his hands of the affair. Although it later came out that Varus' private advice was to banish Antipater, the governor left Jerusalem without making any public statement on the matter.[16]

Herod's death in Jericho at the end of March in 4 BC, triggered the inevitable crisis of succession. The king had finally succumbed to the chronic renal failure compounded by Fournier gangrene of the scrotum (which would account for the 'worms in the privy parts' that Josephus mentions) from which he had been suffering for several years.[17]

Herod had not listened to Varus' advice and Antipater was executed five days before his father's death. The struggle for supremacy at court inevitably dissolved into factional chaos. Under the terms of what was a muddy and unclear will, Herod's 19-year-old son Archelaus was named principal heir, while his two brothers were to become subordinate rulers of territories surrounding Galilee and the Golan Heights respectively. Archelaus was a disastrous choice and it was thanks to him that Judaea segued from client kingdom to province.[18]

But, and it is a crucial point, Augustus had to rubber-stamp the succession before Archelaus could formally take the throne. The king-elect anticipated a rapid imperial sign-off on his new status from Rome, though as a precaution he cannily refused the title or insignia of his father until he had heard from Augustus. In the meantime, however, he jumped headlong into a massive domestic crisis that he had inherited from his father.

The incident of the golden eagle had been one of the low points of the final weeks of Herod's life. Two priests had 'struck a blow for God' and hacked off a gilded stone sculpture of an eagle, a low relief above one of the gates to the temple in Jerusalem.[19] It was both a religious and a political gesture, a blow for the Jewish law which forbade images of living creatures and a statement against Roman domination of their state. The priests and their forty partners in crime were promptly arrested and, on 13 March, the ringleaders were burned alive.

Once Herod had been safely buried, Archelaus was inundated with petitioners who were hoping to benefit from the change in king. He played the perennially populist cards of promising to lower taxes, to remove duties from manufactured goods and to issue an amnesty. With the perception that these concessions indicated general affability, calls then came for Archelaus to remove his father's lackeys from positions of power, specifically those, like the high priest, who had been involved in the eagle incident. As the Passover festival approached, both sides entrenched: Archelaus refused to give in, while demands became more insistent.

During the festival, the king sent out troops to temper what was becoming increasingly ebullient mourning for the two rabbis. Grief escalated, a riot ensued and, according to Josephus, some 3,000 people lost their lives.[20] To this background of civic unhappiness, Archelaus prepared to travel to Rome to claim his throne.

Varus headed south to meet Archelaus before he set sail. This time the governor landed in Caesarea Maritima, later the Roman capital of Judaea.[21] What Shanghai was to the China of the 1920s, Caesarea was to Judea: a westward-looking melting pot of commerce and money. Although it was a new city – it had been twelve years in the building and had been finished only six years previously – the population had already grown to 100,000. Varus arrived at Sebastos, a massive 16-hectare dock, even larger, according to Josephus, than Athens' harbour, the Piraeus.[22]

Although only a tiny amount of the site has been excavated to date, it is already possible to get an impression of the city's majesty and beauty. Mosaic pavements flanked by marble columns of every possible colour – from Italy, from Greece, from Egypt – lined the streets. In front of Varus as his ship passed through two massive, 60m-wide breakwaters, he was faced with the Temple of Augustus, raised on an artificial mound. The discovery of a metre-long, white, marble foot gives some indication of the size of the two statues that the temple housed.

More prosaically, but much more importantly, the wall of warehouses along the southern breakwater, each 30m long, was the city's economic engine. Analysis of amphorae containing traces of garum, the ubiquitous Roman fish sauce, wine and olive oil as well as manufactured goods such as nails, testifies to the health of the city's commerce, while the presence of Chinese porcelain is a witness to its reach.

It is a sign of the governor's equanimity that Archelaus boarded a ship for Rome accompanied not only by his rivals but also by a delegation of diplomats who were demanding the incorporation of Judaea into the empire. History does not relate what the heir presumptive thought of this even-handedness, though he must have been less than impressed. With Archelaus en route to Rome, Varus might have been forgiven for believing that he had bought himself a few months' grace. It was not to be. The empire was faced almost at once with a danger that emerged neither from Archelaus' heavy-handedness nor even from outside the empire: it came from Sabinus, Varus' own financial officer.

'A shining example of the self-important minor official' in the words of one modern historian,[23] Sabinus had proposed the impounding of Herod's entire estate – his money, his property and his fortresses – while the will was being debated. Varus forbade this until Augustus had passed judgement on the Judaean question. As Archelaus set off for Rome, he and Sabinus headed down from Caesarea Maritima to Jerusalem, where Varus secured certain points in the city and garrisoned it with a legion before returning to Antioch.

The moment that the governor's back was turned, Sabinus countermanded his commander's orders, set himself up in Herod's palace in Jerusalem and tried to commandeer his other fortresses into the bargain. Using the troops that Varus had stationed there as well as his own gang of thugs, he attempted to round up as much of Herod's money as they could find. Aside from the fact that he was countermanding a superior's orders, it was a stunningly insensitive move on Sabinus' part, one that would have immediate and violent repercussions.

On the eve of Pentecost, what was obviously a revolt began to play out. Crowds, nominally pilgrims, began to converge on Jerusalem even from outside the kingdom, from as far away as Idumaea to the south and Galilee to the north. This was an organised uprising. The rebels blockaded the city and took up three strategic positions: one group to the north of the temple; one near the palace in the west; and the third to the south. Sabinus found himself not only blocked in; he was isolated from his troops which were stationed on the citadel.

With a growing realisation of the danger he was in, Sabinus sent a stream of messengers to what must have been a deeply irritated Varus, first requesting, then begging for help. In the meantime, Sabinus signalled to the legion to try and push through to the Temple.

Initially the Romans received the worst of it. Although the legionaries made it through the lines as far as the Temple, the Jews caused heavy casualties when a large number climbed on to the roof of the colonnade round the Temple enclosure and bombarded the Romans from above. Only by setting fire to the portico did Sabinus turn the battle in his favour, after which his troops ransacked the Temple.

The sacrilege was enough to strengthen resistance against Rome, and when Sabinus refused the offer of safe passage out of Judaea for himself and his legion, he was besieged in the palace, impotently awaiting Varus.

The debacle at the Temple alone was a diplomatic disaster that would have tested any governor, but the situation that Varus faced was much, much worse than this. Sabinus had triggered a full-blown civil war. The majority of Herod's troops had sided with the rebels – worryingly 2,000 of Herod's veterans in south-west Jordan revolted, converting eventually a further 8,000 to their cause – on top of which the region seemed suddenly to be swarming with claimants to the throne: at least three were recorded.

Varus gathered his army at Ptolemais, now known as Akko. He had brought two legions and four cavalry battalions with him from

Syria and picked up some 1,500 heavy infantry as he passed through Beirut. Fortunately, either through Sabinus' dispatches or more likely from other intelligence sources, the governor had realised the severity of the revolt and had also mobilised Roman allies, who were ordered to bring troops. It does not require too much inter-pretation to realise that the enthusiasm of their attendance had as much to do with hatred of Herod and his family as obedience to Rome.

Dispatching some of his men to secure Galilee and to protect his rear, which they did rapidly and efficiently, Varus marched south with the majority of his men. As a commander, Varus showed his strengths in the march south. He was aware that if he was to have any chance of maintaining the *pax Romana*, then this had to be a clinical campaign. It could not be a free for all that would alienate the population further. He purposely skirted round the city of Sebaste, now Sabastiyah in central Palestine, which had kept itself out of the revolt. The troops there had remained loyal to Rome and so were left in peace.

Varus soon began to find some of his allies more of a hindrance than a help. The two towns the army had camped by en route to Jerusalem had been sacked in the search for booty by his Arab allies. 'Fire and bloodshed were on every side and nothing could be done to halt the pillaging of the Arabs,' writes Josephus.[24] This was hardly the way to capture the hearts and minds of the locals, and so the governor was forced to send them away. After a brief side-journey to Emmaus, which he had burned both in revenge for an ambush on his troops earlier and to secure his flank, he approached Jerusalem from the west.

The capture of the city was almost an anti-climax. Such was the reputation that preceded him, and the size of the army that followed him, that the Jewish forces simply 'melted away'.[25] The rest of the campaign was a straightforward clean-up operation. Ringleaders were arrested and dealt with – some 2,000 prisoners were crucified round the city – and the rebels in south-west Jordan eventually surrendered. Before he headed back to Antioch, Varus sent them to Rome to be dealt with. As for the hapless Sabinus? The last that history records of him is that, rather than face Varus, he headed out of Judaea on a ship.

There is no doubt that the governor's management of what the Talmud calls 'Varus' War' was exemplary from Rome's point of view. His reactions were decisive and quick. He was enough of a tactician to secure his lines of communication and was never caught between enemy forces. Modern sensibilities may flinch at the harsh and punitive manner in which rebels were treated, but if anything this would have endeared him to Augustus. To give some sense of perspective, 2,000 crucifixions would not have seemed excessive compared to the 6,000 crosses and remains of the followers of Spartacus which had lined the Appian Way from Capua to Rome within living memory. In Varus' favour he showed compassion when it was justified and expedient from a publicity point of view.

Following his return, history loses Varus for much of the next decade. His marriage to Vipsania had hitched his fortune to that of Tiberius and with the future emperor in self-imposed exile, it is tempting to read into this that Varus' star was also in decline. A more prosaic reason may be simply semi-retirement. But if he was under a cloud, then it did not last long. Within a few years of his return, in around 3 BC, Varus married for the final time. Wife number three, Claudia Pulchra, was the daughter of another of the emperor's nieces and it confirmed Varus' status within the imperial inner circle. It also signalled a shift in the balance of power in Varus' favour. As well as Augustus' niece, Claudia was also a cousin to Agrippina, whose husband, Germanicus, had just been adopted as the emperor after next.

In AD 6–7, Varus received what was to be his final posting. Now in his late fifties, yet again he relieved Gaius Sentius Saturninus, as he had done in Syria, who had been seconded to assist Tiberius with the campaign against Maroboduus. With five legions, Legions XVII, XVIII and XIX and Legion I Germanica and Legion V 'The Larks', under his command and numerous auxiliary units, some 60,000 men in total, Varus was now in control of Germany. Of what was he actually in charge? Was the region perceived as a province at this time or was it deemed to have the potential to become one? Some, like the eminent historian Herwig Wolfram, believe that a province existed only 'on the papyri or the wax tablets of Roman administrators'.[26] It is a political nuance that is much debated, but it is ultimately insignificant if we are looking at Varus' actions.

A governor's power in his province was practically unlimited. Needless to say this gave him ample scope for corruption. The most high-profile case in recent Roman memory was that of Gaius Verres, famously prosecuted by Cicero in 70 BC. Romans had lasciviously soaked up every tabloid detail of the way the former governor of Sicily had demanded bribes, looted works of art and executed provincials and Roman citizens at will.

Augustus had instituted a number of changes from the status quo under the Republic. Governors were now put on the payroll, supposedly removing the need for administrators to line their own pockets quite so shamelessly. There was also much greater accountability. Contact between Rome and the provinces improved beyond all measure with the expansion of the imperial post. But the behaviour of governors appears to have changed little. The position remained a way to pay off debts and to supply a comfortable pension. One of the leaders in the Pannonian revolt blamed the uprising on the governor. 'It's your fault,' he said to Tiberius. 'You send wolves to guard your sheep, not shepherds or dogs.' Varus himself was charged with financial aggrandisement in Syria. 'He entered the rich province a poor man, but left it a rich man and the province poor,' writes Velleius Paterculus sourly – a charge possibly more aphoristic than accurate.[27]

A governor managed a large staff. In a semi-official capacity, the sons of friends and younger relatives will have petitioned Varus in Rome to be on his staff; for them it was useful experience and a step up onto the political ladder. As well as this, his staff would have been swollen by a retinue of bureaucrats, messengers, slaves and soldiers on secondment. We know at least something about his senior officers. Varus had three legates as deputy-governors, who were predominantly occupied with military affairs. Two of them played significant, if very different, roles in the months to come: Lucius Nonius Asprenas and Gaius Numonius Vala.

Asprenas, Varus' nephew, was the perfect imperial legate. It may seem odd that he sat so firmly on the coat-tails of his uncle, but that was a conventional way of advancement. He was born in around 28 BC but, as is so common, nothing is known about his early life. His wife, Calpurnia, was from a good family and politically a good match. It is not attested anywhere, but it is impossible to imagine that he did not accompany his uncle to Syria, almost certainly as a military tribune. A curious note in Velleius Paterculus accuses him of being an immoral property speculator, appropriating the property and inheritances of those who had died at the hands of Arminius.[28] Although it is odd for Velleius to relate such a piece of gossip (that in itself gives it some credence), such rumours do not appear to have harmed Asprenas' later career. Now in his mid-thirties, he was posted by Varus to Mainz in Upper Germany to command Legion I Germanica and Legion V 'The Larks'.

Vala, the 'quiet and honourable man' presents a very different figure from Varus' slightly shady nephew. Without Asprenas' advantages of relation to the governor and connections to Augustus, Vala had a less straightforward career and was several years older then Asprenas, possibly in his early forties. He was from an upwardly mobile, if not well-known, family that originally came from the region of Campania, south-east of Naples. His father appears to have been a coiner of some repute. For more details we must turn to Horace, who dedicated one of his *Epistles* to him and mentions his 'substantial country estate'.[29]

His age would suggest that his command in Germany was not his first military posting. These were generally two to three years in duration, though it was not unknown for tours of duty to be extended in times of crisis – such as, indeed, the Pannonian revolt. This suggests that Vala was legate and in position before Varus and Asprenas appeared. In itself this is not surprising. It is unlikely that a province's entire senior command vanished on the promotion of a new governor and some continuity of command is to be expected. It is a theory that was given a boost in the mid-1990s when archaeologists began to discover Augustan coins of this period which were countermarked 'C VAL'. Vala was well-enough known both to bother doing this and for the mark to carry weight – something that is unlikely if he had just appeared in Germany.

Going down the chain of command, while nothing is known of Asprenas' camp commanders in Upper Germany, we know that Vala commanded three camp commanders in Lower Germany: Lucius Eggius, Ceionius and Lucius Caedicius. The precise status of the camp commanders, the *praefecti castrorum*, has been comparatively little studied, but their position was based on management of the camps rather than on an attachment to any one particular legion. It is for this reason that Lucius Eggius and Ceionius were both marching with Varus at the time of the disaster. One would have been commander of the summer camp, while the other, at the time of the battle, was preparing to take over some of the forces when they returned to winter quarters. Caedicius himself was in charge of Haltern, preparing the camp for the arrival of the rest of the legionaries in mid-September.

As for Varus' legions, the history of the three ill-fated brigades before the events of AD 9 is frustratingly obscure. The only one we have any idea about is Legion XIX, which appears to have been associated with advances on the northern frontier from the time of Drusus onwards. An impressive iron catapult-bolt, 5cm long, was found at Döttenbichl in southern Bavaria in the early 1990s clearly stamped 'Leg XIX', which places its legionaries there at some point.[30] It is possible that the legion was stationed at Dangstetten on what is now the Swiss border, after the Alps were opened up in 15 BC, though the evidence of a small bronze label found at the camp bearing the number XIX is rejected by some. The legion could have policed the road between the Great St Bernard pass to the Rhine, although it is impossible to reconstruct its movements in anything other than the most sketchy form.

A point often forgotten is that not one of the main historical sources mentions Legions XVII, XVIII and XIX by name in connection with the battle itself; they only mention that three legions were lost. That Legion XVIII was involved is confirmed by the 1.4m-high gravestone of Marcus Caelius, found near Xanten where he had probably been stationed. Set up over an empty grave by his brother Publius, it pictures Caelius in full regimental honours

– five medals on his armour and honorific oak leaf crown, gained for saving the life of a citizen – flanked by two of his slaves. In his hand he holds his centurion's staff, on each wrist he wears a bracelet and on his shoulders are ceremonial rings. The epitaph reads:

> To Marcus Caelius, son of Titus, of the Lemonian district, from
> Bologna, First Centurion of the Legion XIIX, 53 years old.
> He was killed in the Varian War. Let his bones
> be buried here. Publius Caelius, son of Titus,
> of the Lemonian district, his brother erected this.

Although there are dissenters who doubt whether this refers to the Battle of Teutoburg Forest at all, it is generally accepted as such. We know about Legion XIX's involvement from an indirect allusion in Tacitus' *Annals*. He mentions that the brigade's eagle, 'which had been lost with Varus', is found.[31]

Not a single reference to an Augustan Legion XVII, either literary or epigraphic, has ever been found. Both Julius Caesar and Pompey the Great had legions of this number. Coins are also comparatively common of a brigade called Legion XVII 'Of the Fleet' raised by Mark Antony. None of them are the army unit here, which was in all likelihood raised by Augustus in the early 40s BC. In fact there is no evidence at all that there ever was an Augustan Legion XVII. Its presence is attested, however, by its absence in later history from the numerical sequence of legions. Logic dictates that it be associated with its numerical compatriots.[32]

In short, the movements of the three legions before the Battle of Teutoburg Forest is little more than guesswork. The only thing we can say with some semblance of certainty is that they were based on the lower Rhine in AD 9.

Varus' chief duties as governor in Germany would have been first and foremost to secure the province militarily both against external and internal dangers. By all accounts he set to these tasks with great aplomb. He cracked down on crime and arrested robbers, soldiers were garrisoned in undefended communities when asked for, and security details were sent out to escort provision trains.[33]

His second task was the crux of what the empire was about and one of the sticks with which Varus has been beaten by history. He had to introduce the *lex provinciae*, the Roman Empire's code of law. The Roman Empire was always much more about taxes than it was about paved roads and underfloor heating. Varus did introduce a tax system. 'He exacted money as he would from subject nations,' writes Cassius Dio.[34] It is, however, not an especially illuminating passage. The method of assessment, even the speed with which it was carried out, are not mentioned. We are left merely with the impression that the Germans did not like paying taxes, which hardly puts them in the minority.

Along with taxes came the more formal introduction of law and order, proper Roman laws that were the foundations on which a province could be built. Varus seems to have thrown himself into the task. Did he really think, as Florus suggests, that he could tame the savages 'by the rod of a lictor and the proclamation of a herald'? Clearly he did. It is an intriguing insight into the process of Romanisation that the governor led by example. Velleius Paterculus complains that he wasted the summer of AD 9, time that should have been spent on campaign, in holding court and observing the proper details of legal procedure.[35] For Velleius, the trappings of civilisation led Varus into a false sense of security. But as a cavalryman by both training and temperament, Velleius was always more comfortable in the army camp than in the law court. Sitting in session was exactly what Varus was supposed to do.

Varus' third task as governor was by far the most sensitive and follows on from the last point. Control of a province had to be, to a large extent, indirect. It would have been impossible for the Romans to have managed every aspect of every region in the empire without the trust and cooperation of the locals. Governors, therefore, relied heavily on the communities within the province. The challenge was that in less developed parts of the empire, like Germany and Gaul, the people they had to convince of the benefits of the *pax Romana* were tribal. And the best way that the empire had found of doing so was by encouraging urbanism.

Popular belief has it that Varus was in charge of a 300km mili-
tarised zone between the Rhine and the Elbe, one that was barely
touched by man, let alone civilisation. The country was wet in the
north and windy in the south. It was 'either covered by bristling
forests or by foul swamps', as Tacitus snippily dismisses it.[36]
Nothing could have been further from the truth. There had been
a deep and consistent policy of urbanisation that had gone much
further than the *cannabae*, the civilian shanty towns that developed
near a Roman camp, with their pottery manufacturers, wine shops
and brothels.

Most obviously this can be seen in the way that Cologne was
being groomed and moulded into a civilian capital. A shrine for all
of Germany, the Altar of the Ubii, the *Ara Ubiorum*, had been set
up in around 1 BC. Similar to the one erected eleven years previously
by Drusus in Lyons, this iconic focus for Roman Germany had been
built by Lucius Domitius Ahenobarbus. Neither representation nor
description exists, and no archaeological trace has yet been found,
but from images of its sister shrine in Lyons, it is likely to have been
a rectangular altar flanked by Victories on facing columns. What
was important, though, was the very fact of the altar. It projected
the image of Rome and the emperor; it brought the barbarians into
the fold, but with priests who were German.

Alongside the spiritual was the temporal. Elsewhere in the city
there was quite clearly some hefty building work going on. The
6.5m stone-built structure called the Ubiermonument on the banks
of the Rhine, which can still be visited, has been dated to AD 4–5
by dendrochronology. Although its exact role is debated (it has
variously been described as part of the city fortifications and as an
uncompleted mausoleum), the oak-pile foundations covered with
20cm of concrete leave no doubt as to its intended permanence.

Given Cologne's strategic position it is possibly not so surprising
that it was being built up. But excavations since 1993 at Waldgirmes, in the Lahn valley, east of Koblenz, and at Haltern along
the River Lippe, east of Xanten, show that urbanisation was being
pushed beyond the Rhine. Both sites were abandoned in AD 9 and
therefore provide a snapshot of how far Roman urbanisation had

developed up to and during the governorship of Varus. 'Cities were being founded. The barbarians were adapting themselves to Roman life, were becoming accustomed to hold markets, and were meeting in peaceful assemblies,' was Cassius Dio's description. Along with Tacitus' allusions to 'new colonies', traditionally these comments have been dismissed as fictional exaggerations, but archaeologists over the past decade have proved that the Roman historians were telling the truth.[37]

Waldgirmes, in the state of Hesse, is situated only 2km away from what was probably one of Drusus' marching camps at Dorlar. In the late 1990s the foundations of a stone structure were uncovered at the site. Most military camps at the time were primarily made of wood. But what caused the sensation is that, as the 2,200sq-m structure emerged from the soil, it began to look unmistakably like a forum – the heart of Roman civic life. There is evidence here of a clear and deliberate shift from conquest to direct rule.

Although less than half of the site has, to date, been excavated, it is clear that this was a civilian, not a military settlement. It was a theory confirmed by the discovery of an advanced lead-pipe water system and a distinctly urban architecture – store fronts with porticos facing the street and traces of blocks of flats. Industry, too, has a distinctly urban flavour, with evidence found of the production of pottery and value items like statuary and metal objects.

But it is the forum that has justifiably excited archaeologists the most. The 54m by 45m half-timbered building was the heart of the town. A central court, dominated by a monumental gilt equestrian statue of which parts (to date almost a hundred) have been found, gave on to a long hall supported by ten pillars. This, in turn, led to three annexes, a larger, central, 100sq-m room, flanked by two slightly smaller apses, all three likely to have been part of the municipal administration. It compares favourably in size to similar dated fora in Astorga in Spain, Herdoniae in Italy and Les-Fins-d'Annecy in France.

Many of the other finds, the highlights of which include beautiful, multi-coloured glass gems and jewellery as well as the inevitable ceramics, are not just the familiar detritus of Roman provincial civilian life, but the indication of a certain level of prosperity. The amount of Germanic pottery that has been found (some 25 per cent – a massive proportion) suggests a fair amount of assimilation, a sign that German and Roman lived side by side.

The frustrating question remains that of when the town was founded. It is a matter of considerable debate.[38] Dates from the end of Tiberius' first pacification campaigns in 6 BC to as late as the start of Varus' governorship have all been posited. What is not disputed is that although in the end the town of Waldgirmes was to stand for only a short time, the settlement was quite clearly intended for permanence. When the events of AD 9 took the inhabitants by surprise, the town was undergoing a period of reconstruction.

Slightly further north from Waldgirmes, evidence from Haltern suggests that Waldgirmes was not an experiment. Although it is best known as a military site, it is the civilian settlement nearby that confirms the attempt at permanence seen at Waldgirmes. While it is clear that this had evolved out of the lean-tos of the colonists who followed in the wake of the army, an aqueduct with lead piping has been discovered, which suggests that the empire thought a proper water system a worthwhile investment. There are also clear indications that Haltern was turning into a manufacturing base. Entrepreneurial potters frequently and profitably set up businesses next to camps, but here it goes much beyond immediate local use. Samian pottery thrown by the same manufacturer has been found in Neuss, Cologne and as far away as Wiesbaden.

That the process of assimilation was not entirely one-way can be seen in the Main valley at the native German settlement of Gaukönigshofen in Bavaria. Excavations which have taken place since the 1980s have revealed not just the expected smaller metal finds, but a considerable amount of Roman pottery which can be dated to between roughly 5 BC and AD 9. Gaukönigshofen is close to the double legionary camp at Marktbreit, which marks the Roman route of advance east from Mainz, and the fort is quite clearly the source of the tableware, but there is no reason to suggest a hostile explanation for the appearance of Roman pottery in the village. This again implies a broader acceptance of Rome than has been previously suggested.

Seventy years earlier, the great orator Cicero had said that a great general needed four qualities: military experience, bravery, prestige and luck.[39] To date, Varus had proved that he had all of them. A career diplomat with significant military experience was exactly what the Romans needed in Germany. With reports of massive building programmes, altars being dedicated, towns being founded, it is no wonder that Germany was deemed all but taken. Now that imperial attention was on Maroboduus and then the Pannonian revolt, someone who could be trusted in the north was what Augustus needed. Whatever mistakes that Varus was to make in September AD 9, there is no doubt that he was the perfect man for the job.

THREE

Pore Benighted 'Eathen

The Romans had nursed a viper. By almost any possible standards, Arminius was a traitor and a turncoat. The revolt of the
Cheruscan chieftain should not be seen just as an uprising against
hated invaders of his country: it was the mutiny of a Roman officer
against his commanders. Yet how did this 27-year-old manage to
unite enough men to wipe out three legions, hold off the Roman
commander Germanicus, sent to punish him, and then defeat
Maroboduus, king of the Marcomanni?

Arminius' tribe, the Cherusci, dominated the area that roughly
corresponds to the southern part of the modern state of Lower
Saxony, between the River Elbe to the east and the Weser to the
west. The etymology of the name is uncertain, although it certainly
appears to be Germanic. The most likely explanation is that the
tribal name is somehow connected with the word *herut*, meaning
'stag'. Precise boundaries are not possible to pin down and would
have been meaningless to Arminius anyway. Apart from the general
difficulties in identifying a location from the description of classical
historians and geographers, the Cherusci are more difficult to pin
down than most. It also does not help matters that the ancient
sources do not distinguish between the Cheruscan homeland proper
and the wider territory over which they had influence.

Most of the writings that have survived locate the tribe in relation
to its neighbours. Thus for the second-century Egyptian geographer
Ptolemy, they appear to have been the western neighbours of
the Sugambri, with the Bructeri to the south-east.[1] North of the

Cherusci, in the vicinity of Lake Steinhuder, near Hannover, were the Angrivarii, and to the south, so Julius Caesar tells us, they were separated from the great Suebi by the forest the Romans called the *silva Bacenis*, the natural frontier that separated the north German plain from the south.[2] So topographically they appear to have been well protected.

Archaeological research in what was Cheruscan territory remains in its infancy. Because of the nationalist associations that grew up around Arminius in the nineteenth century and up to the Second World War, understandably little work has been carried out on native settlements in Lower Saxony in modern times. Most of the archaeology that has taken place has been of the rescue variety. Indeed up to 1996, only fifty-six settlement sites had been identified in the tribe's territory. The finds at Kalkriese have given research into the period a welcome boost and in recent years a picture has started to emerge of an area much more populous than originally thought. Some 201 settlements have now been found, some of which, such as Hehlen and Schwiegershausen, appear to point to a level of sophistication, though the field requires much more work.

But there is enough evidence to allow us to make some generalised comments. The Roman image of the German countryside was dismissive and patronising. These barbarians were not farmers. The Germans 'are much engaged in hunting; which circumstance must, by the nature of their food, be their daily exercise and the freedom of their life,' writes Julius Caesar. The Germani would rather pick a fight than plough the land and wait patiently for the year's produce, says Tacitus.[3]

In actual fact it was a significantly agrarian countryside based on crops and a wide variety of animal husbandry, predominantly cows, pigs and sheep. Goats and chickens appear less often. Palaeobotanical research can reveal what the countryside at the time was like. In the early Roman period, the plains to the west of the Cologne basin were being cleared to make way for cereal crops, while the grasslands and the heaths were being maintained for cattle. In what is now the state of Hesse, too, there are significant traces of cereal farming, specifically rye, and again some indication of the management of grasslands. This level of farming sophistication, the practice of techniques like crop rotation and fertilisation, does come through in some Roman writings, specifically in the *Natural History* by Pliny the Elder. He singles out the tribe of the Ubii for their techniques of fertilising farmland.[4]

It would be fair to say that the wide and varied German diet was not that far removed from the one of only a couple of generations ago. Beef and pork were meat staples (curiously, surveys suggest that fewer than 10 per cent of bones found on Germanic sites are from wild animals);[5] dairy products were common. Analysis of grains from pollen spectra gives evidence that there was a clear emphasis on barley, oats and some strains of wheat (primarily spelt, emmer and einkorn), while favourite vegetables were predominately peas, beans and lentils. All of this was supplemented with fruits and berries. It is an unresolved curiosity that while Roman settlers in the country grew fruits and spices, there is little evidence of these in German sites. We simply do not know if Germans did not want them, or if they were unable to maintain them.

The countryside was dotted with isolated farmsteads or clusters of farms. Other than occasional stone foundations here or a wooden portico there, the traditional architectural style of rectangular, timber-framed long houses with lateral entrances remained largely unchanged for the entire Roman period. Iron production, too, was both common and of as high a quality as that of Rome, something reflected in the legends that surrounded smiths in later times. Excavations of most sites that can be claimed to be villages show that they boasted their own smithies that churned out weapons, ploughshares and other farm equipment and nails.

Estimating the population of Germany in Roman times is an exercise in guesswork and no definite answer is possible. Nonetheless, it is possible to come up with a plausible estimate for population density by analysing the size of settlements and examining cemeteries. As a rule of thumb, the population of Germany was around a twentieth of what it is today, making it a comparatively populous region in the ancient world.

Nor would it be true to say that the ground was being tilled, crops were being managed and animals were being reared in isolation.

This was not just subsistence farming. The discovery of granaries, specifically in northern Gaul and along the lower Rhine, suggests surplus production. Again this is confirmed by the literary sources. The very first reference to Germans in Roman history dates from the writings of the philosopher and historian Posidonius from the mid-first century BC. Although it was originally fifty-two books long, little of his *Histories* has survived – only a couple of lines about the Germanic diet which are quoted by a later author.[6] But from the reference to their fondness for wine (given that grapes were not yet grown in Germany), it is clear that trading did occur.

Although the Cherusci are mentioned by Julius Caesar, they first assume an importance for Rome with Drusus' second campaign. In 11 BC he pushed through their territory towards the River Weser, an action he repeated the following year. Cheruscan reaction to these incursions is not clear, though Cassius Dio's report that Drusus 'pillaged everything in his path' suggests that there was some confrontation. The Cherusci, either not in a position, or not inclined, to fight back, appear to have reacted by withdrawing across the River Elbe. This would appear to be the event alluded to in Suetonius' biography of the Emperor Augustus, when he writes that the Germans were 'forced back to the far side of the River Elbe'. Two years on, the Cherusci can presumably be included in Dio's comment that 'all the barbarians except the Sugambri . . . made overtures of peace'[7] during Tiberius' campaigns in 8 BC.

Depending on the number of legionaries that the tribesmen were facing, Roman–Cheruscan encounters so far were aggressive or placatory in turn. There was little to distinguish them from the other Germanic tribes. It is not until the governorship of Lucius Domitius Ahenobarbus around the turn of the millennium that we have the first indication of a shift in status, or at least a shift in intent on the part of the Romans. Our only evidence is an opaque line in a fragmentary passage in Cassius Dio's history. 'Later, Ahenobarbus had transferred his headquarters to the Rhine, had failed to secure the return of certain Cheruscan exiles through the efforts of intermediaries and this failure had caused feelings of contempt for the Romans among other barbarian tribes,' he writes.[8]

It would be dangerous to concoct a political history from this, but some points do become clear. Ahenobarbus appears to have attempted to restore Cheruscan exiles. There is no indication whether this was a struggle to do with the broader Cheruscan relationship to Rome or whether some Cheruscans were trying to harness Roman might to solve an internal factional purpose. Nonetheless even though there is no indication of the status of these exiles it does suggest that different parties were at play in the Cheruscan hierarchy almost a decade before the revolt.

For the next three years, as discussed in chapter one, Germany was in the grips of a revolt. Although the Cherusci were players, they do not appear to have been prime instigators. Following Tiberius' campaigns of AD 4 (during which time Velleius Paterculus writes, 'The Cherusci . . . were again subjugated')[9] until the revolt of AD 9, the tribe appears to have been an ally of Rome.

A deliberate aspect of the policy of Romanisation and of conquest was the nurturing of allies among the local tribes. The Romans were doing it with the Cherusci, just as they had done with other Germanic tribes like the Batavians and the Ubians. Alongside steps such as the introduction of urbanism, which helped break down tribal affiliations and was discussed in the previous chapter, Rome promoted leading tribal leaders within Rome's imperial aristocracy. By recognising certain chiefs as allies, barbarians were flattered into becoming emissaries for the Roman way of life. It was a practice that first bound them to Rome, then made them dependent on her. The policy of treating Germanic leaders differently from their warriors both isolated them and distanced them from their own people. In the end, tribal leaders ended up having a stake in maintaining Roman rule. It was a remarkably refined form of divide and conquer.

With great perception, Tacitus himself describes the deliberate steps in this cynical game of political seduction. First of all there was the private encouragement and public aid to build the infrastructure of Roman life: temples, courts and homes. Healthy competition rather than compulsion was encouraged. Then both the Latin language and the toga became fashionable. 'Step by step they were led to things which dispose to vice, the lounge, the bath, the elegant banquet,' he writes with studied irony before famously concluding, 'all this in their ignorance they called civilisation, when it was but a part of their slavery.'[10] Of course Tacitus was here articulating policy with reference to the invasion of Britain. Nonetheless, Varus in Germany followed the same path as Agricola was to do on the other side of the Channel.

Though the obvious weakness of this policy was that the lounge, the baths and the banquets had to be perceived as of value, many chiefs were keen to take Rome's shilling. Numerous examples of what must have been diplomatic gifts have been found. The grave of a local king found near Musov in Moravia in 1988, only 35km north of the Danube frontier, reveals an incredible array of prestige goods, including eight bronze vessels, several of silver, a bronze lamp, two silver spoons, numerous other ceramic and glass items and, above all, a stunning bronze cauldron with the busts of Germanic warriors as handle attachments. In Hoby, on the Danish island of Lolland, excavations of the grave of a chieftain dating to the first century AD revealed a wonderful treasure, including two silver bowls that display the events of the Trojan War in relief. Most significant of all is the ornate seventy-piece silver dinner service known as the Hildesheim treasure, which was found in what was Cheruscan territory and is now on display in the Altes Museum in Berlin. Although its precise role as a gift is debated (for many years it was described as Varus' own dinner service), it is an indication of the richness with which native loyalty was bought.

The role that subsidies played should not be ignored either. Less subtle than diplomatic gifts, in some cases, the Senate simply opened its cheque book. Rome had used cash to shore up allied support in Republican times in the wars against Hannibal and it had also been part of Julius Caesar's foreign policy. More recently it had been used to great effect in Germany particularly. 'We rarely assist [the Germanic tribes] with our arms, but frequently with our money; nor are they the less potent on that account,' writes Tacitus.[11]

Despite what, with hindsight, may seem the obvious flaws of a strategy that centred on winning over the barbarians, it frequently worked. One of the tribes in north-west Germany around the River

Ems remained loyal to Rome throughout this period and beyond. The Ampsivarii chief, Boiocalus, was to suffer imprisonment by Arminius for his allegiance to Rome but remained true throughout —and for the next fifty years.[12] The fact that he was not deposed by either internal or external agents suggests that the majority of his tribe believed there was a distinct benefit to being on the side of Rome. This was hardly the Faustian pact that Tacitus depicts.

With the understandable emphasis on the political and the military, the other weapon at the disposal of the Romans has often been overlooked: they also had commerce. To begin with, the trade was to a great extent one-way. The Germanic tribes allowed Roman merchants in, not to buy from them, but to exchange war booty. The price of free movement was clearly the giving of elaborate gifts. This increasingly created a demand for Roman luxuries. Large numbers of bronze vessels, silver tableware, brooches, wine vessels and even statues have all been found in the graves of German chieftains. The breadth of finds – from Holland, across northern Germany and Scandinavia, into the heart of western Russia – is remarkable.

If trade was initially in one direction, this did not last long. All too soon, the Germanic tribes were trading in their own right and we begin to see a shift away from barter toward monetarisation. Tacitus specifically mentions that the Germanic people bordering Roman territory 'value gold and silver for their commercial utility'. He continues, 'They are familiar with and show preference for some of our coins.' This begs the question what it was that the money was used for in what was presumed to be a mainly barter economy. Yet as Malcolm Todd has written, 'it is increasingly difficult to resist the idea that Roman silver coinage acted as a form of primitive currency'.[13] The wide distribution of coin finds, not just along the Rhine frontier but as far away as the Volga, does suggest the beginning of a monetary economy, albeit a primitive one. In all likelihood, Roman sesterces were used to oil general business and social deals rather than as currency in day-to-day transactions. Certainly by AD 18–19 there was a Roman community deep in German territory in Bohemia, living off the earnings of trade and money-lending, and signs of a healthy import/export market.[14]

The Hermunduri, a tribe which occupied the land to the north of the Danube as far as Thuringia, showed an admirable early entrepreneurial zeal. 'They are the only Germans who trade with us not only on the river bank, but deep inside our lines in the brilliant colony that is Augsburg,' writes Tacitus.[15] It is hard to believe that they were the only ones. There were no governmental roadblocks to interfere with the development of trade, and commerce appears to have remained unregulated. It was not until the latter half of the second century that Rome began to take an interest and specific places for trading were established. How much business had grown by then can be seen in the remains of an especially large and well-preserved trading house, a structure 40m by 14m, found in the mid-1980s in the town of Walheim in Baden-Württemberg, south-west Germany.

So what did the Germans have to offer Rome? Apart from providing access to amber and enthusiastic consumption of Roman wine, other products of trade can be discerned from the philological evidence of Germanic loan words in Latin. What the Romans called *ganta* and *sapo*, for example – geese and hair-dye – were all highly regarded in Roman society. Agricultural produce such as animals, hides and meat were also staples. Take Feddersen Wierde, near Bremerhaven, a site occupied from the 10s BC to the fifth century AD, and some 250km from the Roman frontier. When it was excavated in the late 1950s and early 1960s, it became apparent that although the settlement's earliest phase had only five farmsteads, it looked after some ninety-eight stalls for cattle. This was clearly the hub of a cattle business tapping into what was presumably a lucrative Roman market.

But the commodity which, in many ways, can be said to have done the most to open up Germany was slaves. The use of slaves by German tribes is well documented by Tacitus and a flourishing trade with the Roman Empire emerged. For the Germans this killed two birds with one stone. To start with, it allowed them to gain valuable Roman possessions while at the same time getting rid of prisoners. The deleterious effect that this had on society as a whole was that in the long term, raids would occur specifically to acquire the prisoners to sell on. A similar pattern may be observed in the growth of raids among West African tribes following the arrival of the Europeans seeking slaves in the seventeenth century.

By the later Roman period, the Germans had learned their lessons in economics so well that they were exporting products that had previously been imported. From the second century onwards, the Treveri, who lived round what is now the city of Trier, began not only to dominate the local market in wine, but began to export as far afield as Lyons and Milan. The fourth-century Latin poet Ausonius, in a long paean to the Moselle, writes lyrically about the swelling grapes beside that river, and the remains of two huge warehouses by the Roman port on the Moselle are testament to the importance of the trade in the city. A wonderful carving on the Roman tomb of a wine merchant from Neumagen (now in the Landesmuseum Trier) shows the crew and a distinctly inebriated pilot steering a ship carrying four wine barrels.

This broadly, then, was the environment, the political and economic landscape into which Arminius had been born. As for the man himself, he is difficult to get close to. In many ways, we know more about the food Arminius would have eaten, the kind of house he would have lived in and the weapons he would have used. All of the personal information we have about him comes from Roman sources and not only every date but virtually every fact that will now be discussed has opposing interpretations. Even when some classical writers, like Tacitus, attempt a more balanced characterisation, the fact that it is filtered through Roman eyes, experiences and values magnifies the distance even further. As if this were not enough, what has to a large extent crippled any serious discussion of Arminius is the nationalistic undertones to his revolt that made him into a folk hero in modern times. The very lack of knowledge has allowed writers to project their own mores and ideals on to him. As the historian Dieter Timpe admits, in what remains the only book-length critique of Arminius, this 'has hindered the perception of history rather than facilitated it'.[16]

We stumble at the first hurdle. It is not known what name Arminius was given at birth. It is not even certain what he was called by the Romans, a subject that has been and is still much debated by linguistic historians. Given the convention that auxiliaries of the period generally took on the name Julius, it is plausible that he was called Gaius Julius Arminius. But a further dimension of puzzlement is added since, in the manuscripts that have come down to us, mostly from the ninth century, there is no universal agreement about the spelling of his name. Sometimes he is Arminius, sometimes Armenus. Transliteration from surviving Greek manuscripts does not help either: they retain the same confusion.

Nowadays not much credit is given to the theory that his name is a corruption of 'the Armenian', a nickname, so the argument used to go, that had been bestowed following a period of service on the eastern frontier. It is generally accepted that what has come down to us is a Latinisation of either a familial name or an honorific that he himself used. *Erman* or *ermen* is an old Germanic word meaning roughly 'the eminent' – not an implausible name for a boy born into the Cheruscan ruling elite. Certainly Germanic names were commonly transposed by Roman authors. For example, Tacitus calls Arminius' father Segimerus: the Latin suffix '-us' simply bolted on to the Germanic ending '-mer'.[17]

Slightly surer ground is found for Arminius' date of birth. Tacitus' comment that 'he completed thirty-seven years of life and twelve years of power',[18] in AD 19 suggests that he was born in roughly 18 BC, the year before the Lollian disaster and around the time that the Romans started giving serious consideration to the conquest of Germany.

What little is known of Arminius' background can be related in a few sentences. His father's name was Segimerus and he was part of the Cheruscan ruling elite. Although leadership in general in Germanic tribes was not by kinship – rather it was by an aristocratic oligarchy – the Cherusci give some indication of passing leadership down from father to son. Segimerus' other son, Arminius' younger brother, was called Flavus. Nothing is known of their mother, other than she appears to have been still alive in AD 16.[19]

It has been mooted that Arminius either came to Rome in his childhood as part of a diplomatic mission when his future father-in-law Segestes was given citizenship, or that he spent some of his childhood, like Maroboduus, as a blue-blooded hostage at Augustus'

Palatine School. While both of these are attractive thoughts, and not in and of themselves implausible, there is no evidence either for or against the theory.

It is known for certain that Arminius served in the Roman army, not as a private, but as an officer. From the time of Julius Caesar onwards, many Celtic tribes had supplied the Roman army with auxiliary units. In AD 15 and 16, we know that the Chauci and Batavians, among others, bolstered Germanicus' forces, while even earlier than this, it is known that an Ubian unit fought for Tiberius. There is little doubt that this was a condition of being an ally of Rome. Following the peace treaty that Tiberius signed with the Cherusci in AD 4, the tribe must have been expected to supply the imperial army with troops.

Tacitus states that Arminius 'served . . . as commander of his fellow-countrymen',[20] the senior officer of an auxiliary corps. There is still debate over how formal the auxiliary unit that Arminius led was. The Latin phrase that Tacitus uses (*ductor popularium*) suggests something rather more ad hoc than either a cohort or a cavalry unit but this is only guesswork. The tone of the historian's words may simply be a reflection of the troops Arminius commanded – that they were an ethnically homogenous unit – rather than any kind of slight on the commander's status. While the nuances continue to be debated, what is certain is that Arminius' service record was significant enough for him to have earned not just coveted Roman citizenship but equestrian status.

More than that, we can broadly work out where it was that Arminius saw service, predominantly because he appears to have served with Velleius Paterculus. From the historian's own statements we know that Velleius started his career in Thrace and Macedonia. After stints in Achaia and Asia he served in an eastern campaign against the Parthians and then in Yugoslavia and Germany. Velleius being a few years older than Arminius, it is apparent that the only time that the two could have served together was during the Pannonian uprisings, either after AD 4 or possibly between AD 6 and 8.

We should consider for a moment the status of native soldiers like Arminius who fought with the Romans. It was perfectly normal for the Romans to use native troops, as indeed they did throughout the history of the empire. Primarily they were used in auxiliary units of 500 or 1,000 men, either as lightly armed infantry or as cavalry units. But there is a distinction between units that were recruited from conquered territory and those men who were volunteers. The former were draftees with the same twenty-five years of service ahead of them as legionary recruits. The latter wanted the money and it is to this latter group that Arminius belonged.

Much in the same way that the Gurkha regiments have a relationship and reputation within the British army, so, too, German units had military cachet. They were even used as the emperor's personal and private guards in the early principate, from Augustus to Nero. They were perceived as loyal because they were removed from Roman politics. And so it proved. Their commitment to the cause was seen most clearly in their – admittedly unsuccessful – attempt to protect the Emperor Caligula from his murderers, and their efficiency in maintaining order thereafter.

But a willingness to use them in the military context does not indicate any sense of integration. Just as 'Fuzzy-Wuzzy' was sketched by Rudyard Kipling, so, too, Arminius would have been seen as 'a pore benighted 'eathen but a first-class fightin' man'. Roman prejudices were too ingrained to accept a barbarian as an equal in almost any sphere outside the military. Examples are legion. The Emperor Augustus appointed a Gaul named Licinius as one of the province's financial officers. Even after Licinius had been cleared in an imperial investigation for fraud and mismanagement, he remained on a watch-list because he exhibited 'typical barbarian greed'.[21] This cultural intolerance was still entrenched centuries later, when the future emperor Julian the Apostate wrote a letter to the Senate in Rome naming his cavalry commander Nevitta as consul for AD 362. That Julian was in revolt against his cousin Emperor Constantius II, they could forgive; that he wanted to appoint a German to the Senate, they could not.

The Romans may have resisted this, yet on the German side what is apparent is the desire to integrate. So strongly does the desire to hang on to both Germanic traditions and Roman customs come across, that what may be observed may almost be termed cultural schizophrenia. This can be seen in the burials of auxiliaries of the period. A series of four graves was found in Goeblingen-Nospelt in Luxembourg in 1966. What is known as Grave B dates from between 25 and 15 BC. In it were found weapons (a long, iron sword and elaborately decorated scabbard), riding equipment and a bronze cauldron, all of which are wholly native. But the large amount of Roman tableware, including a bronze Roman wine service, shows how much Roman culture was valued. Another grave, from Putensen in northern Germany, which dates to roughly the time of Arminius' revolt, is of a 30-year-old auxiliary cavalryman. He was buried with the physical manifestations of his relationship with the Roman world; his weapons – short sword, spear and shield – and his spurs are a poignant indication of the status that Roman service conferred upon him when he came home.

It can be seen even more clearly in the images on gravestones. That of an auxiliary called Firmus which dates from the middle of the first century AD is wholly Roman. He is armed in the traditional Roman manner, with a long sword, a couple of spears, a dagger and an oval shield. His slave Fuscus is portrayed wearing a toga, standing, much smaller in scale, at his left foot. Yet the inscription underscores his tribal roots: 'He is Firmus, son of Ecco from a cohort of Rhaetians belonging to the tribe of the Montani'.[22]

Around AD 7, though possibly following the conclusion of the Pannonian war, Arminius left Roman service to return to his homeland. What prompted the move of this – in Velleius Paterculus' backhanded compliment – 'young man of noble birth, brave in action and alert in mind, possessing an intelligence quite beyond the ordinary barbarian'? It is not outside the realms of possibility that Rome had interfered to encourage Arminius' return to act as some kind of standard bearer, an intermediary with the Cherusci.

This is not as shocking a suggestion as it might seem at first. The Romans had a long tradition of manipulating Gaulish and Germanic accession. After all, it is precisely this that Ahenobarbus had attempted and failed to do seven years previously. There is also some elliptical literary evidence of a treaty with the Cherusci at this time.[23] If Varus was attempting to speed up the Romanisation of the province, it made sense for him to want around him as many as possible allies and senior Germanic voices who were perceived to be pro-Roman. The point to bear in mind is that Rome will not have been remotely perturbed either by Arminius' return or his elevation. Why should it? Why would someone who had seen civilisation, tasted its fruits, been promoted within its aristocracy and understood how it worked ever possibly turn his back on it?

While the importance of Arminius to the Romans at the time is clear, the benefits of Roman service to the future Cheruscan leader should not be passed over. Above all, it had allowed Arminius to know his enemy. At its most basic level, from service with the legions, Arminius had become fluent in Latin. His linguistic skills were much better than serviceable. He was comfortable giving speeches in the language.[24] Much more importantly, he had learned how the Roman army worked, seen its tactical innovations in action and had clearly begun to think about how to counter them. Inevitably the emphasis of the majority of archaeologists and historians, indeed this book, is on the conflict between Germany and Rome. Here it is true that the German tribes appeared to be at a disadvantage. But of course for the most part, warfare of the period involved Germans fighting Germans – conflicts which have left no mark on history. Although the Germanic tribes were familiar with the heavier weapons of the Romans, these were never adopted in any wholesale manner. A reason for this may be seen less in any innate technological conservatism, but more in the style of warfare they were used to. Arminius' strength as a tactician and strategist was to find ways of using the very different Germanic manner of warfare to beat the technologically advanced Romans.

How innovative Arminius was can be appreciated if we look at the conventional native style of warfare. The weapon of choice was the light spear, both a throwing and thrusting weapon. Tacitus' detailed description will have been as terrifyingly familiar for a legionary in Julius Caesar's army as for one in Varus' legions, as indeed it was for Ammianus Marcellinus and his colleagues in the fourth century. Military equipment used by Germanic tribes appears to have changed little throughout the period of the Roman occupation and contact. This consistency is a great help to the historian, as the paucity of remains from one period is helped by those from another.

Few use swords or heavy lances, writes Tacitus. 'The spears that they carry . . . have short and narrow heads, but are so sharp and easy to handle that the same weapon serves at need for close or distant fighting. . . . The infantry have also javelins to shower, several per man, and can hurl them to a great distance,' he continues.[25] His observation that they could be thrown a great distance is corroborated by the fact that slings have been found, dating to the pre-Roman Iron Age and from the second and third centuries, to help propel them.

Physical evidence from graves as well as pictorial evidence from reliefs supports this description. Wooden shafts that have been found range from 1m to 3m in length, while the iron heads on average are 20cm in length. In a recent survey of Germanic graves, spears alone appear in 365 cases, shields alone in 339 cases and the combination of the two together in 162 cases.[26] While Tacitus' description is intended to compare the equipment of the Germans with the much more technically advanced kit of the Romans – it is obvious that to him the Germans are not only lightly armed, they appear poorly armed – their weaponry was much more appropriate for the type of warfare that they fought. Speed and agility were favoured over assembly-line pressure.

The failure to mention swords is not an oversight on Tacitus' part; expensive and rare as they were, it is not until the second century AD that they were available in any number at all. In the best weapons cache that has been found so far, dating from the fourth century and discovered in Jutland, we see 60 swords, compared to 200 javelins and 190 spears.[27] They appear to have played a comparatively minor role in combat. This is hardly surprising, given the nature of intertribal warfare. An unarmoured man with a sword and a shield is rarely going to come off better against a man with a spear. This is not to say that they did not exist at all. As mentioned above, some of those whose remains have been found clearly used the legionary short sword as their model and there are some signs of innovation, for example a short, one-edged slashing weapon.

The main protection for the Cheruscan warriors was an ornate shield 'marked with very choice colours', so Tacitus tells us.[28] It is a fact confirmed by archaeologists. Six shields have been found in Scandinavia decorated with faint traces of paint – half with blue, the others with blue and red paint. They were much lighter than Roman models. From the evidence of illustrations on graves, they were made in a variety of shapes and were covered in leather with large metal bosses in the centre, so that they could be used as a defensive weapon as well as for protection.

The question of armour is one that needs to be addressed. Tacitus does say that warriors were 'naked' or 'lightly clothed in a little cloak'[29] and the image of the naked barbarian warrior has remained with us since Roman times. Did Arminius' troops or indeed any Germanic tribesman actually fight in this manner? Practical considerations aside, a quick survey of Roman art in the western Roman Empire suggests that nudity was a convention of heroic art rather than an accurate reflection of what really happened.

Two themes appear most commonly. The first shows barbarian prisoners as captives – inevitably chained, sometimes standing, sometimes hunched down in despair. On a well-preserved statue base, now in the Landesmuseum in Mainz, two Germans, their hands tied behind their backs, strain at the chains round their necks. Grim-faced and naked apart from small cloaks, the two men are pulling in opposite directions. The second image is more martial. Here, reliefs often show a horseman rearing over a prostrate and naked barbarian. It is a theme that can be seen on Rhine gravestones (there is a particularly fine one in the museum in Wiesbaden, that of the cavalryman Dolanus) and as far west as Scotland. The Bridgeness slab, one of the largest and most elaborately carved records found in Britain, was erected by Legion II 'The Emperor's Own' to celebrate the completion of a section of the Antonine Wall in the AD 140s. Here, three naked barbarians lie on a ground littered with weaponry; the fourth barbarian, futilely trying to flee, is on the point of death. A spear shaft is already sticking out of his back; he has spun round in pain, stumbling on to one knee as the Roman cavalry officer, red cloak billowing behind him, raises his determined spear ready for the final kill.

In actual fact, it seems as though German warriors fought wearing trousers and a short cloak, as can be seen in less stylised represent-ations, such as on Trajan's Column in Rome. A more detailed look at the literary evidence backs this up. The Latin word that Tacitus and other writers use is *nudus*, which can indeed be translated as 'naked'. It is after all where we get the English word 'nude'. It can also, however, be translated as 'without armour', which is almost certainly the sense intended. To the Romans, going into battle with-out armour was as good as going in naked. It is not until the fifth century that we find evidence of German use of protection in battle. Then we begin to see the emergence of what is called the Spangen-helm, a conical armoured helmet, often with hinged cheek pieces and a nose guard. Certainly in graves which date to the time of the Battle of Teutoburg Forest, armour is almost completely unknown.

Aware as the Cherusci themselves will have been that they could not defeat the Romans in an open battle, and conscious of recent defeat after defeat, it is easy to understand the enthusiasm with which the tribal hawks latched on to Arminius. Of course, the insights that he brought would have had appeal and even if Arminius had no thoughts of betraying Rome when he returned, it is not difficult to see that he might have been turned soon thereafter.

Arminius may have had a cachet because of his Roman experience but he was not universally welcomed. It is clear that at the time of his return there were at least three factions, or perhaps more accurately, two other nobles vying for influence in Cheruscan politics: Segestes, Inguiomerus and Arminius himself, all three of whom had significant followers. An additional frisson is added, in that all three were related to each other either by blood or by marriage.

Arminius of course represents the anti-Roman point of view. His uncle Inguiomerus wavered between the two parties. Initially he appears to have been pro-Rome, yet after the successes of AD 9 he came over to Arminius' point of view. That allegiance seems to have lasted as long as the threat of Roman reprisals for Teutoburg Forest was real. Thereafter, Inguiomerus was confident of enough influence to speak out against Arminius during the campaigns against Germanicus and in the end he was to betray him.

Segestes remained consistently pro-Rome, views diametrically opposed to those of Arminius. The influence and support that Segestes continued to command is a sharp reminder that Arminius was not leading a universally popular rebellion. The older man comes across as a pragmatist; a Ulysses to Arminius' Achilles. Certainly he was far-sighted enough to recognise the advantages of being considered an imperial friend and ally (the Romans had a technical diplomatic term for people like this – *socii et amici*), and that the offers of citizenship and money to flash should not be rejected out of hand.

Theirs was a relationship that was dripping with dramatic conflict. On one level it was an ideological struggle between pro- and anti-Roman points of view; on another it was between accepting the status quo and challenging law and order; on yet another it can be seen as the conflict between generations; and finally it represented a bitter personal estrangement. After the battle, Segestes' daughter Thusnelda eloped with Arminius while betrothed to another man.[30]

The depth of the rifts within Cheruscan society are personified in the career of Arminius' younger brother Flavus, who followed a much more conservative or orthodox career path. So much so, in fact that, it should be noted that we have no trace of his original Germanic name. His name in Latin is descriptive and means 'the golden-haired one'. The divide between the two brothers is, of course, heightened for literary reasons by Tacitus; however, it highlights not just a family disagreement, but the rift within the Cheruscan hierarchy itself over a relationship with Rome. Not only did Flavus serve with Tiberius (he lost an eye in one of the campaigns after the Teutoburg Forest), he remained loyal to Rome throughout the events of AD 9 and later saw action with Germanicus in his campaigns against the Germanic tribes in AD 15 and 16. Over the years, he had risen through the ranks from the position of private to centurion and was eventually to retire to Rome in some comfort, married to the daughter of the chieftain of the Chatti. During the reign of Claudius, the Romans foisted Italicus, Flavus' son, Arminius' nephew, on the Cherusci. That he was welcomed as chieftain says much about the reputation of Rome; that he was sent off with 'a present of money' says much about Roman understanding of what counted.[31]

Above all what this speaks of is that there was no unity in Cheruscan politics. How did Arminius stay on top? The answer is military might. What kept Germanic society together in the earliest times was the common interests of territory and resources, but what held the tribes themselves together was primarily strong military leadership. Arminius' real power and status rested with his soldiers. Success on the battlefield conveyed status. For the chieftain, loyalty was based on, and grew or declined in relation to, success in battle. As Tacitus succinctly points out, 'The chiefs fight for victory, the companions for their chief . . . fame is easier won among dangers and you cannot maintain a large body of companies except by violence and war.'[32] It was a status that can only have been augmented by the military sophistication conferred on him by having fought for Rome.

The crux of the matter is, why did Arminius revolt? Cassius Dio gives two reasons. First of all, he writes, the Germans were given orders 'as if they were actually slaves of the Romans'.[33] The disadvantages of the change in status from being a friend of Rome to a conquered nation would have been immediately apparent to Arminius and his men. Cheruscans would now have to fight as troops, subject to Roman discipline and conditions rather than as mercenaries. The perceived loss of freedom would have been a difficult and unpalatable pill to swallow.

But it is the second half of Dio's explanation that is the important one. 'Varus exacted money as he would from subject nations,' he continues. It was about the money. Taxes would have hit the tribe hard. More financially sophisticated parts of the empire, like Egypt, had long been used to taxes. Roman rule simply meant the replacement of one payee with another. No matter whether tax had to be paid in cash or indirectly in goods (for example Drusus had arranged that the Frisii pay their taxes in ox hides),[34] the less-developed parts of the empire received a sharp lesson in economics. And as provinces were pretty much self-running, all expenses, such as salaries, building and garrison costs, had to be paid for the province from itself. Naturally in a fledgling province these sums could be high. Furthermore, taxes were likely to increase as the province developed. There was the danger that the bill for roadworks, for buildings and for towns would land in the laps of local worthies. Not only would the Cherusci suddenly have found themselves in the position of having to pay money out, but as they were comparatively wealthy – the tribe's loyalty to Rome had been encouraged with denarii for the last few generations – it was Arminius and his men who would have to carry the strain of these new tariffs.

Resentment would have been fuelled by the continuous presence of the Roman army in their territory. Of course, economically there were some benefits, especially for local businessmen and for nearby villages which supplied the camps with food, manufactured goods or services. The assurance of the first-century orator Dio Chryostom that troops in provinces were like shepherds who guarded the flock of the empire must, however, be taken with a hefty pinch of salt. More plausibly, the poet Juvenal satirises the difficulty in bringing soldiers to court or even getting anyone to testify against them. 'Who is such a friend that he would set foot inside the walls of a military camp?' he asks.[35] It might be a point exaggerated for comic effect, of course, but if it was one that was recognisable in Rome, it would certainly have been even more so in the front-line provinces.

Given this armed presence, it would be surprising if stories of army corruption had not come down to us. In fact, what evidence we have points to widespread, institutional brutality. Threats, extortion, theft and blackmail were common. A private set of accounts dating from the second century sets out:

To the soldier on duty:	2 drachmae, 1 obol
Gift:	240 drachmae
Suckling pig:	24 drachmae

To the guard:	20 drachmae
For extortion:	2,200 drachmae
To two police agents:	100 drachmae
To Hermias, police agent:	100 drachmae
To the [. . .]:	100 drachmae.[36]

For the unnamed man to list his extortion payments so blatantly is an indication of how endemic the problem was. And while we have no direct corroborative evidence from Germany (the above is from the eastern half of the empire), it is safe to assume that the Roman soldiers were not at their most sensitive in the young province after years of warfare.

It was precisely this lack of cultural awareness that lay behind numerous native revolts in the early empire, a fact that points to an inherent weakness in Rome's policy towards the barbarians.[37] It is useful to compare Arminius with, for English speakers, the best-known native revolutionary – Boudicca, the queen of the Iceni. The parallels are quite remarkable. Britain in AD 60, like Germany, had passed the initial phase of Romanisation. The Iceni had been exposed to Roman culture and military occupation for the past twenty years but, as was the case with the Cherusci, taxation and Roman brutality were the triggers for a widespread revolt. Just as pertinently, the British governor Suetonius Paulinus massively under-estimated British discontent, much in the same way that Varus had.

If the issue of why it was that Arminius revolted is straight-forward, the two difficult questions that it opens up are considerably more problematic. Answers can only be tentative. The first concerns the reason behind the timing of the Cheruscan revolt. Certainly with the benefit of hindsight, and even at the time, it should have been apparent that it would have been easier to attack the Romans at almost any other moment in the previous three years. Not only was Varus new to the job in AD 6, but from the spring of that year onwards, Augustus and the empire were distracted by events further south and the Pannonian revolt. A strike against the Romans could well have caused untold damage to the west as a whole. Plausible answers are that Arminius was still finding his feet as leader and consolidating his power or that Roman taxes had not yet begun to bite.

The very fact that Arminius' plot was revealed to the Roman high command suggests that his anti-Roman stance was not entirely popular. It does not matter whether it was self-interest or pragmatism that had kept them loyal to Rome for the past few years, but many, like Segestes, were clearly happy to become stakeholders in a Roman government.

We enter even choppier waters when we consider what it was that Arminius was trying to achieve at this moment. Did he even have something as specific as the liberation of the Cherusci in mind? On the various occasions in the previous generations where there had been revolts, the Romans had always returned in force. It would do Arminius a massive disservice to underestimate him; by no stretch of the imagination was he a stupid man or a bad tactician. After his experiences in the Roman army itself, he was aware that whenever a tribe attacked Roman troops, the imperial reaction was inevitably fast and brutal.

The broader ambitions that emerged after Varus' defeat do not yet come into play. Any consideration of this is coloured by Tacitus' flattering, yet flawed epitaph that Arminius was the 'liberator of Germany'.[38] This is too Roman a perspective. As was to become apparent, Arminius did lead a confederation of tribes against Varus, but neither he nor his allies would have presumed that he spoke for them or indeed had any authority to command them beyond the immediate engagement at Kalkriese. He certainly cannot be spoken of as liberator of a broader geographic area that would have meant little to him. If we look at the geographical reach of Arminius' campaigns, he never went across the Rhine. Doubtless the German historian Harald von Petrikovits is correct to suggest that his aim was simply 'against Roman intention to set up a province between the Rhine and the Elbe'.[39]

Whatever the answer, Arminius must have spent the spring and summer of AD 9 plotting and planning his revolt, at times cajoling and convincing both allies and members of his own tribe to join him. For the Romans, part of the horror of the episode is that, all through this, he stayed close to Varus. According to Cassius Dio, Arminius 'often shared his mess'.[40] Who could consider that a man, a friend who had broken bread at your table could be conspiring against you? Like a good magician, his skill was in misdirection. But by the time the harvest was in and as the evenings began to draw in, all of the pieces were in place. Now Arminius could attack.

FOUR

This Terrible Calamity

P. Quinctilius Varus spent the end of August closing up the summer camp at Minden on the River Weser, a few kilometres downstream from the historic Minden Gap. Contemplating the narrow defile known as the Porta Westfalica, where the river quits the mountains and enters the North German Plain, he had no reason to think that it had been anything other than a successful season. The process of turning Germany into a province appeared to be on track and there had been no military action to speak of. Now, everything had to be packed up, the inevitable civilian camp as well as the military one. Supplies had to be double-checked, accounts settled and business closed for the year before the army headed back to Xanten.

In actual fact, it is not known exactly where Varus had been based that summer, though more than a few have suggested Minden. Like so much about the battle, there is little agreement, either ancient or modern, about what Velleius Paterculus calls 'this terrible calamity'.[1] There is not even any consensus about whether Varus and his men were marching west–east or east–west. Some have him marching towards the Rhine, some away from it. There is even a minority, if a vocal one, which refuses to accept the thesis that Kalkriese is the site connected with the ancient accounts of the loss of Varus' legions at all.[2]

So although it is possible to piece together a plausible account of what happened as Legions XVII, XVIII and XIX stamped towards the abyss, there are discrepancies between all of the classical historians that go well beyond their personal biases. Tacitus describes the battlefield but not the battle; Velleius Paterculus gives a considerable amount of background to the events and Florus adds colour. Only Cassius Dio gives us the details of the battle itself. All of them are wise after the event and none of them were there. Any one modern historian's account can be only a reconstruction selecting elements from the versions that have survived; like a police sketch, the evidence – literary and archaeological – can come up with different answers.

Varus had spent the summer of AD 9 on the minutiae of provincial governorship. It was the setting-up of governmental infrastructure, day-to-day diplomacy, a drudge of community patrolling and escort duty – all that went with a new province. There had been no sign of trouble all summer and the governor had little reason to expect any now.

Some days before departure, Segestes had come to Varus with a ridiculous and outlandish tale of intrigue and treachery. Arminius and some co-conspirators were plotting to overthrow Roman rule. The Cheruscan demanded that the plotters be thrown in chains immediately or at the very least that the governor be on his guard. Varus rejected these demands out of hand. The old man was paranoid, hysterical even. There was no truth to this slander of his relatives and friends. 'After this warning there was no time left for a second,' writes Velleius Paterculus rather piously.[3]

In one sense, only the harshest critic would have no sympathy at all with Varus for rejecting Segestes' warning. He and Arminius had been constant companions throughout the summer. The Cherusci were not only allies and had given no sign of resenting the Roman yoke, but Arminius himself was a well-respected and integrated leader. He was a friend. His brother was a ranking Roman officer. Even Segestes' son was working for the Romans – a priest at the Altar of the Ubii in Cologne. It was not just that Segestes' tale sounded implausible; to him the warning must have appeared a ploy to involve the Romans in some sort of an intra-tribal dispute. Little surprise that, much in the same way that he had refused to act as arbitrator between Antipater and his father, so, too, Varus refused to be drawn in and intervene here.

In another sense, however, Varus can be damned for misinterpreting his intelligence. That Segestes came to the commander suggests that he had what can loosely be called a counter-intelligence network of his own. The Romans had no compunctions about using spies and they did so on a regular basis. Varus himself had used the intelligence services in quelling the revolt in Judaea, thirteen years previously. Painting Arminius' father-in-law as 'M' may be stretching a point, but there is no getting away from the fact that Segestes, either on an official or unofficial basis, had collected what he knew to be important strategic data, analysed it, and come to the conclusion that a revolt was brewing. Varus' failure here was not one of intelligence per se. He knew about the revolt. Where the commander fell short is in not understanding what he was told.

While the burden for the tragedy that was about to play out must inevitably be shouldered by Varus, this distraction of, and narrow emphasis on, the rejection of Segestes' intelligence report in the classical historians hides a much broader Roman blunder. Varus not only misunderstood the extent to which Germany was in any sense pro-Roman or even pacified, he completely failed to appreciate the potential for unity among the Germanic tribes. The degree to which Augustus was at fault here is rarely considered. Had the emperor and the Senate begun to believe their own propaganda that Germany was essentially a province? 'It was a miscalculation of massive proportions, caused by incomplete intelligence on several levels,' writes one modern military historian.[4] The dinners, the close comradeship, indeed everything that was to take place indicates that the idea of betrayal never once crossed Varus' mind.

The trap was sprung with a finesse bordering on genius. Arminius had organised an uprising within the fledgling province to draw the Roman army out. This was a manoeuvre requiring knife-edge precision. It had to be a significant enough incident for Varus to feel he needed to lead the army personally to put it down, but not so serious a revolt as to awaken suspicions either that this was a trap or that it was a precursor to a more concerted national uprising. Arminius' plan was to ambush the Romans en route when they were off their guard. He reckoned that they could be overpowered easily while marching through what they believed to be friendly territory.

Frustratingly, Cassius Dio does not mention which tribe it was that served to draw out the Romans, though it is possible to suggest a plausible candidate. Some may be discounted straight off, as they never broke their oaths of loyalty to the empire. The Ampsivarii were one of the few that were to remain loyal to Rome throughout the revolt; indeed their chieftain was to end up being arrested by Arminius for refusing to join him. The Chauci, whose territory was the north-west German coast, were in a similar position. They had been soundly beaten by Tiberius. Thereafter, during the campaigns of Germanicus, they even supplied support troops to help him. The Batavi, a tribe which occupied the area at the mouth of the Rhine around the modern town of Leiden, had supplied the emperor's personal guards since AD 5 and were used as a base for Germanicus in the campaigns of AD 16, so they can probably also be discounted. It is a similar story with the Frisians, who occupied the modern Dutch provinces of Friesland and Gronigen.

That leaves us with the Chatti, the Bructeri and the Angrivarii. The Chatti, whose homeland pretty much corresponds to the modern state of Hesse, certainly had no love of Rome. They had been perennial thorns in Drusus' side and there is no doubt that they did take part in the rebellion. In fact, they were the first of the tribes to suffer Germanicus' wrath in AD 15, but they do not appear to have been the Germans alluded to here. Their territory was simply too far south for Varus to risk marching on them.[5]

The last two tribes are plausible suspects. Like the Chatti, the Bructeri certainly took part in the uprising and had been consistently staunch opponents of Rome. Based in the general area of the town of Münster, between the Ems and the Lippe, the tribe was in the ascendant at the moment. Although it had been nominally defeated in a naval battle by Drusus, and then again by Tiberius a decade previously, it was a staunch ally of Arminius and played a leading role at Teutoburg. Even Germanicus' campaigns were not enough to quell the tribe's revolutionary tendencies. It was a prime instigator in the uprisings that shook Germany in AD 69–70. At the end of the first century, Pliny the Younger was still able to refer to the Bructeri as 'savage people'.⁶ Again, however, it remains unlikely that they caused this diversionary uprising. Kalkriese is too far north from their territory and a geographically implausible march for Varus to have made.

The Angrivarii remain the best guess. It is credible for Varus to have marched on their territory, which was predominantly between the Weser and the Elbe, just north of the modern town of Hannover. The tribe's identity is confirmed if Arminius' tactical imperatives are considered. As the Angrivarii were to the north of the Cherusci, Arminius' troops did not have to travel far and so there was little risk that the Romans could have suspected what they were plotting. The final corroboration is that the Angrivarii were one of the major objects of Germanicus' wrath.⁷

As the Roman legions marched out, heading north-west, they had no inkling of what was to come. Varus was later to be criticised for not maintaining tactical integrity as he marched, for not ordering the army to march in a state of full war-readiness. The train was scattered with civilians, men, women and children from the camp. As with so much that was written at the time, it is difficult not to see this as wisdom after the fact. It was a march through friendly, not hostile, territory.

Nonetheless, the sight of the Roman army in full marching order, stretching out over some 8 to 10km, must have been an impressive sight. Lightly armed auxiliaries and archers marched first. Their role was to act as scouts, to identify any potential trouble spots and to neutralise them. It is likely that Arminius was part of this vanguard. Certainly it made sense to have those who knew the landscape and the routes go first, to check that all was clear before the army came through.

After some heavy infantry and cavalry, which would act as support troops for the archers and auxiliaries should the van be attacked, came the engineers and a number from every legion, carrying flags. The engineers would work to make sure that the army could proceed as easily as possible, removing logs, cutting down trees, building or rebuilding bridges over rivers and marshland. The army was marching along country paths, not paved, cambered Roman roads. The flag-bearing legionaries were those who would mark out the camp in the afternoon. They had to make sure that the camp had access to firewood for legionaries, fodder for the horses and water for both. They had to take topography into consideration (so that a freak storm did not result in a river flowing through the camp) and strategy was a factor too.

Then came Varus himself, along with his senior commanders, those like Numonius Vala, his deputy, and the camp commanders, Lucius Eggius and Ceionius. To protect what was the heart of the army, the senior officers were shielded by select infantry and cavalry, the best of the best. Traditionally, the senior officers were followed by mules dragging the artillery, as they would have been here. The presence of catapults is attested by a number of bolts that have been found on the field.

Next came the bulk of the army, led by the ensigns bearing the standards. These eagles were the spirits of the legions: 'The king, and the strongest of all birds, which seems to be a signal of dominion for the Romans and an omen that they shall conquer all against whom they march,' in the words of one Roman contemporary historian.[8] The Roman legionaries marched six abreast behind the trumpeters, many wearing the new, segmented armour called *lorica segmentata*. Familiar from recent Roman motion pictures like *Gladiator*, this was a technological innovation which allowed the soldiers both more flexibility and protection. It was also noticeably lighter than the ring armour worn up to now; 9kg, compared to 16kg. Their centurions, among whom we know the names of Marcus Caelius and Fabricius, marched behind them to keep an eye on their men.

The bulk of the army had now passed. An eyewitness who waited around would have seen slaves leading the mules that carried the soldiers' baggage and then more infantry and cavalry units protecting the rear, ready to give warning against any ambush from behind.

The subject of how many men Varus had with him on his fateful march has been endlessly debated. Velleius Paterculus states that 'three legions, the same number of divisions of cavalry and six cohorts' were involved.[9] At face value, that would give a figure of around 18,000 legionaries, some 900 cavalry and a further 3,600 allied auxiliaries. That would account for the figure of 22,500 men which is commonly bandied about. It is of course, at this distance of history, impossible to know what the actual numbers were. Troop figures in the ancient world are notoriously unreliable.

But it is extremely unlikely that all, if any, of the battalions were fighting at full strength. The interim strength report of a cohort which was found at Vindolanda camp on Hadrian's Wall, dating to the end of the first century, gives food for thought. The document says that the first cohort of Tungrians from northern Gaul was 752 men strong, commanded by 6 centurions. Written in business-like Old Roman cursive script, it paints an illuminating picture of the disparity between the paper strength and the actual strength of a unit. Of those 752 men, 46 were on secondment to the governor of Britain's guard; 337 men and 2 centurions were at Corbridge, another camp on the Wall; and 1 centurion was in London on business unknown. It is impossible to read where the others were, but in the end, there were only 296 men left in Vindolanda under 1 centurion – of whom 35 were unfit for duty, either ill or wounded. That leaves 35 per cent of the men on active service. This state of affairs was not exceptional and is corroborated by a daily report on a detachment of soldiers found on an ostracon in Bu Njem in Tripolitania in the third century. Of the fifty-seven men stationed at the fort, over half were away on exercises, sick, or seconded to other projects.[10]

Certainly, logic dictates that this was the normal state of affairs and none of this seems especially extraordinary for any army before or since. If one considers that some of Varus' soldiers were out on patrol or policing duty in other parts of the province, even if one adds in the non-combatants who tagged along – women, children and slaves – a total figure for those who set out from Minden of under 14,000 would be well within the realms of possibility.

Towards the end of the day, Arminius and his auxiliaries, Varus' vanguard, begged to be excused. As part of the advance team, they needed to get away, they said, to mobilise other tribal auxiliaries in support of the general and to clear the way for the Roman army. Again, while those hostile to Varus have seen his acquiescence as a negligent move on his part, it was procedurally common to allow the advance guard to go ahead to smooth the passage of the army. The general was perfectly well aware of the need for reconnaissance in territory like this and as his intelligence sources had failed to give him any advance warning about the tribal uprising, it was reasonable for him to expect Arminius to bring back more-detailed information about what was actually happening on the ground. The problem was that the person he chose to act as scout, to inform and to warn him was the person plotting to attack and kill him.

As Arminius and his Cheruscan auxiliaries rode away from the Roman army, the moment came for the German to cross his Rubicon. The die was now cast. He had thrown off civilisation and his commanders. For the historian Edward Creasy, Arminius' soul was burning at the thought that his tribe would be forced to yield to these 'debased Italians'. That is probably a fairer reflection of anti-Catholic tendencies in nineteenth-century England than first-century Germany. But to what extent was Arminius pondering his destiny? Did he take the fate of the Gaulish revolutionary Vercingetorix into consideration, who surrendered to Julius Caesar and was then ignominiously paraded through Rome like an animal? Or of the numerous other Germans who had set themselves up against Rome?

Arminius rendezvoused with his fellow conspirators who were waiting nearby. Although, by the end of the revolt, many, indeed most, of the tribes of Germany were involved in the uprising, at this point we can be confident of only three: the Cherusci, the Bructeri, mentioned above, and the Marsi, a much smaller tribe which lived south of the Lippe and east of the Rhine.

With Arminius heading off in the late afternoon, it was time to build the camp, the first one seen by Germanicus' men. 'Varus' first camp with its wide circumference and the measurements of its central space clearly indicated the handiwork of three legions,' writes Tacitus.[11] Still, as centurions posted sentries, as the cavalrymen saw to their horses and as the legionaries erected their tents and ate their rations, there is no indication that they were under attack or expected to be. It was the routine of a large army on campaign; it was the calm before the storm.

The attack came the following afternoon. Varus could not know how widespread or perfectly choreographed the revolt was already. The detachments that had been sent to the various communities had already been massacred. According to Roman accounts, the terrain was difficult; more mountainous than Varus and his legions were used to and much more forested. Forward detachments had been engaged in clearing a path for the army, chopping down trees and building bridges. The weather had worsened as they headed towards the Wiehengebirge mountain chain. The lashing rain and wind was quickly becoming a storm. The march slowed to a walk, then almost to a standstill, the storm front off the North Sea extinguishing both light and hope. The ground was slippery, then became muddy, causing wagons to stick. Forward movement became even more difficult as the tops of trees snapped off in the wind, blocking the path.

From *The Tempest* to *Wuthering Heights*, adverse landscape and weather have often been used as a literary device. Certainly it is not uncommon in the classical canon, especially in connection with a disastrous campaign at the edges of the known world. But while the difficulty of the terrain may well be exaggerated, as anyone who has visited northern Germany in the autumn knows, the account of the storms is very plausible.

The Roman force suffered its first defeat east of Kalkriese. To attack the Romans in their camp would have been folly and Arminius had waited for the legions to march out and allowed nature to begin to wear them down. The first assault came when the soldiers, tired, wet and anything but alert were beginning to think of rest and their evening meals. An attack from all sides surrounded the army in the forest. An escape route, the way they had come, had been blocked off. The question of how large Arminius' army was is complicated, but a guess can be attempted. With no reliable literary account as a starting point, it becomes a question of population density. Excavations on Danish islands suggests that 300 soldiers could be recruited from 1,500 people (some 15 villages of 10 homesteads, each with 10 inhabitants), the approximate population density for an area between 10 and 20km in diameter. Arminius could easily have massed an army 15,000-strong, drawing on a mere 750 settlements. While these figures are conservative, it is possible to detect a vague homogeneity in the figures in written sources that goes beyond literary topos. Julius Caesar mentions that Ariovistus' army numbered 12,000 men in the 50s BC. In the 270s AD, the Emperor Probus drummed a force of 16,000 Germans into his army, and in AD 357, the future emperor Julian faced a German army of 35,000 men near Strasbourg under the command of Chondomar, who had melded together six tribes.[12]

The sky, already black with storm clouds, darkened further as the Roman army was showered with German spears. With Roman cavalrymen protected by short-sleeved, hip-length mail armour, the obvious initial target for the Germans was the horses themselves. Arminius knew that in a confined space, cavalry is effectively useless. It is true that, when fighting at close quarters, cavalry have a height advantage, but with wounded animals slipping in the mud, rearing, throwing their riders, galloping uncontrolled towards their own infantry, the Cheruscan had realised what an advantage he could give his men. And any riders who survived would be a liability, their unwieldy swords and shields practically useless as they got in the way of their colleagues.

The Germans also knew that many mounts that were not either killed as the arrows buried and tore their way into them or dispatched by the Roman legionaries in self-defence would die soon afterwards. To all intents and purposes, this was a variation of germ warfare. At a time before immunisation shots, tetanus was one of the most dangerous threats to horses. The disease can take up to three weeks to incubate under normal circumstances, but just over a week is more common, a period that can be hastened to a day or two in battlefield conditions. Some sense of the scale of the problem this would give to the Romans can be seen by the fact that the aftermath of the American Civil War Battle of Gettysburg in 1863 required the removal of 2,250 tonnes of horseflesh.

In this time of mechanisation, it is easy to forget how important horses were. The cavalry units were probably mounted on German or Gaulish horses. These had been drafted into the Roman army for years. Although Julius Caesar dismisses them as 'poor and misshapen', that conclusion should be taken with a pinch of salt.[13] Horse breeding formed a crucial part of Celtic culture and in general their animals were praised for their speed and endurance. Attacking horses was an effective way to immobilise and demoralise an army and cause huge logistical problems.

The Roman troops could make no serious defence. Under normal circumstances, the cavalry would have been deployed as a protective fence with detachments on all sides. But this was impossible in a forest. And it was no easier for the infantry. They were also struggling because of the difficulties in the terrain and hampered by civilians and their baggage wagons. In the confusion and the rain, the number of casualties from friendly fire must have been high. It is curious that Varus appears to have organised his train so badly. Certainly it was one of the more serious criticisms levelled against him by Roman authors. 'The Romans were not proceeding in any regular order, but were mixed in helter-skelter with the wagons and the unarmed, and so, unable to form readily anywhere in a body, and being fewer at every point than their assailants, they suffered greatly and could offer no resistance at all,' writes Cassius Dio.[14]

Yet again, the answer lies in the level of Varus' faith in Arminius. We shall never know exactly when it was that the general realised how misplaced this had been. But certainly it was not quite yet. There was no need for Varus to insist on war-readiness, because he was marching through not just subdued, but actively loyal, territory.

Despite the assault and the shock that it caused, Varus maintained admirable control and presence of mind. He knew what he needed to do. He built a camp, of which sadly no trace has been found. Under normal circumstances, as with everything that the Romans did, there was a procedure to this. Ten men detached from each century carried coloured flags and marched in the front of the army. They were charged with identifying and plotting out a camp every afternoon, the coloured flags signifying the different areas of the camp; the gates, the commander's tent and so on. When the rest of the army arrived, they set to work digging the protective ditches and ramparts, hammering in the wooden palisade, all before meals or sleep could be contemplated.

Here, there would have been no such luxury. The enemy were all around. The cavalry and half of the infantry would have had to stand, battle-ready, protecting their colleagues digging the ditches, building the ramparts and erecting the palisades. Under normal conditions it took three to five hours to complete digging a ditch. Under these circumstances, with the enemy and rain, did they struggle through or did they cut their labours short? Tents should have been put up before work on the ditches and ramparts started, but one wonders whether, in the confusion of battle, this was done.

A sign of how serious the attack was is that Varus insisted that the baggage train be burned or abandoned along with everything that was not strictly necessary. But there is no reason to think that Varus believed that his army would not survive at this stage. He had bought himself a brief respite. There was little chance that the Germans would attack a Roman camp directly. As the senior commanders met that evening to form a plan of action, it is likely that they agreed to aim for a river, where the army could pick up transport to take it to Haltern and then down to Xanten.

The next morning, one day after the attack, the Romans left their camp and began the march towards the oak-covered slopes of the Kalkriese Berg. Arminius will have known with moderate certainty that this was the general direction his opponent would take. It is wrong to suggest that the Romans were being herded in this direction. The point is that there was no need to lure the Romans to their doom or force them into the corridor: they were always going to come this way. It was pretty much the only option open to Varus, where the main west–east routes from the mid-Weser to the lower Rhine converged, avoiding more difficult terrain to the north and the south. Indeed, until 1845 this was one of the main routes through the area and it is preserved on maps up to that time as the Alte Herrestraße – the Old Military Road.

Generally speaking, however, although there was woodland, it was farmed and cultivated rather than wild and ancient forest. This now was not the landscape of thick, dark oaks that the more hysterical ancient commentators mention. The obsession that modern historians have with trying to reconcile the Teutoburg Forest that Tacitus mentions with the landscape could plausibly be the result of a misinterpretation. As has been explained above, while the phrase that the Roman historian uses, *Teutoburgiensi saltu*, can indeed be translated as 'Teutoburg Forest', it may also be rendered 'Teutoburg Pass'.[15] At times, Varus would have looked out to see a damp, agrarian landscape not unlike the Fens of England. It had been farmed for millennia, while wetter, marshier areas were a source of pasture or used for timber. When looking at landscape like this, Tacitus' comment that the Cherusci were 'experienced at fen-fighting'[16] begins to make sense.

As they came round the Kalkriese Berg, the Romans were approaching a narrow pass called the Kalkrieser-Niederweder-Senke, the mountain rising up 110m above the pass to the south, the Great Moor to the north. It would be difficult to think of a more perfect spot for an ambush, now accented by the archaeological traces which let you see how the deceit was accomplished. The analogy has sometimes been used that it is like a lobster pot that allowed the Romans in, but not out. The Kalkrieser-Niewedder-Senke is a narrow corridor, some 6km long and only 1km wide. But because of the high water table at the time, it was only passable at the edges, on the ridges of sand that had accumulated, 200m or so wide. At the same time, with the nearest Roman relief forces some 100km to the south, there was no chance of the alarm being raised.

Varus and his men had been harried all the way. The Germans saw no moral virtue in standing their ground against heavily armoured Roman legionaries. Instead, the constant attack then retreat of the Cherusci began to take its toll. But the losses the Roman forces suffered there were minimal compared to the hell that was now unleashed as they marched into the pass. This is also where archaeology begins to add another dimension to our knowledge. This is the site that has been found. Arminius attacked again, this time with the full weight and anger of the forces with him.

The Cheruscan commander had had the opportunity to line the pass with arc-shaped turf walls and sand ramparts that curved with the shape of the hill. Three have been found to date, with a total length of 400m. Speed was of the essence for him and his troops. From the construction and variety of materials used it is clear that they were built quickly with anything that came to hand (turf predominates where there were meadows, sand at the eastern end, and a mixture of turf, sand and limestone at the western end), all of which suggest that the work had taken at most a few weeks to complete. The style of build of the walls is peculiarly Roman; indeed when they were first discovered it was thought that they were rapidly constructed Roman defensive positions. Arminius had learned the lessons of Rome well.[17]

Despite the speed and crudeness with which they were constructed, these walls were massively effective. Some 4 to 5m wide at the base – something you can work out easily by measuring the space between the drainage ditches that had been dug on the German side and the start of the Roman finds – they were not much more than 1.5m high, though in all likelihood this was raised by a palisade.

It goes without saying that the ramparts did have a defensive role. And as just mentioned, on the inner side, facing the Germans, there were drainage pits. Given the weather, the pouring rain, these must have been significant in the hours before the ambush was sprung, as the natural clay in the soil will have stopped natural drainage. But the walls' primary purpose was offensive. Arminius knew that if his men could attack a fragmented Roman tactical formation, they could beat it. For the Cherusci this was less about matching the Roman *gladius* than 'out-psyching' the legionaries. The forest might help the tribesmen achieve surprise, but it was the basic organisation of the column that needed to be shaped and then ruthlessly exploited. Not only did the very construction of the walls preserve the element of surprise for the Germans, it also managed to narrow the path, to guide the Romans into the dampest, most difficult part of the pass, where the legionaries could be massacred when the Germans leapt out through the gaps they had left in the walls.

It was now that the worst of the fighting took place and the greatest Roman casualties occurred. If the human remains that have been found at Kalkriese provide only a very narrow snapshot of the thousands who died, then it is a terrifyingly high-definition one. Virtually all of the human remains that have been found are of men of military age, between 20 and 40 years old. All of their deaths come from offensive weapons, many of them from sword cuts.

The Roman soldiers were cut down all too easily. Floundering through the pass it was impossible for them to form the impregnable legionary lines that had seen off Hannibal and numerous other enemies. Just as had happened on the previous day, the cavalry units hindered rather than helped. In trying to mount any kind of defence, let alone attack, both types of unit got entangled, crashing into each other. It is possible that Numonius Vala's troops did not even fight on horseback. It was not unknown in forests for cavalry to dismount and fight on foot, certainly in an extreme situation like this. Their disorganisation made it even easier for the German forces.

Arminius may have convinced his warriors of the benefits of Roman ambush techniques, even of using swords, but in terms of tactics it was a different matter. Here the native traditions had the advantage. Speed and agility were what counted and the chief hope of victory was a rapid, overwhelming attack. Could he have convinced them even if he had wanted to change their approach? That is doubtful. The indiscipline of the Germans might have been as much of a recognised literary theme as the softness of the Syrians, but it was their lack of restraint that made it so successful.

A Roman historian who had himself fought the Germans, describes what Varus and his men would have been up against in those first moments: 'The Germans rushed forward with more haste than caution, brandishing their weapons and throwing themselves on our squadrons of horses with horrible grinding of teeth and more than their usual fury. Their hair streamed behind them and a kind of madness flashed from their eyes. Our men faced them stubbornly, protecting their heads with their shields and trying to strike fear into the foe with drawn swords or the deadly javelins they brandished.'[18]

In the face of this assault, there was no time to draw on any of the known and trusted techniques to avoid ambush. Army training recommended that soldiers feign fear and pretend to run away before regrouping. Here, though, their terror was real. They had nowhere to run. They could not re-form. Roman remains behind the wall in the drainage ditches suggest that some legionaries did go on the offensive, scrambling over the top to get at their attackers. Certainly the earth rampart, built without wooden supports, began to collapse even during the battle. From an archaeological point of view this was fortuitous as it protected finds, but in the heat of combat, the disintegration of the walls added to the confusion.

The natural focus of the battle has been on the human element. But another dimension to our knowledge about the battle is added by the animal remains that have been discovered – the few mules that survived Varus' burning of the baggage train. The remains of a mule were found in 1992 – or rather its skull, vertebrae and shoulder blade – along with the pendants and decorative glass pearls that had fallen off their mountings, highlighting the close bond between owner and animal. The iron clapper on the bronze bell round its neck had been muffled with a handful of oats its owner had grabbed from a field while passing, to keep them moving as silently as possible. A tangible sign of the state of extreme tenseness of the Romans who had survived the first day's attack, it is also the analysis of the oats which has allowed archaeologists to date the battle to September. In the heat of battle the mule had broken free from its wagon, still wearing its metal harness, iron ring snaffles and iron rein chains. It fell in front of the wall, which collapsed on top of it, preserving the remains.

Another, almost complete, skeleton of a mule was found in 2000 at the western end of the wall. Frozen in the moment of death, its head facing west and feet south, jaws still clamped on the snaffle, the animal had tried to escape over the wall and broken its neck in the fall. The wall, there built of sand reinforced with sandstone, then collapsed on it, protecting its body both from plunder and from scavenging animals. As Susanna Wilbers-Rost writes, 'In Kalkriese, the collapsed wall has permitted the preservation of snapshots, which are otherwise discovered only rarely in archaeology.'[19]

But the series of finds is not limited to the foot of the Kalkriese mountain, as might be expected of an army trying to push its way through the pass to safety. Traces can be found branching off, away from the main army, in a 2km-wide strip that leads north-eastwards to the edge of the Great Moor. It is clear that one part of the army split off and tried to make a break for it along the sandbars through the boggy forest.

It is tempting to ascribe this attempt to Numonius Vala's flight. In Velleius Paterculus' account, Varus' legate, his deputy, did try to escape, taking the cavalry with him. It is always dangerous to argue from a lack of evidence but there are remarkably few traces of cavalry and horses at the foot of Kalkriese mountain.

Were Vala's actions cowardice and a loss of nerve or a calculated saving of skin? We shall never know. Paterculus, as a cavalry man himself, is damning, suggesting that Vala was deserting the legionaries, trying to reach the Rhine and the safety of the Roman zone. Certainly when Varus' deputy left, he was effectively deserting the legionaries. But it is also possible that he was acting on orders. The cavalry was proving a liability in the narrows of the Kalkrieser-Niewedder-Senke. For Varus to send Vala away might have seemed appropriate, though we are firmly in the realms of speculation here. Whatever the circumstances, he did not make it and his troops were slaughtered to a man. 'Vala did not survive those whom he had abandoned, but died in the act of deserting them,' writes Velleius Paterculus coldly.[20]

The fourth day since they had left Minden brought no let-up from the weather; if anything it got worse. The violent winds made throwing javelins impossible and rendered the surviving Roman archers useless. The legionaries could not even defend themselves properly. The rain had soaked through the leather of the heavy Roman shields into the wood, making exhausted and demoralised soldiers carry even more weight.

It was perfect weather, however, for the Germans. Given their light equipment, the rain and the wind if anything made their guerrilla attacks easier. They could pick off the enemy and quickly retire before the sodden Romans were able to react. Varus and his forces might have been exhausted – they had after all marched through the night – but Arminius was able to draw on fresh men keen for a fight. Overnight, the German ranks had been swelled by other tribes which initially had kept their distance, cautious about throwing their lot in with Arminius. Now, however, they had no such qualms. A much-weakened Roman army and the thought of plunder were enough of an inducement to overcome any misgivings.

Ranks thinned, surrounded by Germans, with even the weather against them, Varus and his senior officers took their final, unimaginably difficult decision. With ever-strengthening German forces and two eagles already captured, it must have been apparent now that the Roman forces had no chance of escape. They would never make it back to safety. The senior commanders were already wounded and there was only the question of how they would die.

Tales of Germanic blood rites were well known and only increased their desperation. Varus and his colleagues would all have heard how priestesses, dressed in white, met those unfortunate enough to be taken prisoner. These POWs would be crowned with wreaths and then led, one by one, to platforms suspended over great bronze cauldrons into which their throats would be cut. It was irrelevant that this dated back centuries. The story was still current, preserved at the time of the disaster in Rome by the Augustan geographer Strabo.[21]

What was worse, suicide or capture? Ceionius, one of the camp commanders, decided to surrender. His colleague, Lucius Eggius, the other legionary commander, had already died in battle. A wounded Varus decided to die by his own hands. Even this, the final gesture of the commander-in-chief, did not pass by Velleius Paterculus' jaded eye. 'The general had more courage to die than to fight, for, following the example of his father and grandfather, he ran himself through with his sword,' he wrote.[22]

In more modern times, Paterculus' comment has usually been reproduced without comment because it chimes with contemporary thoughts on suicide. To Christians, Jews and Muslims, it is a sin. Yet other Roman commentators were more understanding and sympathetic. For Cassius Dio, the action was 'terrible yet unavoidable'; for Florus it was 'noble'.[23] The reactions of all three to Varus' final action encapsulate the classical dichotomy with suicide. While impulsive suicide or some methods, like hanging or drowning, were condemned by Roman society, it was admired for reasons of self-sacrifice or to sponge away shame, just like Japanese *seppuku*. After all, Brutus, Cassius and Mark Antony had all committed suicide, as had, of course, Varus' father.

After their general's suicide, the surviving Roman forces lost all hope. There was no chance of escape. Some joined Varus in suicide, others took their cue from Ceionius and surrendered. The manuscript of Cassius Dio breaks off in mid-sentence, his account mirroring history. 'To flee was impossible, however much one might desire to do so. And so, every man and every horse was cut down without fear of resistance and the . . .'[24]

Arminius had won. The pass was littered with dead men. The few who groaned had passed away or been dispatched in the night. Roman legionaries lay individually and in groups in unnatural positions: their necks were bent back or their heads face forward in the mud. Even the ones who lay on their back were clearly not at rest. The surprise of death on their faces, they stared up at the bleak German sky.

As the battle was dying down, it was time for the mop-up operations to begin. Germanic troops looked to their wounds, tried to discover if their friends were alive and began the honours for their own dead. Their weapons were carefully collected. It was important for burial rites that a soldier's arms were buried with him, something that accounts for the lack of native weaponry found by archaeologists at Kalkriese itself. But for Arminius' opponent, not even the peace of death. Although the body of Varus himself had been partially burned and then buried by his adjutants, it was disinterred and mutilated by the vengeful Cherusci. The corpse was decapitated and Varus' head was sent as a trophy to Maroboduus, along with an invitation to join Arminius in his war against Rome.

Around this time, Arminius divided the eagles among his allies, rewarding those who had supported his campaign and supplied troops. In a last-ditch attempt to save one of the eagles, a Roman standard-bearer had wrenched it out of the ground, concealed it in the folds of his belt and thrown it and himself into the marsh. It was a futile gesture. All three eagles were captured. That of Legion XIX was given to the Bructeri, the Marsi were given a second and the Chauci received the third.

What is often ignored is the strong element of jihad in Arminius' crusade. The blood sacrifice of war captives has long played a prominent role in ritual and it was particularly prevalent in Germany. At the very end of the second century BC, the Cimbri were known for their dedication to sacrifice. They destroyed everything that they had captured. Clothing was torn to shreds and cast away, gold and silver were thrown into the river, any enemy armour was cut into pieces, the tack of the horses was broken up, the horses themselves were drowned in the river, and enemy soldiers were hanged from trees. 'No booty was allowed to the conqueror and no pity to the conquered,' writes the commentator. This practice continued for centuries thereafter. Around fifty years after the Battle of Teutoburg Forest, towards the end of the 50s AD, so Tacitus tells us, the Hermunduri and the Chatti went to war over ownership of a river that bordered their territories. Both sides vowed to sacrifice the enemy's army, 'a vow which consigns horses, men, everything indeed on the vanquished side', he concludes.[25]

Excavations in northern France at Ribemont-sur-Ancre and Gournay-sur-Aronde support these literary accounts and give an unpleasant insight into tribal sanctuaries. Although animal sacrifice was by far the most common ritual offering of the Gauls, the interior of the sanctuary at Ribemont-sur-Ancre revealed the skeletons of around 1,000 men. After their bones had been crushed to expose the marrow (it was believed that a man's soul lived in his bones), they were burned in open-topped ossuaries. A further element to this was the decapitation of the corpse so that the head could be kept as a trophy. Not one skull has been found at the site. If these were sites of ritual that placated and honoured the gods, they were also places that had a secondary role in warning off enemies. At Gournay-sur-Aronde, 2,000 iron weapons and pieces of armour have been uncovered, which were originally arranged as 500 suits of armour and displayed as trophies.

Although the above finds date from the fourth or early third centuries BC, similar cultic and martial elements are apparent in the way that the hapless Roman captives were treated after the battle. It was clear that the site of the victory was an appropriate spot for religious reverence even before the sacrifices. Although not architecturally formalised in the same way, with the construction of a temple, other elements do emerge, particularly in the details of the mutilation. The eyes of some legionaries were put out and then after their deaths, the Germans nailed their heads prominently to the trunks of trees. One of the legionary's last sights was seeing a German soldier cut his tongue out before holding it in his hands with the words, 'At last, you viper, you have ceased to hiss.' He then had the further ignominy of having his mouth sewn shut. It is one of two grotesque vignettes preserved by Florus. Despite the chronicler's love of tall tales, there is the sense that these anecdotes were passed down by one of the survivors. The other is the final heroic act performed by Caldus Caelius. Having witnessed the above, rather than suffer the same indignity himself, he seized a section of the iron chain with which he was bound and brought it down with such force upon his own head as to cause his instant death. His comrade who reported the story back mentioned that his brains and his blood gushed from the wound.[26]

Any hopes that Ceionius and other senior officers might have had that they would be spared or ransomed were soon dashed. In the adjacent groves the Germans soon set up their barbarous stone altars on which they had immolated tribunes and the first-rank centurions. That was the fate that awaited Marcus Caelius and Fabricius, if they were not already dead.

What was going on was the construction, or rather the reinforcement, of what was already a holy site in all likelihood to the Germanic god Donar. Though he was later to become Thor, at the time of the battle Roman authors associated him with Hercules and his cult was centred in the Weser basin. Kalkriese was being constructed as a memorial, as a spot to remember the defeat of the Romans. This is something that Arminius would have encouraged. He would also have been aware that this localisation of the battle would mean that he would be remembered as the leader. It is in this light that we should see the discovery of Kalkriese's best-known find, the 17cm-tall iron cavalry face mask that has become the logo of the museum and site. It stares blankly out of every book on the subject. Originally covered with silver leaf and belonging to auxiliary cavalry from Gaul or Thrace, it is the oldest preserved mask of its kind found so far, compared with other fine examples found in Vechten and Nijmegen in Holland. The feeling of intimidation experienced by every viewer who sees it is deliberate. It was almost certainly leant against the wall. The Germans would have no use for such a ceremonial piece of armour and, after removing the valuable silver leaf, placed it there as a memento mori.

Today there is no trace of this ritualistic aspect of the battle-ground. It must always be borne in mind that the archaeologists have found the detritus, damaged items, pieces too small to scavenge or simply missed. The most valuable archaeological treasures have been found either because they lay protected, under the collapsed wall where scavengers could not get them for example, or where paleobotanical analysis has suggested that the grass was too long and they were hidden from German eyes.

Even though most of what has been found has been smaller items, they still give a sense of the scope of the disaster: helmets, bosses of shields, random pieces of armour or of belts. And of course there are the weapons themselves. The sheer variety highlights the number of troops that were involved: arrowheads and swords, slingshot and spears. Yet the anonymity of the battlefield is occasionally lifted. One fastener for armour is identified as 'Belongs to Marcus Aius, Cohort I, Century of Fabricius'. His name is punched into one fastener with a sharp implement and scratched on to its partner, which was found nearby.

But for all the military objects, it is the domestic and personal items that really have the power to move and give a sense of place: an iron ring carried for luck, its carnelian gem engraved with two full cornucopias crossed over the staff of Mercury, surrounded by ears of corn; a bronze wine strainer; toiletries like a pair of iron scissors and the bronze ring on which a soldier carried the strigil he used to clean himself in the baths; a small silver spoon with a tubular handle; brightly coloured, round, glass pieces, part of a set from a Roman board game; and a bronze hairpin, 13.5cm long, one of few such female items found, reminds us that women are likely to have been among the fallen.

In the days after the battle, all Roman settlements east of the Rhine were overrun. It was not just military sites that bore the brunt of Germanic fury. Civilian ones like Waldgirmes were either abandoned or burned. The rapidity with which events spiralled out of control can be seen in the north-eastern corner of Waldgirmes, where renovation work on four houses was broken off. It is easy to imagine workers downing tools and running for safety. There was no attempt at German inhabitation of the site. Native tribes viewed cities as 'tombs surrounded by nets'.[27] It was as if the Germans were trying to erase every possible trace of the hated invaders and of their civilisation.

Virtually all of the land that Varus had tried to turn into a province had been reclaimed; all of the Roman strongholds 'except one', that is.[28] As Cassius Dio pointedly notes, it was the actions and defence of one camp which prevented the Germans from either crossing the Rhine or invading Gaul. It does not matter that it is distinctly doubtful whether Arminius would have ever considered pushing into the west. At a time of disaster like this, the Romans needed a hero and they found him in Lucius Caedicius, the camp commander of Aliso.

The modern site of Aliso has never been identified definitively, though it has cautiously been equated with the Roman camp at Haltern on the River Lippe since 1900. Certainly Haltern was assaulted and burned to the ground that autumn. It is an issue that may never be resolved unless some further epigraphic evidence is found. Even if the most definite statement that can be made is that current thought tends towards it, the literary evidence of Aliso and the archaeological analysis of Haltern do appear to back each other up. There is no reason to disagree with Colin Wells' comment that 'no other suggestion deserves serious consideration'.[29]

By the time that Varus had made his last stand, Caedicius might already have heard from scouts or refugees about what had happened to his commander and to his colleagues Lucius Eggius and Ceionius. The only point worth pondering is how long the camp commander of Haltern had before the Germans arrived, or whether he was already under attack by Arminius' allies by the time the news reached him.

Caedicius was not the kind of man to panic. He was a *primus pilus*, the commander of the first cohort and the legion's most experienced and senior soldier. Although the literary sources do not mention which brigade he was from, it is possible that he was from Legion XIX. We surmise that the legion was stationed there after the discovery of an ingot with 'CCIII L.XIX' carved into the lead – 203lb Legion XIX. The crude letters on the metal are still quite clearly visible to the naked eye through the glass case in the Haltern museum.

Caedicius appears to have had enough time to get the civilian encampment settled in the safety of the 18-hectare camp, but not all preparations were in place before the hordes arrived. He and his men had not brought in and stored away all of the wood that they had collected. Concerned that the Germans would use the wood to fire the walls of the fort, he pretended to be in need of firewood and sent his men out to steal it, whereupon the Germans removed the stacks of wood.

Initial attacks were repulsed by archers who lined the wooden walls of the fort, supported by *ballistae*, artillery which could throw bolts and stones. The largest of these, what were in effect giant crossbows, were powerful launchers that could fire a 25kg missile up to 500m. The archaeological evidence suggests that, despite this aerial bombardment, the double ring of ditches which protected Haltern – 2.5m across and 3m deep – was soon to fall to the Germans. They seem to have attacked the south gate, filling up the ditches with hastily cut turfs. That the remains of what is clearly a hastily erected barricade have been found suggests that the Romans were able to fight off even this onslaught and push the Germans back.

After the initial attacks had failed, it was apparent to the German soldiers that they had little chance of taking the camp by normal means. Certainly Cassius Dio comments that 'they found themselves unable to reduce this fort, because they did not understand how to conduct sieges'.[30] With what they must have presumed was a Roman relief force on its way, the Germans partly withdrew, deciding instead

His remains were placed in the mausoleum, to join so many of his family who had preceded him. After a decade in the wings, it was time for Tiberius, now 55, finally to take the throne, the position for which he had trained for so many years.

From here on, there was a slow shift in policy towards Germany. Augustus' handwritten will from 3 April the previous year, advised Tiberius not to follow as aggressive a policy of imperial expansion as he had done. It would be hard to guard, Augustus said, and this would lead to danger of losing the territory that had already been civilised.[11] Had the Romans at any stage between now and the end of AD 16 comprehensively beaten the Cherusci, then the Elbe would have been maintained as the border. But before too long into his reign, the new emperor heeded his predecessor's advice and he began to pull back from all forts east of the Rhine.

The Rhine itself was strengthened with the establishment of two more bases: one at Strasbourg to protect one of the main routes into Gaul, and another at Windisch in Switzerland, to guard a crossing of the River Aare. This protection laid the basis for what evolved into the Limes – the Latin for 'path' – the protective frontier that would eventually stretch from Koblenz on the Rhine to Eining on the Danube, a distance of some 570km, and would last up until the third century. The Limes was not a continuous barrier (for that you have to look at either Hadrian's Wall or the Antonine Wall in northern England and Scotland respectively); nonetheless, as seen in Romania and Syria, this line of forts and watchtowers proved an effective border.

The difficulties that now emerged in Germany were the result, for once, not of activities beyond the Rhine but of events in Rome. The news of Augustus' demise had unsettled the empire. Few could recall a time before his reign, and those who could cannot have remembered those years of continual civil war with any fondness. Political uncertainty combined with a lack of military campaigning that year fanned disquiet that became rebellion in several regions. It is essential to understand this revolt and the behaviour of the army, as it casts light not just on the character of Germanicus, but on subsequent Roman military action against Germany in general and Arminius in particular.

Germanicus was overseeing the census and tax collection in Gaul when news of Augustus' death broke on the Rhine at the beginning of September. The uprising appears to have kicked off with the Legion V 'The Larks' and Legion XXI 'The Predators' at their summer camp around Cologne (they were normally stationed together) but soon dragged in Legion I Germanica and Legion XX 'Valiant and Victorious' with them – in other words the whole of Lower Germany. Fortunately for the commander, discontent appears to have been confined to this region. 'The troops under Silius, with minds still not made up, watched the issue of mutiny elsewhere,' writes Tacitus.[12]

What could Lucius Poblicius have made of this? Then a new and young recruit to 'The Larks' from Italy, he was many years away from the incredible wealth that would allow him to leave the mausoleum that is one of the centrepieces of the Roman-Germanic Museum in Cologne. Was he egged on by Plautius Scaeva Vibianus, one of his legion's military tribunes? Did Gaius Ventienus Urbiqus, trumpeter with Legion I take part? How far through the legion did it go? Was even Gaius Deccius, the Legion XX's veterinary surgeon involved?[13] Inevitably the focus of history is on the leaders, the commanders and the politicians who shape the momentous events of history. These names and their stylised images on gravestones take the attention off weightier matters for a moment and give an intimate and personal colour that these incidents all too often are lacking.

There was no one single reason for the revolt, but a common underlying factor appears to have been the fallout of the military emergency created by Varus. The mass enlistment to replace those who had fallen at Kalkriese resulted in a large number of draftees unsuited to military life. The impatience with hardship that Tacitus credits them with has the ring of truth about it; complaints about harsh discipline (an infamously strict centurion in Pannonia was nicknamed 'Cedo alteram', or 'Bring another', because when he broke a stick over a hapless legionary's back he called for another, then another), bad pay and excessive deductions from what was left, and the rigours of square-bashing.[14] Even at the best of times it is clear that the army was not the route to riches. The pay record of an auxiliary soldier stationed in Egypt from the second half of the first century makes this abundantly clear:

Gaius Valerius Germanus from Tyre received the first salary instalment of the third year of the emperor, 247½ drachmas out of which

Hay	10	drachmas
For food	80	drachmas
Boots, socks	12	drachmas
Saturnalia of the camp	20	drachmas
For clothes	100	drachmas
Expenditure	222	drachmas
Balance deposited into his account	25½	drachmas
And had	21	drachmas

Makes a complete total of 46½ drachmas.[15]

It is not easy to put the 250 sesterces payments (drachmas were on parity with the Roman sesterces – the 2½ drachma deduction presumably a currency exchange charge) into a context that is understandable today. The 46½ sesterces that Germanus had in his account was the equivalent of 465 asses, the bronze coins in common usage. To give some indication of purchasing power, a litre of good wine cost four asses and a week's worth of grain around twelve asses. It is easy to see how even the slightest increase in deductions or delay in payment would cause resentment.

More specific were the complaints about length of service. Under Augustus, legionaries were supposed to serve for twenty years – sixteen in the ranks and four as veterans. With the constant campaigning of the past years, and the pressure to push back the boundaries of the empire, service times began to stretch. In Cologne, veterans who had thirty years under their belts were losing their sense of humour.

Germanicus' deputy, Aulus Caecina Severus, seemed unable to cope as normal military and disciplinary structures splintered in the city. Tacitus was convinced that it was the sheer scale of the disturbance that 'broke his nerve',[16] though there appears to have been more to the story than that. Caecina's behaviour is certainly questionable and not for the first time either. He had behaved similarly indecisively and ineptly during one of the Pannonian campaigns seven years previously. Yet there is no doubting the extreme nature of the revolt. A self-regulating commune emerged as centurions were lynched and either thrown out of camp or tipped into the Rhine.

When Germanicus did return from Gaul, he was faced with a barrage of protests. To emphasise their complaints about the length of service, some veterans grabbed his hand and pushed his fingers into their mouths so that he could feel their toothless gums, while others showed him their bent and broken limbs.

Even if Germanicus, strictly speaking, had no authority with which to make any concessions, he miscalculated badly. Rather at odds with his reputation as an intuitive commander, he now displayed such a lack of any real sense of his troops that he almost lost his life into the bargain. The frenzied soldiers tried to acclaim him as emperor. Objecting to this *lèse-majesté*, he tried to leave the camp, but protesters blocked the way. Theatrically Germanicus pulled his sword and ordered the men to return to normal duty or he would kill himself. It was an oratorical gesture, not uncommon in Rome, but the soldiers took him at his word. While some indeed did hold back their commander's hand, a significant number called his bluff and urged him on. One legionary went so far as to offer his own sword, saying that it was sharper. Humiliated, Germanicus had to be rescued by friends and hurried to his quarters.

A semblance of order was achieved sullenly, unwillingly and predominantly by forging a letter from Tiberius agreeing to the rebel demands. Legion I and Legion XX caved in, returned to normal duties and were marched back to their camp in Cologne. Legion V and Legion XXI took more convincing. They did not knuckle down until Germanicus and the high command had bribed them out of their own pockets. Only then did they calm down enough to march back to their winter camp in Xanten. With Lower Germany soothed, Germanicus turned to the continued rumblings in Upper Germany.

It quietened down more easily. When asked to, three brigades, Legion II, Legion XIII and Legion XVI, all accepted the oath of allegiance. Legion XIV 'The Twins', which was later to win glory during the revolt of Boudicca in Britain in the 60s AD, took more persuasion. But to bring the affair to as rapid a conclusion as possible, as soon as they began to hesitate, the legionaries were immediately offered the same financial and discharge inducements as the army in Lower Germany.

Many must have hoped that this would have drawn a line under the unfortunate incident, but tempers flared up again with the arrival in Cologne of two envoys from the Senate in the first week of October. Knowing nothing of the mutiny, they had in fact come bringing Germanicus official condolences on the death of his grandfather, rumours inevitably circulated that the Senate had come to remove the concessions recently granted. A mob from Legion I and Legion XX began to riot and the chief envoy was almost lynched.

It was clear that imperial control was just a veneer. It says much about the state of the city that Germanicus went so far as to send Agrippina and his 2-year-old son, the future emperor Caligula, away from Cologne, to a friendly local tribe. It was a calculated and ostentatious charade designed to bring the soldiers to their senses. The stunt appears to have worked and although the details are unclear, the rebellion in Cologne began to peter out by mid-October.[17]

There still remained the problem of how to punish Legion V and Legion XXI. The two brigades were, after all, the ringleaders of the original disturbances. Germanicus' solution may have had the advantage of allowing the legions to wash their own dirty linen in private, but it is hard not to get the sense that the commander was absolving himself of all responsibility. He sent Caecina in Xanten a blunt dispatch that he was en route with a strong force; either punish the guilty or he would massacre the rebels indiscriminately.

Caecina dealt with the problem with a decisiveness he had lacked in Cologne. He plotted with those loyal to him to butcher the mutineers. Some of the revolutionaries fought back, so when Germanicus arrived in Xanten towards the end of the month the camp was an abattoir. Attempting to draw a line under the incident, Germanicus sorrowfully concluded that this was a disaster not a cure.

Despite the lateness of the year, it should not come as a surprise that there was now a campaign. Germanicus' talk of avenging Varus and his three legions was in one sense a blind: this operation's secondary purpose was revenge and restoration of Roman power across the Rhine. It was all about keeping control of his own forces. Let the soldiers – some 12,000 legionaries made up from all four brigades in Lower Germany – take out their aggression on the Germans rather than on either each other or the senior command. It is an interesting point that Germanicus also took 13,000 auxiliary infantry and 4,000 auxiliary cavalry with him, presumably as their loyalty had never been in doubt. As one German historian has it, 'Germanicus improvised the autumn campaign to restore discipline to his legions in Lower Germany.' Yet it did not harm his case that the tribe he had targeted was the Marsi, one of the conspirators at Teutoburg.[18]

It was an unattractive if solid campaign of slaughter, a depressingly familiar approach to natives even in the twentieth century and rationalised by the colonial historians. By the end of October, he and his army set out across the River Rhine from Xanten and attacked the Marsi in the Lippe/Ruhr area. The tribe had presumed that the death of Augustus and the subsequent mutinies had meant that they were safe for that year. They were caught off-guard. Timing his arrival to a German festival, Germanicus split his army into four and then ravaged the entire area for an 80km radius. His army then returned, with comparative ease, to winter quarters. Morale had been restored.

If the Romans were distracted for the latter part of AD 14 with domestic matters, so, too, Arminius had his own internal problems. The breach that had always been threatened in the Cheruscan high command now made itself felt in a power struggle. Inevitably the rift was over the relationship with Rome. Following his success at Kalkriese, Arminius appears to have attempted to consolidate his own position and in doing so he needed to oust his father-in-law, Segestes. Initially, at least, things appear to have gone his way and by the end of the year he had confirmed his status within the tribe, while Segestes was marginalised.

In retrospect, that year will have seemed one of calm for the Cherusci, at least as far as their own relationship with the invaders was concerned. It was all about to change. The Roman campaigns of the next two years were driven by vengeance and the need for military exorcism. Tiberius' post-Teutoburg caution and security imperatives were replaced with a much more aggressive stance, specifically aimed at revenge on Arminius. It is clear that Roman intelligence had absorbed reports of a division between hawks and doves in the Cheruscan camp that could be exploited if rapid action were taken.

The winter of AD 14/15 must have been spent on logistical matters – this was no campaign taken on impulse – and it is clear that Germanicus' aim was to break up Arminius' coalition. First and foremost he planned to attack the three main anti-Roman tribes in turn and forcibly remind them of Roman superiority. At the same time, as the opportunity presented itself, Arminius was to be isolated from his allies. While Germanicus led the main force, Caecina was to act as a defensive buffer. He was to stop Arminius coming to his allies' aid and to prevent the Marsi from joining in (which says much for the success of the previous year's campaign). The weather was in Germanicus' favour. An unseasonably dry winter meant that the Roman commander could set off early in AD 15 against one of Arminius' southern neighbours, the Chatti. He crossed the Rhine with a massive force: all eight legions, many auxiliaries and a significant native levy.

Germanicus rehabilitated a fort that his father had used on Mount Taunus to use as a base for the campaign. Although absolute certainty is impossible, it is generally believed that this was the camp of Friedberg. Germanicus, together with Gaius Silius, commander of the upper Rhine army, then marched on the Chatti. Germanicus caught them by surprise and killed them all. 'So suddenly did he come on the Chatti that all the helpless because of their age or sex were at once captured or slaughtered,' writes Tacitus.[19] It seemed to have been a definitive assault. The tribe's capital of Mattium was razed (it has not been identified, and although it has traditionally been associated with the Alterburg, near Niedenstein, this seems wrong) and those Germans who did not surrender vanished into the forest.

There is some indication that Germanicus may have had more than retaliatory action at the back of his mind as he set out. Lucius Apronius had been ordered to follow in the army's footsteps, building roads and bridges. This raises the possibility that Germanicus was still considering a more permanent conquest at this stage. Another high-flier, Apronius, along with Caecina and Silius, was a core member of Germanicus' team. He was eventually to rise to a successful governorship of Africa.

Over the winter, Roman intelligence had been able to report that the pro-war party was dominant in the Cheruscan camp. Segestes was under physical as well as political attack and had been trapped by his son-in-law in what was essentially house arrest. His base of support had not been entirely eroded, as somehow he had managed to get word to the Roman general. It is an indication of the danger in which he found himself that his son agreed to lead the diplomatic mission. Segimundus had absconded from the Altar of the Ubii in Cologne, where he had been a priest, and had joined Arminius six years earlier. Understandably, Tacitus refers to his 'hesitation'[20] at what kind of reception he could receive at the Roman camp.

The benefits from the defection of such a high-profile Cheruscan were enough to divert Germanicus from hunting down the remaining Chatti. It was an entirely successful raid. His army wheeled north, fought its way through to the besieged Segestes and rescued him. Not only had the Romans saved an old ally, but much of the loot that had been taken from those who had fallen at Teutoburg and given to Cheruscan warriors was recovered. Best of all, the Romans had their first material success against Arminius – they captured his pregnant wife, Thusnelda. At some point over the past months, the divisions within the Cheruscan camp had become so marked that Segestes had been forced to kidnap his own daughter. The success of the raid allowed Germanicus to be magnanimous. Past sins were forgiven, while Thusnelda was locked in the gilded cage in Ravenna, rapidly becoming the place of exile for former

Germanic royalty. Some months later, in Ravenna, she gave birth to a son, Thumelicus.[21]

After the diversion of Cheruscan politics, Germanicus set his sights on other pro-Arminian tribes, this time the Bructeri, Arminius' northern neighbours. Based in the general area of the town of Münster, between the Ems and the Lippe, the tribe was in the ascendant at the moment. Although nominally defeated by Tiberius a decade previously, it was a staunch ally of Arminius and had played a leading role at Teutoburg. The attack was a complete success. Germanicus planned his confrontation carefully – it was a combined assault, with cavalry, infantry and the fleet arriving from different directions – and the Bructeri were slaughtered. Best of all, the first of Varus' three lost eagles was recovered: that of Legion XIX.

The time that Germanicus spent attacking the Bructeri and, as described in the Introduction, in following his desire to bury Varus' dead on the battlefield gave Arminius time to remobilise. In one sense, the rescue of Segestes and the capture of Thusnelda was one of the worst moves the Romans could have made. Roman interference had managed what Arminius appears to have failed to achieve in the previous year. It had unified the Cherusci behind him. Certainly his biggest coup was in convincing his uncle, Inguiomerus, formerly a supporter of Rome and an ally of Segestes, to join his cause. Internal politicking was now forgotten, as not only the Cherusci rallied to him but neighbouring tribes were recruited to his banner.

The rest of the campaigning season was dominated by inconclusive guerrilla warfare, as Arminius harried Roman troops and Germanicus failed to tempt the Cherusci to the battlefield. Late in the season, Germanicus decided to return to winter quarters. He took his four legions and the cavalry back to camp, following the river so that he could make best use of his fleet. Two of his brigades were caught and almost wiped out by sudden high winter tides along what is now the Dutch coast. Their commander, Publius Vitellius, the grandfather of the future emperor Vitellius, had disembarked with Legion II 'The Emperor's Own' and Legion XIV 'The Twins' so that the coast-hugging ships would have fewer difficulties in shallow waters. They were caught completely unawares. 'Men were swept away by the waves or sucked under by eddies; beasts of burden, baggage, lifeless bodies floated about and blocked their way,' writes Tacitus.[22] After an uncomfortable night on higher ground without food, water or fire they were eventually rescued.

This was uneventful compared to what the rest were to endure. Caecina and his four legions were sent back by the more conventional path, which had probably been in use for the past two decades. Built during the command of Lucius Domitius Ahenobarbus, the route dubbed 'the Long Bridges' was hardly ideal. 'It was a narrow road amid vast swamps . . . on every side were quagmires of thick clinging mud or perilous with streams,' is how it is described.[23] Even allowing for Tacitean hyperbole, it does not take much imagination to consider the state of the wooden bridges after – at the very least – six years of neglect and northern European winters.

As they marched towards the Long Bridges, the Romans realised that Arminius had anticipated their route and that the surrounding hills, normally covered in forests, were actually covered in Germans. Caecina decided to set up camp. Half of his troops were set to building a marching fort as others rebuilt the roadway.

They were attacked throughout the afternoon, bombarded with missiles and harried whenever Arminius saw an opportunity. The terrain showed up the weaknesses of the Roman military. Bogged down in the swamp as they were, it was slippery and impossible to march. The Roman heavy armour sucked at them, slowing them down even further. Recognising this, Arminius' men then dammed several streams to flood the already waterlogged plain. Up to their waists in water, the Romans found it impossible to throw javelins back at the Germans.

Night brought some relief, though not for Caecina. While the Germans caroused through the night, the Roman commander suffered nightmares. In Tacitus' chilling account he saw Quinctilius Varus, covered with blood, rising out of the swamps and calling to him. In his dream, Caecina fought him off, refusing to come to him and fighting away the old general's hand as it stretched out to him.[24] For all of the literary quality of the account, the story does have a ring of plausibility about it.

The next morning, shaking off his nightmares, Caecina had a plan. A path between the mountains and the swamps allowed for a marching line, albeit an extended one. He formed up his four legions into what would have been a familiar hollow square: Legion I Germanica at the front, Legion XXI 'The Predators' and Legion V 'The Larks' on the left and right flanks respectively while Legion XX 'Valiant and Victorious' protected the army's rear.

Something went wrong. Possibly Legion XXI and Legion V misunderstood their orders, but they began to run rather than march towards the open ground. Certainly, given their actions during the revolt, a wilful disobeying of orders is not out of the question. Either way the baggage train was exposed, unguarded and stuck in the mud. This was the moment that Arminius chose to attack. He cut through the column, targeting the horses. As wounded and dying horses lashed out, throwing riders and trampling those on the ground, the Germans aimed for the eagles. It was a close call and not even the commander escaped unscathed. Caecina's horse was killed under him and he was thrown; it was only the swift action of soldiers from Legion I that saved him from capture or death.

It must have been small consolation, but the loss of much, if not all, of the baggage train almost certainly saved them. As the Germans looted the spoils, Legion I and Legion XX were able to reach the more open ground and they all dug in. It cannot have been pleasant. To start with, they were hampered in digging as they had lost some of their tools. Their tents were gone and they had no medical supplies. Cold, wet and dirty, at least they had the comfort of food – Roman legionaries habitually carried provisions on their backs.

An episode that evening gives some idea of the fear among the Roman forces. In the night, a horse broke free of its halter and galloped through the camp. Thinking the Germans had launched a night assault and broken through their defences, the legions panicked and 'most of them sought the Decuman gate'.[25] Tacitus' dry comment refers to the gate at the back of the camp, away from the enemy. It took Caecina, standing in the gateway, facing off his own men, to calm the soldiers down.

Trapped, tired and tense, Caecina was in danger of re-creating his own Teutoburg battle. Indeed it was only Cheruscan disunity that saved the Romans. Arminius wanted to allow the four legions out of their camp and then ambush them again. It was the technique that had worked so well six years before and was by far the best way that had been found of neutralising Roman technical supremacy. His uncle, Inguiomerus, however, disagreed. Arguing that the Romans were all but beaten, he proposed a full-frontal assault.

Inguiomerus' view prevailed, a sign both that the cracks in Cheruscan unity had been papered over rather than filled and that Arminius' position was not as unassailable as many have presumed. The Germans attacked. It was exactly what Caecina had been hoping for. With only limited resources he distributed the horses that remained with the army to the best of the cavalry. When Arminius and his men attacked the camp, the Romans rallied, their trumpets blaring. The Germans found themselves trapped in the fort. Attacked from the rear by galvanised Roman troops, they were routed and slaughtered throughout the day. Although Arminius himself was unscathed, his uncle was severely wounded.

Caecina's return to quarters was a moment made for celluloid. Although that last battle had seen off the German threat, the Roman troops that had been left in Xanten had worked themselves into a panic, as only intermittent and unclear news reached them. First, they had been terrified that Legion II 'The Emperor's Own' and Legion XIV 'The Twins' had been wiped out with Publius Vitellius. Now, just as six years earlier, a large and furious German army led by Arminius seemed to be marching on Gaul and the only camp in their path was Xanten.

As Roman soldiers went to pieces and tried to destroy the bridge across the Rhine, it took Germanicus' wife, Agrippina, to stop them. She stood on the German side of the Rhine, welcoming the troops back in person. Over the next weeks she became the lady of the lamp, distributing clothes and medicines to those who had lost everything or were wounded.

For all the symbolism of the moment, it was one which was to have repercussions. It is certainly indicative that the next we hear of Aulus Caecina Severus is six years later, when he proposed legislation banning wives from accompanying their husbands on campaign. 'A train of women involves delays through luxury in peace and through panic in war, and converts a Roman army on the march into the likeness of a barbarian progress. Not only are women feeble and unequal to hardship but, when they have liberty, they are spiteful, intriguing and greedy for power,' he said.[26]

He had presumably spent the previous years suffering jibes about how his army had been saved by a woman. But rather more seriously, Agrippina's actions had not gone unnoticed in Rome. Were the emperor's troops still so unsettled that it had taken a woman to stop a near mutiny and certain panic? Did this woman now have more influence with the soldiers than the officers? Than the generals? And all of these questions and mutterings around the emperor were fanned by jealous advisers.

To halt the spread of frontier nervousness, the year's campaign was portrayed as a victory. Lucius Apronius, Aulus Caecina Severus and Gaius Silius were all decorated and their commander was granted a triumph in Rome. But apart from the prosaic fact that Germanicus had come no closer to capturing or defeating Arminius, he had suffered major losses and his deputy had almost ended up a second Varus. Even more disturbing had been the behaviour of 'The Predators' and 'The Larks'. The time that Germanicus spent that winter tending to the pastoral needs of his men suggests that he was not unaware of these potentially explosive ramifications either. Indeed the only person for whom the year might be deemed a success was Arminius. Although he had been thwarted in his end-game, he had both won a great deal of Roman booty and inflicted significant losses on them.

For the Romans, the following year had to be decisive. The strain on the resources of the western empire was beginning to tell and Tiberius had more immediate problems on the other side of the empire in Armenia to worry about. While the Rhine army was being rearmed and remobilised, Germanicus did not neglect intelligence matters. In the meantime, the defection of Segestes' brother had been arranged and Segimerus (not Arminius' father) and his son were escorted to Cologne. Like Segimundus, the latter was unwilling to go over to the Romans. As an active participant at Kalkriese, indeed one of those who had defiled Varus' corpse, he had concerns about his reception, but again propaganda benefits for the Romans outweighed thoughts of revenge.

The strategy this year was very different. Germanicus planned a predominantly marine expedition and much of the spring was spent in rapidly constructing a fleet that could drop the army right in the heart of Germany. This obviated the need for a long and potentially casualty-rich march, as well as maintaining an element of surprise. Tacitus suggests that the existing Rhine fleet was boosted by a thousand ships of all shapes and sizes: some flat-bottomed assault craft, some with decks to carry the artillery, others kitted out to transport horses.[27]

The rendezvous point was set for the territory of the Batavi, a tribe which occupied the area between the rivers Rijn and Waal around where the modern town of Nijmegen is now situated and which, conveniently, was a significant supplier of auxiliary troops. While the army was being mobilised, a flying column was sent under Gaius Silius to make sure that the Chatti did not attack them from the rear (bad weather hampered Silius, but he did manage to kidnap the chief's wife and daughter), while Germanicus, who had received news of an attack on a Roman fort on the Lippe rushed north with six legions. The spirit of Varus still haunted them. The tribes had destroyed the barrow containing the bones of Legions XVII, XVIII and XIX that they had built last year, and torn down an altar that had been built by Drusus.

By now the fleet had made it to the mouth of the River Ems. Peculiarly, they landed on the wrong side of the river, so were delayed for a few days, building bridges. Another brief distraction was caused by a revolt at their rear by another tribe, the Angrivarii, but nothing else halted the march north. Soon Germanicus and his army were camped on the left side of the River Weser, opposite Arminius and his troops, which were massed on the right side.

Here, Tacitus describes how Arminius and his brother Flavus shouted at each other across the river; the former berating the latter for his slavery at the hands of the Romans. It may even reflect a real incident. What is interesting is Tacitus' comment that the conversation happened in Latin, a reminder to his readers, and to us, that Arminius had once been a Roman auxiliary officer.[28]

Germanicus found himself trapped in a stalemate. Arminius would never attack, and he was unwilling to commit to a crossing without a bridgehead on the other side. Several cavalry attacks were launched. The Batavian allies forded the river but they failed to draw the Cheruscan army into an ambush. The chieftain was killed in that action and the Roman cavalry had to come to the rescue to stop a rout. But it was a successful enough distraction to allow the Romans to cross the River Weser.

Intelligence reports suggested that Arminius and his allies had mobilised nearby in a sacred forest dedicated to their god Donar and were planning to attack the Romans at night. Thus forewarned, the Romans were able to ensure that the attack did not take place that night. Instead, a Latin-speaking German shouted over the Roman ramparts, offering all deserters almost half their annual salary a day as long as the war lasted, together with wives and farmland. All this did was to galvanise the legionaries and had as little success as a tentative attack that morning on the Roman camp.

The military foreplay was now at an end. It was about to come to pitched battle – Arminius' final confrontation with what he called the 'cowardly runaways from Varus' army'. The exact site of what has become known as the Battle of Idistaviso remains uncertain. Tacitus' description of the battlefield itself is detailed – it was between the River Weser and a range of hills with a forest to the rear – but does not allow more precise identification and archaeological traces are still to be found.[29]

That it had come to pitched battle is curious. What had made Arminius so outstanding as a commander so far was his recognition that he could not compete with the Romans on a level playing field. However much of an advantage the Germans had had topographically by knowing the countryside, or emotionally because they were fighting to free their own land, Arminius had always managed to minimise the effect of Roman military technological supremacy. It is tempting to suggest that he had been overruled by his fellow commanders, as he had the previous summer. Whether it was this or simply confidence, Arminius' battle formation showed how much he had developed as a military thinker. Despite the fact that this was his first set battle against Rome, his deployment was professional and notably Roman in style. He and the Cherusci kept to the higher ground, with other tribes to the fore, the River Weser to his left, and forest to the right to keep the Roman attack front narrow.

The gods favoured the Romans though. As the battle started that morning, Germanicus saw eight eagles fly into the woods. 'Follow the Roman birds, true gods of our legions,' he said.[30] It gave the legionaries the encouragement they needed as they prepared themselves for battle. Allied auxiliaries from Gaul, Switzerland and Bavaria, along with the foot archers to give them covering fire, marched at the front. They were followed by Germanicus himself with four legions, the best of the cavalry and a couple of cohorts of praetorian guards. The remaining four legions, horse archers and other allied battalions brought up the rear.

The battle itself, which cannot have lasted for more than an hour or so, is difficult to untangle, other than in the broadest outline. Against their orders, the Cheruscans charged, while Germanicus sent the best of his cavalry round to fall on the German flank and rear. The legionaries and the two cavalry arms began to tighten their grip on the German horde, which began to weaken and crumble. Arminius tried to rally the troops and himself led the head-on attack towards the Roman archers. He would have broken through, too, had it not been for the native auxiliaries blocking his way. Injured in those first moments, he smeared his face with his own blood to disguise his face, regained control of his horse and charged off to safety.

As it became obvious that the Romans had won, and with notably few casualties (the majority were killed in that first German assault), the legionaries routed and slaughtered the remnants of the barbarian army during the rest of the day. Many of those who were not slain tried to escape by swimming across the River Weser, but either archers or the strong current saw to them. Tacitus records the blackly humorous detail of Roman archers taking pot shots at Germans who had hidden themselves in trees.[31] Those who were not chasing down Germans raised a commemorative monument on the battlefield, inscribed with the names of the tribes they had just defeated.

It was the sight of the smug and gloating monument to foreign dominance that reignited the spark for battle the Romans thought they had just extinguished. Even tribesmen who had planned to withdraw across the River Elbe heard Arminius' call to arms. In a curious moment of historical symmetry, this battle was a mirror image of Teutoburg Forest.

The Germanic tribes had planned an ambush along the route the Roman army was marching. A narrow path was chosen, hemmed in by river and forest and within a narrow, swampy plain. Rather than have his warriors build a wall, this time Arminius could use one that was already there – an earth rampart that had been built as a territorial boundary marker between the Cherusci and one of their neighbouring tribes – and he ranged his foot soldiers there. The cavalry was hidden in the woods, ready to take the Roman army in the rear.

But this time the Roman commander both had and used his intelligence, turning the enemy's position to his own advantage. His infantry was split in two: half to charge those in the forest, the other to attack the wall behind which the Germans were hiding, while the cavalry was sent to secure the path and the swampy plain. Initially the legionaries sent over the ramparts came off badly, but an organised withdrawal, followed by a protective bombardment from slingers and artillery, soon allowed the Romans to make a second attack.

Germanicus himself was one of the first over the top. He had even removed his helmet to make himself more visible to his own troops. In contrast to Kalkriese, the forest here hindered the Germans. Hemmed in as they were, they could not make use of their spears and were forced into close combat, where the Roman short stabbing sword became lethally advantageous. With Arminius himself conspicuously subdued on the battlefield (the wound from Idistaviso clearly more serious than anyone had imagined), the Romans soon had the day. As night drew in, one legion built a camp, while the rest of the army 'glutted themselves with the enemy's blood'.[32]

After signing a swift non-aggression pact with a nearby tribe, Germanicus erected a second memorial to his victories. It was now time to return to winter camp. Some legions, as in the previous year, went overland. The majority, however, went by sea. Once again, they were caught out by the weather, though much more seriously this time. The Roman fleet sailed down the River Ems without incident, but storms broke out when the flotilla hit open sea. Some ships were sunk, others were scattered, and some were blown so far off course that they ended up as far away as Britain.

An eyewitness was Albinovanus Pedo, whose poetic description of the storms was quite rightly described in ancient times as 'inspired':

> . . . now they think the vessels
> Are sinking in the mud, the fleet deserted by the swift wind,
> Themselves left by indolent fate to the sea beasts,
> To be torn apart unhappily.
> Someone high on the prow struggles to break
> Through the blinding mist, his sight battling.
> He can discern nothing – the world has been snatched away.[33]

Germanicus' fleet eventually staggered into port, some ships towing others, clothing used for sails in others, those that could make it often with only a few rowers. But it was still not over. Galvanised by accounts of the sea disaster, the Chatti and Marsi rose up again. Gaius Silius dealt with the former, while Germanicus himself attacked the latter. The year's campaigning ended on a high note. After a tip-off from the Marsi, a commando raid managed to recover the second of Varus' eagles.

On that inconclusive note, Roman involvement on the eastern side of the Rhine ended. Germanicus' plea for one more campaign fell on deaf ears and he was recalled. Why the halt now? Despite the desire of ancient authors to read this as imperial jealousy, the much more prosaic reasons were the immense financial and manpower pressures the previous years had imposed on the empire's finances. The German historian Erich Koestermann believes that Germanicus knew what he was doing and lays the blame squarely at the feet of

Tiberius. He suggests that the campaigns of AD 15 and 16 were a complete waste of money and resources: the emperor should either have had the courage of his convictions and finished the war or should never have started it.[34] It is a blunt view and not entirely fair. Tiberius should not be wholly blamed: Germany was, after all, an inherited problem for him.

The difficulty that now arose was what to do with Germanicus. From the perspective of Rome, he had achieved very little. The final shrine that Germanicus had ordered to be erected on the River Weser boasted: 'The army of Tiberius Caesar, after thoroughly conquering the tribes between the Rhine and the Elbe, has dedicated this monument to Mars, Jupiter, and Augustus.' But that solitary sentence smacks of self-deception rather than achievement. Germanicus could not be replaced, and therefore the most elegant solution was to present the campaign as a victory. The German historian Dieter Timpe points out the self-justifying argument by using the analogy from Aesop's fable of the fox who cannot reach the grapes and so decides that they must be sour.[35] There was no public demonstration of a lack of belief in the empire, no great disavowal of the dream, but Romans only rarely ventured across the Rhine again.

Germanicus himself was fobbed off with the delayed triumph for the wins of AD 15, held on 26 May AD 17, and a second consulship. A sop it might have been, but that did not detract from the glory of the occasion as the Roman public cheered the spoils that were carried through the city, entertained by tableaux representing mountains, the rivers and battles and, of course, the opportunity of gawking at the prisoners.[36]

Some of the stains from the Varian disaster had been washed away with the recovery of two of his eagles. So important was this that a coin dating from the reign of Germanicus' brother, the Emperor Claudius, depicts Germanicus with the legend: 'After the recovery of the eagles and victory over the Germans'. Their recovery was also enough to warrant a memorial: the so-called Arch of Tiberius. A single-span arch which stood in the Forum between the Temple of Saturn and the Basilica Julia, it no longer survives (though its foundations were discovered in the first half of the nineteenth century) but representations of it can be seen on a relief on the Arch of Constantine.[37]

Rome's conquering hero was sent out east, where he was to die under somewhat dubious circumstances in Antioch, three years later, on 10 October AD 19, at the age of only 33. The sheer depth of what one modern historian has called 'frenzied mourning throughout the empire' was confirmed in the spring of 1982 with the discovery of two bronze tablets in the town of Siara, near Seville in southern Spain, called the Tabula Siarensis. One of the most significant epigraphic discoveries in modern times, they contain the remains of several decrees relating to honours for Germanicus after his death. The first fragment concerns the erection of several arches in his memory, one of which, pointedly, was to be set up in Germany near that of his father. Dedicated by the Legion XIV 'The Twins' just beyond the bridge over the River Rhine from Mainz, its remains were found in 1986.[38]

The most apparent sign of Germanicus' failure in Germany is that Arminius was still at large. His wife and son might have been paraded through the capital in chains, taunted by Romans, but the Cheruscan was still very much a potential danger. And yet, he was never to come up against Rome again. Arminius' defeat at the Battle of Idistaviso had been a turning point for his own power. Cheruscan warriors began to move east in the search for new homes, far away from any future Roman threat. News of Germanicus' recall had not yet reached them, and even if it had, who was to say that another, even more bellicose commander might not be sent out against them? This migration inevitably brought the settlers directly against the Bohemian king Maroboduus, who had made himself unpopular with both Germans and Romans by his isolationist foreign policy over the last seven years.

With the external threat of Roman attack removed, Germanic rivalries flared into hostilities within a year. Arminius would never have contemplated any moves against Maroboduus while Romans were marching through German territory. He was much too canny a general to be seduced into a war on two fronts. He now had no such qualms. In many ways the cause of the war that now broke out was ego. The two German leaders were fighting for the hearts and minds of their fellow men.

Arminius was still sounding the clarion call of freedom. It was a seductive call, partly because he had effectively succeeded in pushing the Romans back to the Rhine and partly because the loyalty he was counting on was one that the tribesmen would have recognised. He was trying to tighten the bonds of traditional tribal allegiance. Maroboduus, however, was the ruler of a real empire. The political structures that he was trying to institute were precisely those the Germans had so recently fought against.

The cold war continued until several of Maroboduus' tribal subjects on the Elbe shifted their allegiance to Arminius, and the Cheruscan leader's uncle, Inguiomerus, went over to the Bohemian commander. The reason for the latter's move is opaque. Tacitus' suggestion that the uncle refused to submit to his nephew's command as it was beneath his dignity has the air of an excuse.[39] Whatever the real reason, these political chess moves were enough to tip the balance of power.

There is something grimly comic in the thought of the battle that the two fought in AD 17 somewhere north of Bohemia. For all of the effort that the two, very different, commanders had made in distancing themselves from Rome, the battle itself was fought in classic Roman style. Although it was a close call, Arminius was deemed to have won. Maroboduus found himself increasingly deserted by his allies and had to turn to Tiberius for help. A diplomatic solution kept Maroboduus in power for a year, but his authority had been so undermined that a young revolutionary captured his residence and treasury and deposed him. He was forced to come to Rome a supplicant, 'like the serpent under the spell of his salutary charms', writes Velleius Paterculus. It was a trip from which he was never to return. He spent the remaining eighteen years of his life sinking quietly into senile dementia ('He lost much of his renown through an excessive clinging to life,' writes Tacitus) in Ravenna, the same city as Thusnelda and her son. He died in AD 37.[40]

For Arminius, this should have been the greatest moment of his life: the consolidation of his power. He had won. The Romans had been pushed back to the other side of the Rhine and his greatest rival was gone, caged up in Ravenna. But he was not up to the task. Arminius fell for the very reasons he had attacked Maroboduus, in trying to meld the tribes into a single nation. He was 'aiming for royalty', writes Tacitus.[41] By giving up his call for freedom, Arminius gave up the source of his power and became simply another oppressor.

With admirable political straightforwardness, the chief of one of the Germanic tribes wrote a letter to Tiberius that was subsequently read out loud in the Senate. If poison were to be sent, he wrote, then he would make sure that Arminius was removed permanently. The emperor rejected the plan. This was not the kind of behaviour for Romans, he sniffed. Poison was for barbarians. The battlefield was the Roman way to do things.

Tiberius was right. That was how barbarians did things. Arminius was faced with a civil war and although he had some initial successes, he was soon murdered by a member of his family in somewhat murky circumstances. History has not preserved any more details; we do not know who killed him or how he died.

It is a tidy coincidence of history that the same year that saw the death of Germanicus saw the death of Arminius, too. In the end the Romans were denied the satisfaction of a hand in their enemy's demise. His death, or perhaps more accurately the internal feuding that led to his murder, appears to have weakened the Cherusci chronically. By the time that Tacitus was writing his *Germania*, they were no longer players, on the periphery of Roman interest. 'Once good and upright, they are now called cowards and fools,' he says. When the geographer Ptolemy was map-making in the second century, they had shrunk even further – just a small tribe, south of the Harz mountains.[42]

Arminius succeeded only as long as he was on his holy mission. As soon as he began to demand authority for its own sake, he had bitten the apple and had to be cast out. It is the eternally tragic motif of power corrupting and absolute power corrupting absolutely.

Within a generation all that was left was the memory of Arminius. He survived in song and legend, yet that has proved to be the most potent part of him. So seductive was this that even the Romans began to come under the spell. His obituary at the end of the second book of Tacitus' *Annals* is one of the most extraordinary pieces of Latin prose to come down to us. In a few sentences, Tacitus manages to capture both the admiration and revulsion the Romans had for their most successful opponent with incredible pathos: 'Make no mistake, Arminius was the deliverer of Germany, one too who had defied Rome, not in her early rise, as other kings and generals, but in the height of her empire's glory. The battles he fought were indeed indecisive, yet he remained unconquered in war. He lived for thirty-seven years, twelve of them in power, and he is still the subject of song among barbarous nations, though to Greek historians, who admire only their own achievements, he is unknown, and to Romans not as famous as he should be, while we extol the past and are indifferent to our own times.'[43]

SIX

Germany's Might

The Nazis' show of *Entartete Kunst* – degenerate art – to ridicule Modernism in the summer of 1937 stands out as one of the twentieth century's more ridiculous and desperate exercises in censorship. The exhibition of 650 paintings by artists such as Paul Klee, Emile Nolde, Max Ernst and Ernst Ludwig Kirchner is now justifiably revered and was the century's first blockbuster art show. During the two months it was on show in Munich, it was seen by some 2 million visitors, a larger draw than any exhibition before or since.

But that summer's contrasting exhibition, the *Große Deutsche Kunstausstellung*, the Great German Art Exhibition, predominantly featuring works personally selected by Adolf Hitler, is largely forgotten. It opened the day before, on 18 July, to inaugurate Munich's House of German Art, the first official building erected by the Nazis. Its opening was marked by an elaborate pageant called 'Two thousand years of German culture'. The town's Prinzregentenstraße was lined with 160 pylons, some 12m high, crowned with an eagle and a swastika. From the station to the centre of town, 243 flags were flown from flagpoles 10.5m high. Hundreds of thousands of spectators watched as 3,000 participants, 400 animals and a procession of huge papier-mâché heads, borne by people dressed as Rhine Maidens and Cheruscan warriors, paraded through the streets of the city.

It was here, in the Nazi era, marching through Munich, that the apotheosis as well as the nadir of the image of Arminius can be seen. But the metamorphosis from mutineer to Teutonic superman is a long one. Over the years Arminius had been an excuse to attack Rome, then France, and eventually the whole of western Europe. He had been embraced by Protestants, then nationalists and finally by the National Socialists.

The transmission of the Battle of Teutoburg Forest is so wide-ranging that this chapter will predominantly look at the way that Arminius has been politicised and how that in turn has influenced German nationalism. Of course it must be borne in mind that there is little consistency of imagery. Arminius was all things to all men. But it is possible to draw out some general themes. Richard Kuehnemund is right to point out that, for all of the nuances and complexities of the stories that have woven their way round the Cheruscan chieftain, two leitmotifs run though the entire corpus of literature about Arminius. The first is the message that death is preferable to slavery; the second that strength lies in unity.[1] Taken together, these themes illustrate that Arminius has always been a symbol of nostalgic longing, of a proud, free Germany.

It should not be forgotten that Germany was never entirely Romanised. While the provinces that the Romans called *Germania Superior* and *Germania Inferior* comprised the southern and western *Länder* of the modern states of the country, the north and east remained free. Nonetheless, connections continued even after the fall of the Roman Empire; indeed it is arguable that relations grew even closer after its collapse, based on strategic and cultural interdependence. When Charlemagne, the King of the Franks, was crowned emperor of the Holy Roman Empire on Christmas Day AD 800, it was by Pope Leo III and it was in St Peter's in Rome. This is not to say that it was always a happy relationship. Medieval history is littered with spats between the emperor and the pope, each vying for the political upper hand.

As mentioned in the introduction, Arminius' modern life starts with the rediscovery of Tacitus' *Germania* in the mid-fifteenth century. Although it is a mere 25 pages long, some 750 lines of Latin in modern editions, it is easy to agree with one modern scholar who calls it 'the christening present of the ancient world to the peoples of the future'.[2] A less charitable point could be made that if we consider the ratio of its length to its devastating political effect, it has given both Mao's *Little Red Book* (twenty-five pages) and *The Communist Manifesto* (forty-one pages) a run for their money.

Medieval manuscript-hunters had been aware of the manuscript's existence in Germany for some thirty years previously, but it was not until 1455 that it was finally repatriated to Italy from the library of the abbey at Hersfeld, along with some works by Suetonius. The humanist cleric Aeneas Silvius, later to become Pope Pius II, was the first to allude to the text after its discovery. In a condescending letter, replying to complaints about papal taxation from the Bishop of Mainz, Silvius used the *Germania* as proof of how far Germany had evolved from its barbaric state under the guidance of the Church and that, no, the taxes would not be remitted. It is fortunate that the letter was not published more widely.

When *Germania* was published in Venice in 1470, and in Nuremberg three years later (its first translation into the vernacular did not occur for another twenty-six years in Leipzig), it was the literary sensation of the century and caused a furore on both sides of the Alps. So popular was it that by the end of the Thirty Years War in 1648 it had run to twenty-six editions. Until then, Germany had been a country without a past. There was a broad presumption, fed by the obvious physical evidence of the remains in what had been Roman provinces, that Germany was a child of the Roman Empire. Most scholars believed that Germany was one of the heirs of the classical tradition. But this was the moment of birth of a true national consciousness.

In 1492 Conrad Celtis delivered an inaugural address at the University of Ingolstadt. In that Bavarian town, the scholar and first German poet laureate of the Holy Roman Empire let Tacitus through the door of scholarship. He, in turn, was then able to start the twin fires of German patriotism and national consciousness. Celtis was the appropriate heir of Arminius in many ways. The son of a winemaker, he claimed to have been born in the 'middle of the Hercynian forest'. Simultaneously he tried to distance the ancient Germans from the true barbarians further east ('brutal as beasts of prey', he called them), while pushing his country away from the corrupting decadence of Rome. It is an emotive call to his fellow countrymen to remember their own nobility and their own antiquity, far removed from decadent Italians. 'German men, take on that ancient spirit of yours with which you so often terrified and scared the Romans and turn your sight to the four corners of Germany and think about her torn and broken territories,' he said.[3]

New editions of *Germania* began to pour out of the country's presses and were soon joined on the bookshelves by histories of the country and its peoples. The effects were almost instantaneous. First, an awareness of a common ancestry began to emerge that was to foster national consciousness and already hinted at unity. Second, there was the presumption that past and present are inextricably linked. In other words, it was taken for granted that a classical author like Tacitus could be used to solve modern arguments of race and, significantly, territory. But most important of all was the self-realisation that the Germans had never been beaten by the Romans. All three ideas converged in the works of the Alsace-born humanist and theologian Jakob Wimpfeling, whose 1501 *Germania* is a forceful tract, pointing out the differences between the unsullied north and the diseased south. It also puts the view forward, one that was to have repercussions, that the Rhine should not be seen as the boundary with France.

Underpinning this was the rediscovery of Tacitus' *Annals*, the first six books of which were published in Rome in 1515 (ordered by Pope Leo X). That same year, the German humanist Beatus Rhenanus discovered Velleius Paterculus' *Roman History* in the Benedictine monastery of Murbach. Although Rhenanus complained that the manuscript was 'so monstrously corrupt that no human ingenuity could restore all of it', it was subsequently published in Basel in 1520.[4] That edition also boasts the first modern pictorial representation of the battle. The images of Varus and Arminius are labelled, one of the last times in which that was to happen.

These discoveries, what was now a wealth of classical source material, moved the arguments on to a more personal and combative level. With his reports of Arminius, the 'deliverer of Germany', as Tacitus called him, who 'in war remained unconquered', became the instant focus and hope for German aspirations. As this occurred, Arminius stopped being a half-remembered, semi-legendary figure and started becoming what one modern academic calls: 'a sharply delineated historical personality'.⁵ This is not to say that his mythic qualities are not brought to the fore. As he comes out of the billowing smoke of legend, he emerges dressed in new robes, the ideal man and the defender of liberty.

Under the German humanists, such as Ulrich von Hutten, Arminius stopped being a tribal leader from the dim and distant past, laying the foundations for his image as a national hero. The Cheruscan is resurrected as the embodiment of Germany, a unifying force, the symbol for the will internally to unify and externally to make a stand against invaders.

In 1522 Ulrich von Hutten wrote the first dramatic account of Arminius, though it was not published until several years after his death. His aim was both to glorify Germany's past and to call for unity against a common foe. In *Arminius*, the Cheruscan is 'the most free, most invincible and most German of them all'.⁶ Hutten's hatred of Rome was as virulent as that of Arminius. Hutten's inspiration was the classical Greek satirist Lucian of Samosata and his *Discourse of the Dead*. In the original version, set in the underworld, Alexander the Great, Scipio and Hannibal argue over who deserves the title of the greatest general of all time. Hutten introduces Arminius into that ancient argument. With Tacitus as his second, the Cheruscan argues that he has been unjustly ignored. Inevitably in the dialogue, Arminius comes out top: he had fought the Roman Empire at its peak, he had done so with no thought of personal gain and, symbolically, he had won. King Minos, who sits as judge in both Lucian's and Hutten's versions, declares Arminius the winner.

An important point to bear in mind, though, is that Hutten was arguing only to Europe's educated class. There is no attempt here to engage the common man. Hutten wrote in Latin and his work was not translated into German until 1815. The first wholly German representation of Arminius appeared in 1543, when Burkhard Waldis published *Illustrierte Reimchronik*, tales of the twelve greatest ancient Germans, written in entertainingly bad rhyming couplets:

> Arminius, called Hermann in our tongue,
> a warrior hero, strong and brave and young,
> mature and true in action and in word,
> born in the Harz, a noble Saxon lord.[7]

But as Arminius was increasingly being groomed as a nationalist hero, he also found himself adopted by another cause. October 1517 heard the hammer-blow that echoed round Europe as Martin Luther questioned the sale of indulgences and nailed his ninety-five theses to the door of the Castle Church in Wittenberg. With Arminius co-opted as a champion for the Protestant cause, the wars between Rome and Germany immediately became a parable for the struggle between Catholic and Protestant. What Arminius did was to give both authority and focus to the country's long-simmering dispute with the papacy.

At the same time, the sixteenth century also saw the increased Germanification of the story, as Arminius turned into Hermann. There remains some confusion about when this happened. The most likely answer is that it was Martin Luther himself. It remains one of the more controversial and debated name-changes in linguistic history. One modern historian claims that 'the name [Arminius] certainly has nothing to do with the name Hermann'.[8] This is nonsense. As discussed in chapter three, Arminius is a perfectly logical Romanisation of a name which has definite primitive Germanic elements and Hermann is a logical enough back-resolution of that Latinised name.

Linguistics aside, up to now, Arminius had mostly inhabited the intellectual planes and religious nuances of Latin-based polemic. With the seventeenth century, he began his move from the ivory towers of European academia and started to reach out to the masses.

Daniel Caspar von Lohenstein's immense, apparently shapeless and nigh-on unreadable novel *Magnanimous General Arminius, or Hermann* may be seen as the first attempt to do so. Although unfinished at the time of the author's death at the age of 48, it was published four years later – all 3,076 quarto pages of it – in 1687. Nowadays as little discussed as it is read, it stands as a parable for the social and political situation of Germany after the ravages of the Thirty Years War.

Of the eighteen books which make up the novel, only four concern themselves directly with Arminius, though elsewhere other characters contribute to the background about his childhood and so on. It is Book I that contains the heart of the story. Much more than is seen in later literary versions, Varus is the catalyst and arguably the central character in Lohenstein's novel. As a Roman he exemplifies the enemy, while his seduction of a Germanic princess provides the moral reason of the revolt. From the outset, the familiar figures are drawn with exaggerated characteristics: Varus is voluptuous, Segestes is selfish, Thusnelda is noble, Maroboduus is fickle and Arminius is heroic.

There are fewer attempts in the novel to reconcile the views of the ancients with the mores of his own time, though Lohenstein knew his Tacitus and Velleius Paterculus intimately. Instead his Arminius betrays the great baroque theme of the beauty of the human soul and sets up the ideals of heroism in the face of fate.

Arminius also now began to move out of Germany. The first French version of the play, *Arminius ou les frères ennemis*, by Georges de Scudéry, which focused on the relationship between Arminius and his brother, appeared in 1643. This was followed in 1685 by the stage smash hit *Arminius*, written by Jean-Galbert Campistron. Here the battle for freedom is background to a love triangle between Arminius, Varus and Thusnelda (Isménie in the play), and so popular was it that it played twenty-nine times in the next fifteen years.

Understandably, though, here nationalistic tendencies are kept to the background and, in the grand scheme of things, this was little more than a foot across the Rhine. Almost as if the past few centuries had been a period of gestation, required for the idea of Arminius to take root, he began to grow and to flourish in the Germany of Frederick the Great. The Prussian king was one of the chosen children of the Enlightenment, an accomplished musician and philosopher, a friend to both Voltaire and Bach. His era was one of a great flowering of culture. It was the time of artists like Goethe and Schiller, while thinkers like Johann Gottfried Herder led the charge against the supremacy of classical culture, calling instead for native culture from the vernacular arts.

In this enlightened environment, Arminius began to change, particularly in the hands of Johann Elias Schlegel, the author in 1740–1 of the first full play on the subject of Arminius, called *Hermann*, written in Leipzig when he was in his early twenties. Gone are baroque flourishes and broader moral themes; instead the characters are recognisably human. The play's main theme of the division of Germany into pro- and anti-Roman parties is reflected in the fact that most of the action takes place in a sacred grove before and after the battle. Dialogue focuses on the relationship and rivalry between Hermann and Segest. An intriguing nuance is that Flavus, Arminius' brother, takes a much more important role, having fallen in love with Thusnelda, though the love theme is not the core of the play. Segest is in many ways the central character, prepared to use the weak Roman commander and sell out his country.

Hermann is a statement of independence rather than a call for autonomy, a quiet announcement rather than an aggressive declaration. Arminius is advised by his father to be guided by traditional German virtues (loyalty, magnanimity, love of freedom) and to protect his native land. Written only a few years after the accession of Frederick the Great, it is clearly influenced by that era. Arminius is being shaped, not to be a despot, but rather to be the first servant of the country.

If Schlegel is the dominant apologist for Arminius in the first half of the eighteenth century, the lyric poet Friedrich Gottlieb Klopstock made the second half his own. Sandwiched in between, a number of Arminius poets flourished. Justus Möser's 1749 tragedy *Arminius* is a curiosity because of what it says about Germany at the time. It had little influence (it was never performed), but with its call for a prince to unite the country it holds up a mirror to a fragmented and disunified state pinning its hopes on Frederick's rule. Most of the other works are barely of interest, even to specialists.

But Klopstock raised the argument on to another plane. After the ravages of the Second World War it is difficult to see his obsessions with Norse mythology and his frequent use of words like '*Volk*' and '*Vaterland*' as anything other than sinister, despite the fact that his inspirations were more religious than political. In his youth, Klopstock wrote about Henry I, the German king who beat the Magyars at Lechfeld in 955, but from the 1750s onwards he fixated on Arminius. Not counting his many odes on the subject, half of his dramatic output deals with the themes of Arminius: *Hermann's Battle*, published in 1769; *Hermann and the Princes* in 1784 and *Hermann's Death* in the late 1780s. To call them plays as they are understood today is a misconception. The style of Klopstock's dramas is called *Bardiete*, deliberately anachronistic and supposedly in the style of the ancient Celtic bards.

It is his second play that remains the most interesting for readers today. The first play is, to modern eyes at least, a clumsy piece extolling the virtues of a united Germany, and the third is dramatically masterful, focusing on Hermann's downfall, yet strangely dull. *Hermann and the Princes* takes a much more compelling approach, focusing on the inner strife and jealousy that surrounded a successful Hermann. It is set in AD 15, several years after the events of the Teutoburg Forest and during Germanicus' campaigns of revenge, at the moment when the Germans are debating whether to attack Caecina's camp. The play opens, significantly, with the Cheruscan chief absent. All of the other princes are sitting around, arguing the benefits of Arminius' plan to lure the Romans into the swamps. The play's tragedy lies in that it becomes clear that the princes would rather accept defeat than follow Hermann to another victory. It is a depressingly modern message: heroism and self-sacrifice can always be trumped by human selfishness and cynicism.

Klopstock's great theme is patriotic fervour. Although still not overtly political, he is resolutely national. One chorus of his first play, *Hermann's Battle*, praises the strength of a united nation:

You are the thickest, shadiest oak
In the innermost grove
The highest, oldest, most sacred oak,
O fatherland.

The key word is oak, a symbol for the battle, for Teutoburg Forest, indeed for Germany itself. Much in the same way that writers had been luxuriating in this kind of woodland nativism, we see the gradual evolution of the oak as a symbol for Arminius and his struggle in paintings of the time, just as medieval artists used the lion to symbolise St Jerome. The importance of this imagery and sylvan idealism is reflected in the Göttinger Hainbund, the Grove Leagues set up by students at Göttingen University in the early 1770s to spend nights in forests dreaming of a new Germany, and in the blue 100-mark note that, even a century later, portrayed Germania holding the emblems of commerce and industry, while watching battleships speed into the middle distance from under an oak.

An almost innocent idealism comes through in visual arts of the time. Philip Clüwer's engravings of early Germans were reprinted in several books from the early seventeenth century onwards. It cannot be an accident that his *Germanic Couple* recalls Adam and Eve. There is certainly something static and unthreatening in *Hermann's Triumph after his Victory over Varus* by the court artist Johann Heinrich Tischbein the Elder, painted in 1758. As his men march past after the battle, some eagles held aloft, Arminius stands under an oak on a slight hill. Right arm raised, left hand on his hip, he is speaking to his men. To modern eyes, he looks a little incongruous, especially because of the red tights and pink singlet, but he is without doubt the hero.

Tischbein's painting is a general comment on heroism. Others focus much more on human aspects. The illustrator Daniel Nikolaus Chodowiecki, in a book from 1782, has Arminius in the moments after the Battle of Teutoburg Forest. Standing again under an oak tree with Thusnelda looking on and surrounded by druids, some of whom are holding Varus' eagle standards, Arminius kisses a young boy mortally wounded in the battle. Despite the glorious victory the Cheruscan leader has the humanity to give his attention to an individual. The charming *Thusnelda Crowning Hermann* by the Swiss neoclassical painter Angelika Kauffmann, painted in 1786, similarly focuses on the individual. She puts Thusnelda, seated and dressed in white, centre-stage, but yet again she is under an oak tree.

The shift to the more aggressive, less innocent imagery can in many ways be blamed on Napoleon Bonaparte. Nothing did as much to galvanise German intellectuals to think about what it meant to be a nation and to articulate the idea of German unification than French aggression towards Germany at the start of the nineteenth century.

Arminius' desire for freedom was clutched at by a nation that was politically fragmented, economically ruined and militarily humiliated. These stirrings were perhaps best articulated by the philosopher Johann Gottlieb Fichte. After being disgraced at the hands of the French at Jena following Prussia's ill-advised declaration of war on Napoleon in 1806, Fichte delivered a series of lectures, his *Addresses to the German Nation*, in Berlin on the steps Germany should take towards a recovery. In his idealisation of his country and his countrymen, Fichte develops and refines Rousseau's theme of the noble savage. His fourth address ponders why it was that the German nation and Arminius rejected Rome. With flair, he concedes Roman brilliance, their refinements, their laws and their titles. But, Fichte concludes, 'All those blessings which the Romans offered meant slavery to them because then they would have to become something that was not German, they would have to become half-Roman. They assumed as a matter of course that every man would rather die than become half a Roman, and that a true German could only want to live in order to be, and to remain, just a German and to bring up his children as Germans.'[9]

With Fichte's words echoing round the country, the German playwright Heinrich von Kleist began work on what remains the highest dramatic interpretation of the Arminius theme in literature: *Die Hermannsschlacht*. It was written between May and December 1808 for an intended performance in a Vienna that was mobilising against Napoleon.

It is the first overtly political representation of the battle. In an extreme reaction to extreme times, Kleist calls for total sacrifice in times of total crises. The play is shaped to be a piece of propaganda (the author himself admits at the beginning that 'it is meat for the present'), yet it is also the period's most intriguing literary representation of the struggle in the Teutoburg Forest. The Romans become mouthpieces for Kleist's views of France's conquering intentions. From their point of view, the Germans are to be despised and their nationalist goals are to be ridiculed.

An interesting nuance is that Marbod (Maroboduus) is brought into the story. If Kleist's own time began to see the expression of Greater Germany, while Hermann stands for Germany, then Marbod is Austria. It is significant that at the end of the play it is Marbod who decisively beats Varus. Despite his victory, Marbod rejects Cheruscan homage and instead proposes that Hermann become leader of a united Germania. The question of who does ultimately succeed to power is left open.

This is much more overtly political than the Arminius of the eighteenth-century poets. With themes of honour and integrity, Schlegel's Hermann is an idealisation. In Klopstock's trilogy, Arminius is only political in the sense that he is a national figure. But in Kleist we see a seismic shift. Forget any thoughts of gentility or Hamlet-style soul-searching. Kleist's Hermann is an aggressively driven character. He is happy to get his hands dirty. He is an indignant and angry man; he is also a secretive, duplicitous operator. In other words he is a recognisable political character. The message he sends is that all means are acceptable if they achieve the ends of an independent Germany. All morality can and should be sacrificed in the interests of the national cause. Above all, there can never be any compromise with the Romans. 'Hate is my duty and anger is my virtue as long as they defy Germany,' Arminius says.[10]

This shift in literary representations of Arminius is mirrored in art. In the eighteenth century, he is the ideal citizen, the ideal hero, the ideal man. But after Napoleon's humiliation of Germany there is a shift from this chocolate box romanticism to much more aggressive, slightly sinister representations. If it were possible, paintings become even more overtly political following the Rhine crisis of the 1840s. The French government had suffered a humiliating diplomatic defeat in the Middle East. To divert the attention of its citizens from this foreign-policy debacle and to restore national pride, France declared its intention to recapture the left bank of the Rhine from the Germans and to re-establish the river as the country's natural eastern border. The German response to this sabre-rattling was defiance.

Lorenz Clasen's *Germania on Guard at the Rhine* from 1860 is possibly the best-known example of the broader genre, but several artists focused specifically on the story of Arminius. The most arresting example is Wilhelm Lindenschmidt's particularly martial *Hermannsschlacht*, painted at some time in the 1840s and now in the Staatliche Kunsthalle in Karlsruhe. A barely armoured Arminius astride a white horse, a shimmering sword in his hand, is anointed with divine light. Despite the bodies of several warriors that feature in the bottom of the picture, and the chaos surrounding the Cheruscan leader himself, there is no doubt of the outcome. They may be pressed but the Germans will win.

Friedrich Gunkel's *Die Hermannsschlacht*, from 1864, takes a similar approach. Arminius, sword in hand, on a rearing white horse about to charge down some archers, is contrasted with a Roman, back to the viewer, falling off an injured black horse. There is the same crude, yet effective, use of light throughout: the Germanic army on the left of the painting, charging forward, is bathed in light, while the Romans, crouching, retreating and dying on the right, are in semi-darkness. Again the outcome of the victory is made clear. After Arminius, the viewer's eye is drawn to action in the bottom right corner, where two legionaries are carrying off a wounded comrade.

After German success in the Battle of Sedan in September 1870, which crushed the Second French Empire of Napoleon III and led to the establishment of the German Reich under the watchful eye of the Iron Chancellor Otto von Bismark the following year, the arrogance of a young, victorious nation comes through. In Karl von Piloty's 1875 *Thusnelda in the Triumphal March of Germanicus*, Arminius' wife and son stand uncowed before the Romans. They will never be beaten and have no intention of bowing to anyone. Friedrich Tüshaus's *Battle between Germans and Romans at the Rhine* from 1876 shows the Romans at the moment of a rout. The intentions in the image are all too clear: any invaders of Germany will be pushed into the Rhine.

The above examples are all by private artists. They reflect the political mood around them. But Arminius now began to appear in state-sponsored art; the connection was explicitly made between Arminius as the representative of the German people and the modern German state. An attempt had been made in 1848. An Arminius memorial coin was handed out on the occasion of the opening session of the first German parliament in Frankfurt, but the institution's failure makes this a one-off. Between 1870 and 1873, however, the painter Peter Janssen was commissioned to decorate the town hall of Krefeld in North Rhein-Westfalia, with a series of eight paintings on the theme of Arminius. They are impressive pieces of art. As well as the obvious themes, such as the battle itself and Thusnelda in Germanicus' triumph, one painting is of the goddess Germania, spear in hand, leaning on a shield, telling Drusus that he may not cross the Elbe. Another is of Maroboduus captive in Ravenna, being gawked at by his guards. The paintings survived Allied bombing during the Second World War; nonetheless it says something about their original nationalistic intentions that they have never been returned to the walls of the town hall.

The emergent confidence resulted in a huge flowering of the arts as the youthful nation found its feet. A new country meant new museums and new literature that could all be funded by a rapidly growing economy, and that had an audience as the population of the cities boomed. Berlin's population grew from 400,000 in 1800 to 4 million by 1900. At the same time, there was a tiny, yet significant shift away from the classical humanistic education. It was eventually voiced at the highest level by Kaiser Wilhelm II, who wrote on the school reforms of the 1890s that 'we must educate young Germans, not young Greeks or Romans.'[11] The politicians were using the Germani to make the distinction between 'them' and 'us'. Of course they were capitalising on what, in retrospect, was a distinct trend. The trickle had started earlier. A journal entitled *Thusnelda*, devoted to the study of Germanic history, had been founded in 1807, followed in 1814 by one called *Hermann*. It is also possible to point to the numerous Arminiusstraßen in Germany. For example, the one in Moabit, the working-class district of Berlin, was named in 1879.

It would be easy to regard the reverence accorded Arminius as a purely German phenomenon, but of course many European countries throughout the first half of the nineteenth century were searching for a national hero. Over a similar period, Britain saw the growth of the cult of Boudicca, and in France there was that of Vercingetorix, both of which provide counterpoints to Arminius. The ways in which these three Celtic heroes were represented in statues in the individual countries highlights very different approaches to nationalism and the past. Britain's offering on Westminster Bridge is understated and unprepossessing; the French statue at Alise-Sainte-Reine commemorates the heroic but futile. But the Germans celebrated the valiant and victorious. There is little doubt that the Hermannsdenkmal on the Grotenburg near Detmold is a most dramatic physical representation of the Arminius myth, a sign of muscular Germanism.

Suggestions for a heroic statue of some sort in Germany to celebrate the Battle of Teutoburg Forest went back centuries, but these ideas did not begin to coalesce until 1838, when Joseph Ernst von Bandel took on the job. 'My memorial shall have but one object, the figure itself,' he wrote. A devoted German patriot, von Bandel reveals himself as something of a mystic in his account of how he found the spot where he was to build his monument, two years previously:

It was early on a beautiful morning in September, 1836, that I started to ascend the highest peak of the Teutoburgian forest, the Grotenburg. At the foot of the mountain I found by a little pond a twelve-year-old boy who agreed to take me to the top. He proved a talkative companion, and led me through thick and thin to the old stone wall. The higher I went the more surprised I was at the beauty of the mountain form. At last we came to the top of the peak, which was then entirely free from trees of any size, for only stunted pines showed themselves from the thick sweet-broom. The beeches and oaks just down the mountain were dead, partly from old age and partly from the beating of the storms. Only the lowest part of the peak was fresh and green with oaks and beeches. I knew this mountain peak, which lifted itself, cone-shaped, in the midst of the deepest valleys of the range (the poor Romans who were caught fast in these ravines even Jupiter himself could not rescue) as a fitting place for my memorial. From it one could look into all the valleys, and upon it a statue could be seen at the greatest distance. I found on the summit a pile of stones, and I said to my little conductor, 'Here, boy, will I build a monument.' Whereupon he looked at me as if he were astounded.[12]

Bandel was not to know then that his vision would take thirty-nine years to realise – the rest of his life. Cruelly, like a monumental Beethoven, he was denied sight of his own genius, going blind in his final years. He started work in 1838, financed by donations not only from Germany, but also countrymen who had emigrated to Britain (Queen Victoria's consort, Prince Albert, subscribed) and the United States.[13] Although the impressive base was by then finished, by 1846 work had stopped for financial reasons. The work was given a new lease of life after the 1860s. The future Kaiser, Wilhelm I, supported it and the new German parliament underwrote a considerable part of Bandel's vision. It was finished in 1875 in the afterglow of France's humiliation by Germany in the Franco-Prussian war, and it was officially dedicated on 16 August with a vast pageant, Kaiser Wilhelm in attendance.

Any visitor can see why it so easily grabbed the public imagination and has appeared on all manner of advertising from cigars to bottles of beer ever since. First, it is huge, as imposing as the Washington Memorial. There is virtually no ornamentation on the cylindrical dome-like base of the statue. Into the cylinder are cut ten Gothic-style niches that are flanked by triple-branching columns topped with oak-leaved capitals. Not only do they stop the effect from being too austere and subdued: the choice of oak reflects the myth and Germany's *Urwald*.

Upon the dome-shaped top is Arminius, 'rising' in Bandel's intentions 'from the mountain as naturally as the fir trees, so that upon it my Arminius may seem to stand free in the heaven'. Dressed in a short-sleeved tunic, a wide belt with sword chain and a winged helmet, the figure, 26.5m in height, is built up of more than 200 beaten-copper sheets (bronze was too heavy). These were then riveted on to great iron cylinders which were bolted on to a socket plate.

Standing on a Roman eagle and fasces, Arminius has his left hand resting on a shield. His right arm is raised and in his hand he holds a sword: Nothung, Siegfried's blade. Specially built by Krupp, it weighs 550kg. The words 'German unity is my strength' are engraved on one side, 'My strength is Germany's might' on the other. And the sword is not pointing south, as might be expected: it is aimed at France. Even without Tacitus' epitaph for Arminius inscribed into one of the niches, a more blatant expression of nationalism is hard to consider and is unimaginable without the confidence given to the country by the reforms of the Iron Chancellor, Otto von Bismark.

When the German poet Heinrich Heine returned to Germany in 1843, after a time at a spa in the Pyrenees, he wrote his series of poems *Germany: a Winter's Tale*. A joy to read, it is a witty attack on all things Prussian, mocking, in no particular order, the Church, the monarchy and German nationalism. Naturally enough, he visited the half-finished Hermannsdenkmal:

> This is the Teutoburg Forest
> as described by Tacitus,
> and this is the classical swamp
> where Varus got himself stuck.

> It was here that the leader of the Cherusci,
> Hermann, the noble thane, defeated him,
> and German nationality
> was victorious in all this mud.

If Hermann and his blond hordes
had not won the battle,
there would be no more freedom
and we should all be Romans!

In our fatherland there would only be
Roman customs and language;
there would even be Vestal Virgins in Munich,
and the Swabians would be called Quirites.

Despite the satirical tone that mocks nationalist pretensions, Heine does confess in the end that 'I contributed to it myself.'[14]

If Fichte's rhetoric at the turn of the century was the overt face of this growing national identity, Arminius found himself pulled at the same time in another, slightly different direction, into that of the people and people's history advocated by Herder. The nineteenth century saw a growing interest in folk songs; myths such as the Ring Saga that were so to influence Richard Wagner, and fairy stories by such proselytisers as the brothers Grimm. These back-to-nature ideals saw the ancient Germans as 'almost the [American] Indians of antiquity'.[15] Jacob Grimm, a professor of philology as well as a publisher of folk tales, was one of the first academics to put Tacitus' *Germania* on a university syllabus, where it remained, as much holy writ as set text. For all of these, the forest is both a place of change and of surprise, but also of resolution. Indeed it is virtually impossible to think of the Grimm tales without picturing a forest. The whole of Wagner's *Ring* cycle can be seen to be about the wooden spear which Wotan carves from Yggdrasil, the ash tree of Life. Arminius was being absorbed, more quietly, by Romanticism.

Even though many have tried to find a connection between Siegfried and Arminius, it is curious that the Cheruscan chief was not explicitly co-opted by Wagner.[16] It would have fitted his themes perfectly. Nonetheless, the conflict has inspired a large number of operas but, as one commentator has written, 'few of the composers will be familiar even to a devoted student of opera'.[17] It is to be regretted that although the classical composer Christoph Gluck was moved by the settings he made for Klopstock's dramas, he never set down the music, nor were they ever to become an opera. Some thirty-seven different operatic Arminiuses appeared in the eighteenth century, and a further eighteen in the nineteenth and twentieth centuries. Domenico Scarlatti and Johann Adolph Hasse are among the few composers who will have been heard of and, in both cases, the operas are much stronger musically than dramatically.

Only two have been recorded in modern times and inevitably both are called *Arminio*. The former, which counts as the first German opera, though sung in Italian, was written by the composer/violinist Heinrich Ignaz Franz von Biber at the end of the seventeenth century (the exact date is disputed) in Salzburg. The other is George Frederick Handel's *Arminio*, written in the autumn of 1736 in a particularly fruitful period of the composer's life. While, musically, it will satisfy the most jaded *barocchisti*, it is incomprehensible even by the shaky standards of opera – a matter not helped by the fact that the composer seemingly arbitrarily cut around a thousand lines of text from Antonio Salvi's libretto. Suffice to say that the plot exists only in the composer's imagination and that all's well that ends well.[18]

If Arminius kept a polite distance from so-called high culture, he found his niche in popular songs (the exception is Schubert's 'Hermann und Thusnelda', a song for two voices and piano and based on a text by Klopstock). Two written in the mid- to late nineteenth century, one by Albert Methfessel and another by Viktor von Scheffel, are still sung today. 'Gab's darum eine Hermannschlacht?' ('Was this why Hermann won the day?') was especially popular during the Second World War, while 'Als die Römer frech geworden' ('Some Romans once got uppity'), by Viktor von Scheffel, remains well liked to this day (several of the author's friends recall singing it in their youth) and the song-name sees regular use in newspaper headlines and as the title of lectures.[19]

During the reign of Wilhelm II, up until the end of the First World War there was what one modern writer has called 'an isolated intermezzo' in Arminius imagery.[20] Certainly it is true that in trying to position himself internationally as the successor to Augustus, the

Kaiser was an enthusiastic admirer of Rome. Nonetheless, it is not strictly fair to see the period as a timeout. The 1,900th anniversary of the battle in 1909, for example, saw massive celebrations all over Germany. During the First World War, Arminius was drafted to remind the people of the sacrifice that was needed of them in a 1915 play called *Die Varusschlacht* by Adolf Römheld, while in the academic field 1900 had seen the publication of a commentary of Tacitus' *Germania* that comes in at an almost grotesque 750 pages. Wilhelm II could no more halt imagery of Arminius than Canute could push back the sea. For nationalism to exist, there has to be some idea of a nation. By now Arminius was firmly in the public domain. The damage had already been done.

Nationalism was only ever going to increase rather than recede in a Weimar Republic that felt embittered and humiliated by the terms of the Treaty of Versailles. The bellicose defensiveness that this had engendered saw yet another upturn of interest in German culture and history. Stripped of its land, with a ruined economy and social fragmentation, the country took refuge in the past, in what was called *Deutschtum*, or German-ness. One aspect of this was the growth of walking clubs and a reaffirmed idealisation of the forests. The Hermannsweg, the 156km-long Hermann Way, which starts at the Rhine and passes the Hermannsdenkmal, remains one of the most popular walking routes in Germany to this day. But it was also an ideal that was reflected in novels, music and art at the time. As the historian Simon Schama notes, this 'all ensured that the Heimat had never seemed so leafy'.[21] But the radicalisation of the German soul, their *Volksseele*, that had been identified by Herder was no longer an unchanging absolute; rather it was now increasingly thought to be under threat from non-German forces.

The growing, black undercurrent, however, becomes ever more apparent throughout the period. The pastoral reverence of students and youth was preparing to pull on the jackboot. The celebrations in August 1925 of the 50th anniversary of the Hermannsdenkmal became the focus for 50,000 young ultra-nationalists to march on the monument, dressed in historical costumes and waving flags. Only two years previously, *Die Hermannschlacht*, the earliest surviving motion picture about the battle, was filmed. Shot in 1922 and 1923, and premiered in the Detmolder Landestheater in February 1924, it was made on location in and around the Externsteine in the Teutoburg Forest. As many as a thousand extras were used in the battle scenes of the film, which had been deemed lost until a copy turned up in the Moscow Archives in 1992. A tone of defiant hopefulness is seen at the beginning:

> Then comes a day of vengeance, when we thrust
> Our deadly enemy from the Saar and Rhineland shore
> Then shall we from our slavish fetters burst,
> be free and German as our fathers were. [22]

But following the Wall Street Crash of 1929, both unemployment and Nazi support boomed. Within only a year, Nazi representation in the Reichstag went up from 12 to 107; within three, unemployment had gone up from 1.3 million to 5.1 million; and within four, Adolf Hitler had completed his seizure of power and this patriotic zeal became considerably more unpleasant.

The sharp contrast from previous defensiveness to self-assured arrogance can be seen, if we stay with cinema, in the semi-documentary 1935–6 film *Ewiger Wald* (Eternal Forest), directed by Hans Springer and Rolf von Sonjewski-Jamrowski. Produced by the Nazi Culture Group it is an 'allegory of our history and life' that draws the parallel between the eternal forest and the eternal people. Broken into episodes, accompanied by a banal semi-poetic voiceover, the first part presents the Battle of Teutoburg Forest. This arboreal farrago is primarily of interest nowadays to cineastes. The special photography credit went to Ernst Kunstmann, who worked not only with Fritz Lang on *Metropolis*, but also with Leni Riefenstahl on both *Olympia* and *Triumph of the Will*. What makes the film important is that the shift in tone is markedly more assured and less apologetic, seen in the film's final line: 'The people, like the forest, will stand forever.'

German prehistory was becoming overtly political. The Nazi Party's ideologue Alfred Rosenberg went so far as to describe German prehistory as the 'Old Testament of the German people'. Archaeology was now a direct political tool and many scholars were to become both fellow travellers and the unwitting mouthpieces for the new political reality. Typical was one of the first academic dissertations to look at the Arminius motif in literature, which was published in 1937. It is a serious piece of scholarship and remains a useful work to this day, but within a few pages it is apparent that the author is overly obsessed with questions of race and the relationship between Führer and Volk. Other subjects were not immune either. A 1936 article about Gothic art begins, 'Since Arminius the Cheruscan's resistance against Rome, the German tribes have been fighting the same battle: the battle for German right and German freedom.'[23]

Nay-sayers were given short shrift. Those who had the temerity to suggest that the Germani were hardly what one would call the bringers of culture were dismissed. Eduard Norden, the professor for Latin studies at the University of Berlin, was widely excoriated when his book *Alt-Germanien* was published in 1934 for daring to use archaeological and anthropological evidence to question the accepted party line on German prehistory. The Reich's Deputy for German Prehistory and the leading Nazi archaeologist in the field, Hans Reinerth, described such views as 'the great ideological enemy of national prehistory'.[24]

Between 1928 and 1941 the number of academics in prehistory at German universities grew from thirteen to fifty-two. The groundwork for this had been laid by the writings of Gustaf Kossinna. Originally a philologist and librarian, then professor at Berlin from 1902 until his death in 1931, he was one of the first scholars to make prehistory an academic discipline. In a lecture in 1895 he asked the chilling question, 'Where in the present day territory of Germany are we dealing with Germani and where with non-German people?'[25] The expression of the notion that the boundaries of the ancient Germani had political relevance for the borders of the modern country as much as the distinction between German and non-German people was to have profound consequences. It is not possible to overemphasise Kossinna's importance. He was so influential because he was deliberately writing for the people.

He took prehistory out of the lecture theatre and brought it into the salons of Germany, so much so that his best-known work, *Die deutsche Vorgeschichte* (A Prehistory of Germany) went through eight editions between its publication in 1912, and 1941.

What lay at the core of the Nazi attraction to Arminius was less his opposition to Rome and more Tacitus' comments on German ethnicity. His one sentence, 'I agree with those who deem the Germans never to have intermarried with other nations; but to be a race, pure, unmixed, and stamped with a distinct character', has arguably done more to change Europe's landscape than any other. It, of course, matched Nazi ideology of a pure race perfectly and was articulated throughout the period almost verbatim. To take just two examples, Walter Groß, head of the Nazi Party's Office of Racial Policy, speaking before an audience of women at a rally in 1934, said, 'In our Reich, we are separating that which belongs to us, because it is blood of our blood, from that which does not belong to us, because it is foreign.' Julius Streicher, in his final editorial in the Nazi Party newspaper *Der Stürmer* in 1945, wrote, 'The German people are the last stronghold of European civilization, thanks to the continuing effect of the German people's inherited Germanic blood.'[26]

Despite this, Arminius was never to be central to Nazi thought – as with everything that Hitler attempted, expediency overrode idealism – but he stayed within shouting distance, dressed up as a blond-haired Nordic pin-up. After Hitler's seizure of power in 1933, German youth began to be portrayed as the heirs of ancient German warriors and the Cheruscans were just one of the many totemic figures to the Nazis that could be called upon to support their perverted view.

It goes without saying that Adolf Hitler himself admired Arminius. He mentioned him several times in private conversation, on one occasion calling him 'the first architect of our liberty'.[27] But if there is the feeling here that Hitler was in one sense paying only lip-service to heritage, he had recognised the value of early Germanic history for propaganda purposes. Even in *Mein Kampf*, written in the early 1920s while he was in prison in Landsberg Castle, the Führer had written, 'The lighter its scholarly baggage and the more exclusively it is directed towards the feelings of the masses, the more effective its success will be.'[28] That he never forgot this can be seen in the fact that he commissioned eight tapestries, 5.4m by 10m, from Werner Peiner, one of the best-known National Socialist painters. These were to be the artistic centrepieces of the new Reich Chancellery. The intention was to place the German Reich in a historical context for visiting dignitaries, and the theme for one of the tapestries (all of which were martial in nature) was the Battle of Teutoburg Forest. In the end, the factory in which the tapestries were supposed to be produced was never built, but in one sense the tapestries did exist throughout the Third Reich, because the art press continually published articles about them.

It would be wrong to see the interest in Germanic prehistory just as a political tool or even as solely an educated-middle-class issue. There was a continuing awareness of prehistory that went right through every level of society. As well as displays in museums, touring exhibitions and the emphasis on the teaching of prehistory in the school curriculum, Arminius had become part of popular culture. For example, in 1934 the Dresden-based cigarette company Eckstein produced a series of cards celebrating German history from Hermann the Cheruscan to Charlemagne, six of which illustrate events from the battle. The Hermannsdenkmal is given a particular prominence in an illustrated map of Germany published by the German Railways Information Bureau in the 1930s for British tourists. Covers of women's magazines displayed prehistoric themes, and Arminius was an image that was exploited on holiday brochures. Even household products emphasised their connection with the Germani either in their name or their advertising.

Arminius had travelled so far that it is now fair to identify Arminius' effect on popular culture. Novels about the Cheruscan became such an industry in their own right that between the end of the First World War and that of the Second World War, more than thirty novels were published, virtually all of them using the words 'liberator', 'hero' or 'the first German' somewhere in the title. It is irrelevant that from a literary point of view this phenomenon was an issue of quantity, not quality.[29]

Paul Albrecht's 1920 novel *Arminius-Sigurfrid* is a straight-forward retelling of the story, albeit mixed with elements of the Siegfried myth and written in the florid style popular at the time. The novel's title is taken from the conceit that Arminius changed his name from Sigurfrid when he joined the Roman army. When it was republished in Berlin in 1935, however, Albrecht added an introduction. 'If we have understood our mission correctly, then we must start again where the First Empire also started, to build up the edifice of Germanic greatness and get rid of any building-blocks that were alien,' he writes. Kossinna's lessons had been well learned.

While some novels toned down the nationalistic tub-thumping (Walter Heichen's *Thumelicus, Arminius' Son*, published in 1939, for example, tells the story of Arminius' heir from gladiator to freedom fighter in a comparatively straightforward manner), many more welcomed the spirit of the age with right arm held aloft. Hjalmar Kutzleb's 1933 novel *The First German: a novel of Hermann the Cheruscan* wholly captures the thoughts of the Nazi period: the glorification of the leader, the strength of the people and the denunciation of lesser races. One of the Jewish characters, inevitably a merchant, is particularly unpleasantly drawn. At one point Arminius says, 'Maybe it would be good if we wiped him and his type out before they eradicate us.' Its concept of the nation is entirely contemporary. The themes of *Lebensraum* come to the fore to the extent that at one point Arminius hatches a plan to invade Britain. It is a chilling novel for anyone with a sense of history.

Yet others appear even more extreme in this day and age. Freerk Hamkens' 1934 *Hermann the Cheruscan: a tale from early-Germanic history* is a particularly pernicious literary example of the Arminius myth, not just because it is more overtly political than the previous example (if that were possible) but because it is written for children. From a historical point of view it follows the events described by the ancients closely. It begins to diverge only after the death of Augustus. The campaigns of Germanicus and the capture of Thusnelda are compressed into a single year – AD 14 – while the suicide of Thusnelda is pure fiction.

The stench of Nazi theories on German culture permeates the book; the long prehistory of Germany is emphasised, as are ideas of German glory. 'If we need land and we don't have any, then we take it. We will ask nicely. And if they don't want to. Well then, war!' It is a direct transmission of the policy of Nazi expansions. The messages to its young readers are about being true to yourself and your people. It ends semi-poetically, 'People die, tribes fade. You will die as they did. I know one thing that lives for ever: reputation, won in death.' This is political brainwashing masquerading as literature.

All of this came to an abrupt end with the end of the Second World War. Naturally enough, postwar Germany was keen to suppress discussions of national heroes. But there are practical reasons, too, that went beyond the public rejection of Kossinna's theories and the prosecution of leading Nazi archaeologists like Hans Reinerth, who became a scapegoat for the profession. Germany – indeed all European countries – had managed to lose an entire generation of archaeologists and classical historians. Those who had not been killed or had emigrated were involved in exonerating themselves. The institutions themselves had not escaped damage either. A significant number of museums and sites were badly damaged; the best-known example is the Römisch-Germanische Kommission in Frankfurt but smaller ones, such as Haltern, which had direct relevance for any discussion of early Roman involvement in Germany, was bombed in 1945. Within this ideology-free environment, Arminius and the Germanic tribes suddenly found themselves isolated and ignored. They were sent back into the forests.

SEVEN

A Second Troy

At the end of the Second World War, Cheruscan warriors who had marched to the sound of the Reich that would last a thousand years, found themselves disarmed, disbanded and toothless. The enthusiasm that the Nazi regime had engendered for archaeology, through its massive investment in it, refused to go away. Some 130,000 tourists still ascend the Hermannsdenkmal near Detmold every year, such is its popular resonance.[1] The passion for ancient history in Britain that was generated by scholars and popularisers like Mortimer Wheeler and Leonard Cottrell had its counterpoint in Germany with C.W. Ceram. His *Gods, Graves and Scholars* remains in print and is as popular today as it was when it was first published in 1949.[2] But there is no mention whatsoever of Germanic archaeology.

A deliberate, unthreatening gloss was placed on Arminius. School-books in Germany unduly emphasised the evidence that there is for German cooperation with the Romans. Arguments that related to the purity of the Germanic tribes and discussions of Arminius' bloody resistance, which had been so much a part of German consciousness from the time of Frederick the Great until the dictatorship of Hitler, were played down. In an interview debating the role of pride in one's homeland (*Heimat*) and nationalism/patriotism, the German historian Hans-Ulrich Wehler rails against what he calls idiots who believe that 'Arminius and Charlemagne were German and that the German nation marched from the time of the migrations into the present.'[3]

Uncomfortably, German prehistory has been made to sing Schiller's *Ode to Joy* and to show itself to be in harmony with the political goal of a united Europe. So sensitive a subject is it deemed to be that only two special museum exhibitions dedicated to early Germanic history have taken place in the country since the war: the blandly titled 'Excavations in Germany, 1950–75' in Mainz in 1975; and then nothing for twenty-seven years, when 'People, Times, Regions' took place in Berlin in 2002, some twelve years after re-unification.

Germany's prehistory had become so unthreatening that it was even the subject of humour, at the hands, of all people, the French. In the 1963 comic book *Asterix and the Goths* (the third book in the series), France's relationship with Germany over the past century is caricatured – one of Asterix's German opponents looks distinctly like Otto von Bismark – as the plucky Gaulish warrior and his indomitable friend Obelix travel to Germany to rescue their druid. Although Arminius is not mentioned by name, the plot hinges on German desires to invade both Gaul and Rome, poking fun at the fear that had defined Germany's relationship with its southern European neighbours since the time of Marcus Lollius.

Within Germany, however, few attempted to engage in any seriousness with the theme. Anselm Kiefer, the leading exponent of German neo-Expressionism, is the exception. He is one of the rare exceptions; throughout his career, his work has mapped out Germany's psyche since the end of the war. He remains an artist who provokes and who is wary of any view of the world that is 'vulgarly Manichaean'.4 One of his best-known pictures is the 1978 work *Ways of Worldly Wisdom – Arminius' Battle*, a print with woodcuts of generals, politicians, philosophers and writers who eulogised Arminius. These portraits surround a fire that alludes to the furnace that engulfed Germany as a result of its nationalism, as well as the flames that burned so many books during the Nazi period. It gives a glimmer of hope, too, representing the new Germany that rose out of the ashes past.

But Kiefer is a lone voice. Much more commonly, Arminius had become an avowedly commercial character, an innocent figure of fun, appropriated for advertising rather than politics. He was more likely to be seen wielding a salami than Nothung, to have croissants rather than horns sticking out of his helmet. The Cheruscan commander has been used to endorse almost any kind of product imaginable, from food to banking services. Even at the museum in Kalkriese today, Thusnelda strawberry jam, Varus waffles and Hermann sausage are all for sale.

With the collapse of the Berlin Wall at the end of the 1980s and imminent German reunification, however, journalists began to reach for Arminius in greater numbers, especially whenever they wanted to sound alarm bells about German might without mentioning Hitler. In 1990, *Time* magazine analysed the implications of German unification for Europe by leading with the story of Arminius. A piece headlined 'Anything to fear?' reminds readers of the 'curse of their history' and suggests that it is 'a fact they may resent, but cannot ignore'. This has remained a convention to this day. As recently as 2003, in reaction to a minor diplomatic spat between Germany and Italy, the Italian journalist and author Roberto Pazzi took the opportunity to dredge up the ancient ambivalence between the two countries that started with the Battle of Teutoburg Forest. Italy is the 'warm maternal centre of Europe, the place where the egg of Greek civilisation had come to be hatched'; Germany is 'barbaric', a country that nurtured both Arminius and Charles V's Lutheran soldiers who 'entered the eternal city, raping and murdering nuns and priests' in 1527.[5]

But the question that the great German historian Theodor Mommsen had posed at the end of the nineteenth century was still waiting for an answer. Where had the battle taken place? As mentioned in the introduction, the search for the actual site of the conflict had become a cross between the quest for the Holy Grail and a cottage industry. Both academics and interested amateurs put forward some 700 theories that placed the battlefield pretty much everywhere in northern Germany and ranged from the balanced and believable to the simply bonkers.

With the benefit of hindsight, it should have been obvious that Kalkriese was the site of the battle, though with other spots clamouring for attention, it had been overlooked. In 1716, a local theologian called Zaharius Goeze with a particular interest in numismatics mentioned the large number of Roman coins that had been found in and around Kalkriese. Half a century later, in 1768, there was further mention of the number of coins that had been found as farmers in the area dug turf and tilled the land. One local field was even called the *Goldacker*, the 'field of gold'. Certainly the local landowners, the von Bar family, whose connection with the area stretched back centuries, had managed to amass a substantial collection of Roman gold and silver coins, the majority of which dated from the reign of Augustus. Fortunately, although the collection was stolen by Allied soldiers in 1945, it had been properly catalogued.

When Mommsen examined the collection, he concluded that the area around Kalkriese was the site of the battle. One reads his account with a slight jolt at how accurate his conclusions were. He identified the site at the south edge of the Great Moor and north of the Wiehengebirge correctly, spotting the tactical advantages that the relatively narrow pass would have given Arminius.[6] But his thoughts were conspicuously ignored, primarily because of the lack of any evidence of a battle. After all, so said the nay-sayers, hordes of coins found in northern Germany were hardly that rare an event.

It was not until the summer of 1987, almost a century later, that Tony Clunn, a major in the British army with the Armoured Field Ambulance and keen amateur metal-detector enthusiast, was able to confirm Mommsen's suggestion. When he started sweeping the area, no one believed that he would find anything. Not a single Roman coin or artefact had been found in the county for the past thirteen years. Undaunted, Clunn discovered the old military road marked on maps and decided to concentrate on one area of it. Soon his metal detector began to react to something under the soil. Clunn's account of that moment is riveting:

I cut away a square of turf, checked that first and, when I did not get a signal, continued carefully to clear out the black peat from within the hole. I rechecked the signal tone then picked up a handful of soil. No signal in the hole. Painstakingly, I sifted through the contents in my hand, but I could see nothing resembling a solid object as indicated by the signal. I sifted through again and then I saw it: black, small . . . and round! The merest glint of silver. It was a perfect silver coin, blackened with age, with the same black hue as the peaty soil: a Roman denarius. I saw the proud aquiline features of Augustus Caesar on one side, and on the other, two figures standing behind battle shields and crossed spears. I could hardly believe it. I stood transfixed, savouring a combination of disbelief, excitement, and the pure exhilaration of finding such a wonderful 2,000 year old artefact from ancient Rome.[7]

Within a fortnight, he had recovered a total of ninety-two coins. The region's head of archaeology, Wolfgang Schlüter, suggested that Clunn concentrate his search in the area around Kalkriese. At this stage, it crossed no one's mind that the site of Varus' defeat had been discovered. In fact, as Clunn turned up coin after coin over the next year, it was generally believed that what had been found was the horde of a merchant or some soldier.

It was not until he dug up three lead, oval-shaped objects in late 1988 that it became apparent that Clunn had unwittingly stumbled on something significant. The objects were slingshots used by Roman auxiliary troops. This was enough to remove the doubt once and for all, that the area Clunn was examining did not just have a trade connection, rather there was a military link here. Even though nothing had been found, as yet, to link the site to Varus, it was time to turn the excavations over to the professionals.

They began to dig in 1989, in a field called the Oberesch, which fortuitously turned out to be one of the main battlegrounds of the Varian disaster, if not the climax of the battle itself. The following year was one of slow realisation, as the sesterces began to drop regarding what it was they were dealing with. It was the excavations of the next twelve months that began to remove lingering doubts that what had been found was the site of the Battle of Teutoburg Forest. 'Varus wanted to be found,' said Susanne Wilbers-Rost, now lead archaeologist at Kalkriese, but who had then just been brought on board.[8]

The first artefact to bring the excavations in Kalkriese to wider national and international attention was the discovery of what at first looked like a rather unpromising, dark brown lump. On cleaning it turned out to be a stunning cavalry mask. The rapidity with which that has become the logo for the battlefield is testament to its quality and power to move after all these years. It was also regarded as an important enough find to appear on a stamp in 2001. Although several elements of German Roman history had appeared on special issues in previous years, from Drusus' Monument in 1962 and Xanten in 1975 to one celebrating the 2,000th anniversary of the town of Cologne in 2000, a lack of any physical remnant of the battle meant that Arminius' victory had never been celebrated, until now.

Perhaps the most impressive knock-on effect of this discovery was the attempt the following year to put a face to the cavalry officer mask, using evidence from the mask itself and human bones found nearby. Quite rightly they captured the national imagination. Finally, a real image, not one from a relief, coin or gem, nor a visage frozen in marble, a statue staring whitely and somehow inhumanly into the middle distance. Richard Helmer, professor of medicine and expert in craniofacial identification (he identified the bones of Josef Mengele), was able to reconstruct the face behind the mask.

The auxiliary who had worn the mask was nearing the end of his military service. A strong and powerful man, indicated by the thickness of the base of the skull that was found on the battlefield, he was 35–40 years old. He must have been looking forward to retirement. From a forensic study of the inside of the mask it was apparent that he had distinct scars on his nose and chin, the mementos of previous battles. The brown hair and eye colouring are supposition, based on a presumed Mediterranean heritage. Nonetheless the overall effect is both startling and moving as you come face to face with someone who was there, who saw what happened.

Back in the 1990 archaeological season, the second high spot of the year was the discovery of what was thought at first to be a Roman fort. In all likelihood, it was mooted, this was a marching camp of some kind. After a couple more months, the archaeologists began to realise that the majority of the Roman finds lay in front of the wall and not behind it. The legions had been the ones who were attacked at this spot. By the end of 1992, Wolfgang Schlüter was able to make a definitive statement that this was the site of the famous battle.

Of course there were numerous battles and skirmishes all over Germany throughout the Roman period. Without epigraphic or literary evidence from the site itself, what makes the archaeologists so sure that the battle they are still uncovering is the same Battle of Teutoburg Forest mentioned in the sources? The answer lies in the coins that have been found – more than 3,000 to date, 400 of them on the Oberesch itself. There was no doubt at all that the conflict that took place here did so during the early principate. First and foremost, all coins found, from the relatively small number of gold coins to the vast number of silver denarii coins or copper coins, can be dated to the reign of the Emperor Augustus. No coins from a later emperor have been found, which means that battle that happened here took place before AD 14.

But is it possible to narrow it down within Augustus' reign? He ruled for a long time and not only did he mint coins throughout, but as we have seen in previous chapters, Roman soldiers tramped pretty continually across Germany from the time of Marcus Lollius' debacle with the eagle of the Legion V for the next thirty-one years.

From the style and images used on the coins, as well as the mint marks, it is possible to be more accurate about the period in Augustus' long rule from which the discovered coins date. Around a fifth of the coins found are from a specific series minted in Lyons known as Lugdunum I, which dates from 8 BC onwards. These feature images of Gaius (born in 20 BC) and Lucius (born in 17 BC), Augustus' grandchildren, adopted as sons and heirs to the throne and celebrated throughout the empire around the time the series was minted. From a chronological point of view a *terminus post quem* is given, as both men died young: Lucius in AD 2 and Gaius two years after that.

Of the coins that were excavated in the pass, none come from the previous series that the Lyons mint produced (struck in 14/13 BC) or the subsequent one, which came into circulation between AD 10 and 14. So the latest coins that have been found date to between 2 BC and AD 1, which easily gives a date for the battlefield of between 2 BC and AD 10 – exactly what one would expect to find if this was the site where Arminius won.

The types of coins found confirm the military nature of the site and back up the evidence of the weaponry that has been uncovered. First of all, the majority of those discovered are copper coins, called asses, the currency the soldiers would most commonly use. But the overwhelming evidence is that the majority of these coins were countermarked – some 96 per cent of them. Countermarked coins were exclusively given to soldiers on certain occasions – before a campaign or on the accession of a new governor – and are a hall-mark of a military zone. They rarely turned up in civilian hands. The countermarks used, 'AVG', 'IMP', 'C VAL' and 'VAR', would seem most obviously to be read as 'Augustus', 'Imperator', 'Caius Numonius Vala' and 'Publius Quinctilius Varus'.

It is the last one of these that clinches it. The 'VAR' countermark was only used for the few short years that Varus was governor. No other major conflict during the governorship of Varus is reported. The sheer variety of military finds suggests that a huge combined force was involved in a battle here, something that would certainly not have gone unreported. There was no doubt: part of the Battle of Teutoburg Forest had been found.

Now that the site had been rediscovered, the inevitable desire to celebrate such an important event was tempered by the problem of how to incorporate Arminius' victory back into modern German mythology, especially in a country that had been newly unified. Gone, inevitably, were all traces of nationalism. More-serious broadsheets commemorated the spirit of discovery, of adventure that harked back to the glory days of archaeology. So the *Neue Osnabrücker Zeitung* headlined an article 'Excavations in Kalkriese a second Troy'. The confusion is more apparent in the way that it was presented in the popular press. Here, the battle was the conflict between 'David and Goliath'; it was a case of the first world being beaten by the third world and the victory of the German guerrillas should be seen as an 'early Vietnam'.[9] There is no mention anywhere of conquering predecessors and the glorious German heritage.

This more tempered and subdued tone can be seen in the frequent allusions to the events of AD 9 in historical novels throughout Europe from the 1990s onwards. That these were not now refracted through a nationalistic prism means that the history itself had a chance to shine in its own terms. In France, Anne Bernet has the prefect of Judaea taking part in the battle in her 1998 novel *Les mémoires de Ponce Pilate*; in Germany, Jörg Kastner has written a series of novels about the era since 1995, starting with *Thorag oder die Rückkehr des Germanen* (Thorag, or the Return of the German); and in Britain's *The Iron Hand of Mars*, Lindsey Davis's popular Roman detective Marcus Didius Falco is sent off to the wilds of Germany in AD 71 and ends up spending a night in the Teutoburg Forest.

By far the best of this genre are David Wishart's 1995 novel *Ovid* and Iris Kammerer's *Der Tribun* (The Tribune) from 2004, both of which deal with the Battle of Teutoburg Forest directly. The former is a hugely entertaining conspiracy theory that links the exile of the poet Ovid to the loss of the three legions under Varus. As well as witty characterisations of individuals like Asprenas, what makes it stand out is the generally sympathetic portrait of the Roman governor. He is corrupted and betrayed by Arminius, but he is not wholly incompetent. A real sense is also given of the way in which the subject became one to be avoided in the polite society in Rome. In Iris Kammerer's book, Gaius Cornelius Cinna, the great-grandson of Pompey the Great and the tribune of the book's title, is sent on a secret mission to warn Varus of the Cheruscan conspiracy. Captured and knocked out by a Cheruscan noble, he finds, when he regains consciousness, that the Battle of Teutoburg Forest is history and the three legions have been lost. In the author's note, Kammerer explicitly states that her intention was to reconstruct what happened and to remove the German patriotism and nationalism which has grown around the story.

The issue that had to be addressed, that in many ways goes to the heart of Germany's relationship with its own history, was how to present the site to the public. Certainly some solution had to be found. A farmhouse and its outbuildings had already been taken over near where the archaeologists were working, but something considerably more formal was needed. From a practical point of view alone, they were in danger of being overwhelmed. The jerry-built information centre was being swamped: some 50,000 visitors had come by the end of 2000.

The new, purpose-built museum and park of Kalkriese opened two years later, towards the end of April 2002 – on the 21st, the traditional founding date of Rome. Landscaped by Swiss architects Gigon & Guyer, with the exhibition space designed by Paris-based Integral Concept, all at a cost of 14 million, it consciously distances the battle from purely a German past. It is difficult to think of a monument more removed from the martial grandeur of Bandel's fantasy in stone. The site has been sympathetically and intelligently managed.

As you pass through the gate, almost the first thing you see is a slightly disconcerting tower to your left, at the south-eastern end of the park. It is a vast, vaguely intimidating structure, 37m high and made of what turns out to be huge panels of rusted corten steel on top of a steel frame. As you climb the tower, random openings frame views of the countryside, not allowing an overview of the site until you reach the top. The choice of structural material for the tower is no accident – a reference to the weaponry used and found – nor is its resemblance to a military watchtower.

At the base, a single-storey museum sticks out at right angles. It is by far the least successful aspect of the entire site. Intriguing from a design point of view, the permanent exhibition fails at a practical level. The curators decided not to replicate the standard layout of archaeological museums; instead they present a deliberately fractured narrative, presenting titbits of information without necessarily providing answers. There is no doubt that this approach emphasises how much our knowledge of the battle remains fragmentary but, while undeniably beautiful, this approach does rather mask the objects themselves. Visitors have to go on hands and knees to see some objects, or peer at coins displayed in semi-darkness.

It is with some relief that you go into the actual park. The battlefield itself is cleverly laid out. The course of the Cheruscan walls is described by a long, curving row of vertical steel tubes. The tubes themselves stand closely together when they replicate an archaeologically attested path, slightly distanced from each other when their course is more speculative. The route along which Varus and his men marched is presented by a series of flat plates, upon which are etched comments from classical authors on the events that unfolded here. These plates, shaped like shields, appear only at irregular intervals, to underline the constant attacks from the German troops. A network of narrow, wood-chip paths suggests the routes by which Arminius' men continually attacked and retreated. The use of different materials is deliberate. It underlines Varus' misunderstanding of Arminius' nature and refers back to the sylvan traditions of the early Germans, without overwhelming.

If all of this appears too allusive, a long, broad rectangular excavation trench in the centre of the park, running roughly north–south and encased in a metal wall, shows the lie of the land in AD 9. Here, for the first time, the visitor has an inkling of what the three Roman legions were faced with. The sandy ground becoming waterlogged pond at the end is (even artificially created here) unpleasant terrain, while the re-created Cheruscan wattle rampart at one end, roughly 1.5m high, shows how overwhelming Arminius' ambush was. The reconstruction brings it home in a way that Cassius Dio cannot.

Scattered over the park are three small pavilions, each one devoted to seeing, listening or understanding. These fantastic steel structures, disconcertingly referred to as 'perception instruments', are intended to augment the visitor's thoughts and experiences of the site. The 'seeing' pavilion, the first you come to, has a camera obscura lens bulging eye-like out of its front. Inside the little chamber, the device provides a distorted, inverted fish-eye view of the park. The 'hearing' pavilion is the most effective of the three. Through a massive galvanised-steel ear-trumpet that sits on top, looking similar to the gramophone of His Master's Voice, sounds are picked up from all over the park. Inside the wood-panelled room, disorienting noises of horses and men in battle are played. In the 'understanding' pavilion

at the end of a winding path, the most isolated of the three structures, looped television clips of contemporary conflicts are simultaneously shown on nine screens. The gnomic comment inscribed
on the wall, 'war is not history – why?' links the battle back to the
twenty-first century.

The museum and park at Kalkriese have been sympathetically and
intelligently designed. Whether or not it finds favour with individual
visitors is a separate issue and a matter for personal taste. Without a
doubt, a valid solution of how to present the battle has been attempted.
And yet, where it fails to satisfy is where all museums, rather all ancient
sites, fall down. Visiting the museum and park at Kalkriese brings to
the fore the essential question of what it is that we are looking for,
what was it that the visitors, for example all the 120,000 who visited
in 2005, were hoping for after the   7 entrance fee had been paid?

An inevitable element of voyeurism creeps into any visit to a military
field of conflict. The relief that one is not there in person is tinged
with the human curiosity about who did what to whom and where.
Recognition of this is most apparent at the site of the Battle of the
Little Bighorn, where General Custer and the 7th Cavalry fell in 1876.
Red granite markers now indicate the exact spots where commanders
fell, white ones where the rank and file died in eastern Montana.

But we are also hoping for some kind of enlightenment. We
want the voices to speak to us from the grave. This is the reason
that we go on pilgrimages to Flanders and to the beaches of
Normandy. Through family stories, the national communion every
Remembrance Sunday, and the wearing of poppies, all of which is
augmented by documentary footage and movies, these conflicts are
still real and fresh.

But that is not possible in Kalkriese. You strain to hear the
marching boots of the Roman legionaries or the battle cries of the
Germans. As individuals it is difficult for us to form any kind of a
personal connection with either Arminius or Varus. We know too
little about them and there is too much historical distortion. At the
site itself, despite the best attempts of the architects, there is not
even any sense of place. The landscape itself has changed beyond
all measure in the intervening two millennia; even the paths of the

roadways are different. And, of course, the isolation of the ambush is impossible to re-create.

Part of the problem is that, in wariness of the outcry and public soul-baring that would inevitably have ensued, the role that the battle played in shaping national identity is toned down. Historically, museums, certainly the European ones with large classical collections, have promoted an element of national identification and have celebrated a nation's might. So pervasive a concept is this that, in the New World, a fictional classical past has been used deliberately to confer legitimacy. It is no accident that the national museums in both Australia and the US are overtly neo-classical in style. It should be borne in mind that this imperialistic element to museums is by no means a solely nineteenth-century phenomenon. The past is still regarded as important for conferring a sense of worth. Perennial Greek tantrums over the return of the Elgin Marbles or the increasingly vocal anti-European sentiments by the museums of Egypt are indications of that.

Kalkriese's inoffensive multiculturalism, a site that was discovered by a British amateur and landscaped by a Swiss company, and with a museum designed by a French firm, takes the edge off the battle's nationalist subtexts. This allows modern Germans to visit without a sense of guilt, yet combines to give it a slightly bland texture. The park and the structures are as far removed from the martial grandeur of Bandel's Hermannsdenkmal as it is possible to get.

But in the end, the site succeeds precisely because of this deliberate distance. Rome's greatest defeat has a resonance, not just because it is about the emergence of a German national consciousness or because it is a part of the common history of the English and German-speaking peoples today, but because it stands as a testament, recalling Carl von Clausewitz's caution to strategists, as often ignored as it is cited: 'The first, the supreme, the most far-reaching act of judgement that the statesman and commander have to make is to establish the kind of war on which they are embarking: neither mistaking it for, nor trying to turn it into, something that is alien to its nature.'

The lessons of the Battle of Teutoburg Forest have never been learned. From the defeat of Napoleon to the opening salvoes of the

First World War, the British Empire faced an army on the battlefield on only four instances. On all other occasions, it came up against enemies who refused to fight with conventional tactics. This was the reason for the number of humiliating defeats the British army suffered, from the Indian Mutiny to the ambush in the Khyber Pass during the First Afghan War in 1842. Any suggestions that the army needed an unorthodox military design to fight enemies who refused to play by her rules would have been met with the same arrogant distain in nineteenth-century London as it would have been in first-century Rome.

Even at the time of writing, the same tragedy is unfolding once more. In the summer of 2005, the British journalist and military expert Max Hastings trenchantly observed what was going wrong with the war in Iraq. It was hard to believe, he wrote, that Washington's objective to create a viable local government and institutions to run Iraq as a unitary state was achievable within an acceptable time-frame. He then pointed out that intelligence was proving a critical weakness. And finally, whatever military successes American forces had achieved, Hastings saw no sign that the US army was winning the critical battle, for the hearts and minds of the locals. 'The experience of ordinary Iraqis with the US military is at best alienating, at worst terrifying. There is no hint of shared purpose, mutual sympathy and respect between the armoured columns rolling along the roads, intermittently belching fire, and the hapless mass of local people, caring only for survival.'[10]

Germany in AD 9, Afghanistan in 1842, Iraq in 2005: it is the same story; the same warnings from history ignored. That is reason enough for the importance of the museum and park at Kalkriese. It is the equivalent of the fool in a medieval court or a dwarf in a Renaissance canvas. It is a repository of human memory that reminds us of the folly of grandeur and the absurd fates of those who seek power.

APPENDIX

The Finds

Few would dispute that the range of finds uncovered by archaeologists at Kalkriese has been incredible. It is, however, necessary to understand the limitations of what has been discovered. First and foremost, what archaeologists have uncovered is what was left after Arminius' men had stripped the battlefield. This was clearly done efficiently. Tacitus writes that when Germanicus visited the site, all that was left was 'fragments of weapons'.[1] It is also worth reiterating that what has been found is almost entirely Roman. As the victors, the Germans took their equipment and that of their fallen comrades home with them. What was left was either missed or unusable.

Second, battles rarely occur within a neatly defined area. Finds have been plotted in a huge area around what we think of as the site of the battle. That area is estimated at some 50sq km, a reflection of skirmishes, smaller ambushes, or perhaps Roman soldiers trying to escape with their lives.

For the most part, the attention of archaeologists has primarily been at the foot of the Kalkriese Berg. Their work has been carried out in the narrow pass called the Kalkrieser-Niewedder-Senke, between the mountain to the south and the Great Moor to the north. What we have is a bright light that has been shone narrowly on only part of the battle, albeit arguably the climax of the ambush. To put this into some perspective, it is a little like trying to tell the story of the Normandy landings in June 1944, only really having evidence of the assault on Omaha beach.

Appendix

A further point worth emphasising is that excavations are still ongoing. Although the number of objects uncovered in the last few years, between 2002 and 2004, has declined (the exception is a fine agricultural knife that was found in 2003), our understanding of the site and the battle is likely to continue to change and develop. At the time of writing, studies are being carried out on the increasing number of bones, both human and animal, that have been found, as well as palaeobotanical research on the environment.

Outlined below are the highlights of the objects that have been found so far.

WEAPONS

Swords and Daggers

The three main weapons of the legionary were the sword (*gladius*) and the dagger (*pugio*), together with the heavy javelin (*pilum*) discussed below. Evidence of all three has been found at Kalkriese. During this period, the main type of sword used is called the Mainz sword, a twin-bladed short-sword, the blade up to 60cm in length and 7cm in width, which had a broad waist with a blade that tapered to a long point. Legionaries wore it on their right side, centurions on their left. While the point – as much as 20cm long – clearly meant that it was designed for stabbing, it was an effective slashing weapon as well. Between 1.2kg and 1.6kg in weight, it had replaced the heavier Spanish sword in around 20 BC.

Scabbards were conventionally manufactured from sheet iron or bronze (sometimes silvered) over wood, and often embossed with decorative images. A system of four rings allowed them to be attached to a leather strap. By far the best example is the so-called Sword of Tiberius, found in Mainz and now in the British Museum. The tinned and gilded scabbard shows Tiberius ceding a military victory to Augustus by handing him a Victory statuette, as two gods, Mars and Victory, look on. It is believed to have been commissioned for a senior officer to commemorate a victory during one of the campaigns in Germany, possibly those under Germanicus between AD 14 and 16.

Every legionary also carried a dagger on his left side, a useful back-up to his sword. In design terms, these are swords in miniature, with blades up to 35cm long. Again, like swords, daggers had scabbards with four rings, which would here be attached to the belt. Throughout the period, the scabbards themselves were metal plates that were lined with wood.

At Kalkriese, less immediately obvious evidence for swords and daggers has been found. Any blades that survived the battle were stolen. One of the arguments that Inguiomerus employed for wanting to storm Caecina's camp in AD 15, rather than wait and ambush the soldiers, is that the weaponry would not be damaged. Later on, before the battle with Maroboduus, Arminius boasted that his men were carrying 'weapons wrested from the Romans'.[2] It should not be surprising that every metal element other than the swords themselves has been found: bronze and silver mountings on sheaths, bindings for the scabbard, sheath brackets and guards. Of special note are the complete mountings of a sheath of silver with settings for precious stones, and one sheath bracket with a garnet gem, 2cm long, engraved with the image of a woman. What evidence there is, is from smaller, individual parts. As for daggers, the bronze rivets that would have held the blade on to the hilt have been found, as well as a very fragmentary iron blade.

Missiles

All Roman legionaries, at least until the third century, carried a heavy javelin (the *pilum*). Numerous reliefs, from Trajan's Column in Rome to the Tropaeum of Adamklissi in Romania, show these familiar missiles, up to 2m in length and weighing around 2kg. They were an effective first-strike weapon (Virgil describes how 'the Italic shaft of cornel lightly flew along the yielding air'),[3] thrown before the legionaries followed up their assault with the sword. Although a *pilum* could be hurled up to 30m, its effective range was really only 15m.

The *pilum* assault had a twin use. Apart from killing enemy soldiers, its secondary purpose was to hinder them. In an innovation developed by Gaius Marius, the Roman general and politician at the turn of the first century BC who is credited with turning the army into a professional fighting force, the points of the *pilum* were designed to bend on impact so that they could not be used against the legionaries.[4]

Julius Caesar noted the chaos that this could cause. 'It was a great hindrance to the Gauls in fighting', he wrote, 'that, when several of their shields had been by one stroke of the [Roman] javelins pierced through and pinned fast together, as the point of the iron had bent itself, they could neither pluck it out, nor, with their left hand entangled, fight with sufficient ease; so that many, after having long tossed their arm about, chose rather to cast away their shield from their hand, and to fight with their person unprotected.'[5]

The best preserved *pila* so far have been found at the camp of Oberaden. Not just the metal shanks and heads have survived, but also the parts of the wooden shafts. At Kalkriese, only one *pilum* tip, 16.9cm long, has been found so far, in 1995, but several *pilum* collets have been discovered. Made of iron and some 4.8cm tall, these reinforced the joint between the head and the wooden shaft that was typically made of ash or hazel.

Generally one of the weapons of auxiliaries and cavalry auxiliaries, several lance spearheads of varying sizes have been also found, the longest of which is 20.5cm long. One of the most intriguing discoveries is the protective end for a lance, a so-called butt-spike. During a march, lances were usually stuck into the ground, and the spike protected against splintering of the shaft.

Several other missile finds point to the wide variety of soldiers in Varus' army. A three-winged arrowhead found in 1993 attests to the presence of archers; and it was the discovery of three slingshots in 1988 that identified Kalkriese as a military site. Although no individual unit is known in the Roman army, slingers are depicted on Trajan's Column and it is presumed that they made up an element of the auxiliary units. Certainly it was generally believed that the best-known slingers came from the Balearic Islands and Crete – Virgil refers to the 'whirl of hempen-thonged Balearic sling'.[6] Slingshot was made of tin, stone or lead; three lead ones have been found at Kalkriese, each one of them 3.7cm long. Finally, one of the more curious discoveries is several iron bolts with massive square heads. As these have also been discovered in greater numbers in camps, it is generally presumed that they are bolts from a light catapult, though no trace of one has yet been found.

ARMOUR

Evidence of two types of armour that were worn by Roman soldiers has been found at Kalkriese. Two S-shaped hook fasteners indicate that some of the soldiers were wearing chain-mail, what the Romans called *lorica hamata*. Made from small rings – as many as 30,000 – chain-mail was standard issue for legionaries throughout the Republican era and into the early principate. The metal rings could be as small as 3mm, each one linked through four others, two in the row above it and two below. Few examples have survived, and those only in fragmentary form. The best representation is from a statue of a Gallic officer dating to the late first century BC, now in the Musée Calvet in Avignon. From the surviving inscription on the fasteners that were found in Kalkriese, we know that this was the type of armour worn by Marcus Aius. One fastener says, 'M Aius [cohorte] I [centuria] Fabrici[i]'; its partner, 'M Aii [cohorte] I [centuria] Fab[ricii]'. The first inscription translates as, 'Marcus Aius of cohort I, of Fabricius' century', while the second is, 'Belongs to Marcus Aius of cohort I, Fabricius' century'.

Until the excavations at Kalkriese, it had been presumed that the shift from mail to plate armour did not appear in earnest until the reign of the Emperor Claudius. Evidence of widespread usage does not appear until the Roman invasion of Britain, some thirty-three years after the events discussed here. But in 1994 came the discovery of an 18.8cm iron plate with a bronze buckle, and a number of buckles and hinges of the armour, some silver-plated but for the most part tin-plated; this has pushed back the dating of its introduction to the reign of Augustus.

Possibly entering Roman military usage via the gladiatorial arena, general use of plate armour, what is called *lorica segmenta* (the term was not used until the Renaissance), was a significant innovation. Considerably lighter than chain-mail (9kg, compared to 16kg) it afforded much greater protection against missile attacks.

The earliest form of *lorica segmenta*, which would have been worn by legionaries under Varus, is now known as Corbridge A. From the discovery in 1964 of two complete sets of armour in a wooden chest buried below the floor of a timber building in the camp of Corbridge, just south of Hadrian's Wall, we know that this armour consisted of forty plates. The collar and shoulder units were made up of twenty-four plates, and the torso was protected by sixteen semicircular iron strips, which were positioned horizontally and riveted on to straps.

In the dying days of the Republic, there had been a gradual shift in shield shape; away from a curved oval shape towards the familiar curved rectangular shield. It is known from the only surviving example of this type of shield (from Dura Europos in Syria) that they were just over 1m long and more than 80cm wide. They were constructed from what was effectively a type of plywood, normally three layers of thinly planed wood, glued together with the grain of each sheet at right angles to its neighbour, for added strength. This would make them 5cm thick. The wood could be protected by a removable leather cover. The remains of one of these from this period, for example, have been found at Vindonissa. One major improvement from Republic times was that shields were much lighter, down from 10kg to 5.5kg. To strengthen the shields they were often edged with metal, and to make them more effective as an offensive weapon they typically had a hemispherical boss in the centre. It is these two elements that were found at Kalkriese in 1992, together with an iron reinforcing bar that was often placed on the inside, to stop the wood from splitting. Gilt sheet-silver elements decorated the front of the shield, both patterns and a unit's insignia, and fragments of these, too, have been found, though not in a state that they can be reconstructed.

Helmet

From fragments that have been found, it is apparent that the style of helmet used by soldiers in Varus' army is the Imperial Gallic or Wiesenau-type. The former name is used by English-speaking scholars, the latter by those in mainland Europe. A particularly fine example was found in Oberaden, and is now on display in the Westfälisches Museum für Archäeologie in Münster. Lined with felt for comfort, this helmet is characterised by a broad neck-guard, ribbed and angled to deflect blows, and a brow peak, both of which provided significant defence against downward sword blows. The protection came at a cost. First of all, they were not light, weighing over 2kg. The second downside is that peripheral vision for soldiers wearing the helmets was not great. Archaeologists at Kalkriese uncovered a complete iron plume-holder (a well-preserved example, some 7.5cm tall) in 1991, and have also found crest knobs and a bronze helmet handle, 8.1cm long.

Military belt

A Roman soldier's leather belt, called the *cingulum*, identified him as much as his sword. Augustus was known to punish centurions by making them stand outside his tent without their belts, while Juvenal describes soldiers simply as 'armed and belted men'.[7] Belts were often richly adorned and used to carry a dagger (the sword was normally carried over the shoulder on a separate leather strap). At Kalkriese, numerous buckles of bronze have been found, one measuring 2.4cm across and displaying evidence of silver-plating being worthy of note. As well as attaching their dagger to their belt, soldiers could hang an apron of between three and eight leather straps from it, reinforced with small bronze plates and acting as protection for the groin and lower abdomen. Although the leather itself had corroded away, a complete set of sixteen plates was found in 1990, each of them 1.5cm wide, together with a belt end.

Appendix

The Iron Mask

Found in the winter of 1989 in front of one of the Cheruscan walls where it had been buried, the 16.9cm-tall iron cavalry face mask is justifiably one of the most reproduced Roman artefacts ever found; 16.2cm wide at the top, narrowing to 8.2–8.4cm at the chin, it has become the symbol of the museum and site at Kalkriese. Originally covered in silver leaf – presumably removed by a plundering Cheruscan – it is the oldest such mask ever found, compared with other impressive examples found in Vechten and Nijmegen in Holland and Emesa in Syria. This is just the frontispiece of a face helmet that covered the whole head and face and in all likelihood was connected to the helmet at the top with a hinge and straps at the side. Its owner was probably a senior commander in an auxiliary Gallic or Thracian cavalry troop serving with the Romans.

OTHER PIECES OF MILITARY EQUIPMENT

To keep their cloaks together, crucial for some degree of comfort in the damp German autumn, Roman soldiers clipped them on the left shoulder. Given the size of the clips that they used, it is not surprising that a number have been found on the battlefield. These are all bronze and iron, in three different styles. Some are safety-pin types and omega types, the latter styled in the shape of the Greek letter. The majority that have been uncovered, however, are Aucissa brooches, a distinct style with a highly arched bow. These have been found all over the Roman Empire and their name comes from the fact that many are inscribed with the word 'AVCISSA', presumed to be the name of the manufacturer. Although none of the Aucissa brooches that have been found in Kalkriese have this name, the best one in this style is 6.2cm long and is decorated with a pine tree motif.

Remarkably, three hob-nailed boots, called *caligae*, were found in 1990. Although the leather had rotted away, the nails retained their pattern in the sand. From evidence in other parts of the empire, it is clear that there was an element of standardisation in nailing

202

patterns, which broadly conform to patterns in sports shoes now. Each shoe in Kalkriese had around ninety nails. Even though no upper leather has survived, it is clear that these were the classic military boot, providing support for the ankle and foot and allowing ventilation. Although marching in cold, wet Germany would have been miserable, as has been pointed out, 'at least the Roman soldier was spared the horrors of trench foot'.[8]

Several fragments of *phalerae* have been found. These were typically regimental honours, medals worn on a harness. Representative examples can be seen on Marcus Caelius' gravestone, though they were not issued just to officers. At Kalkriese, a small number of bronze and lead *phalerae* have been found. By far the best example discovered is 4cm across and shows the profile of a man, typically held to be Augustus. What makes it especially worthy of note is that it has the distinct air of the mass market about it.

HORSES AND MULES

Numerous small elements of horse tack point to the significant presence of cavalry at Kalkriese. As Georgia Franzius has cautiously pointed out, 'horse tack does not necessarily derive from the military, but it does appear naturally in a military context'.[9] Noteworthy are two pieces of an iron hackamore bit, as well as small, round bronze decorations from the bridle and protective amulets such as a bronze phallus pendant found in 1989.

Two mules have also been found, one in 1992 and the other in 2000, two of the many hundreds of animals which will have borne the burden of legionaries' kit. Around the bones of the first were found the remains of its harness: ring snaffle and iron reins some 60cm long, bronze pendants and decorative glass pearls that had fallen off their mountings. The iron clapper on the 16.6cm-long bronze bell round its neck had been muffled with a handful of oats that its owner had grabbed from a field while passing, to keep them moving as silently as possible. It is the analysis of that vegetation that has allowed the battle at Kalkriese to be dated to September of AD 9.

BUILDING EQUIPMENT

A large number of other objects have been found on the battlefield, though for the most part these can be ascribed either to non-military units of the army or were part and parcel of what a legionary carried on his back on campaign. Even if the various innovations that lightened the load, like the *lorica segmenta*, are taken into account, a legionary was still carrying roughly 23kg of weight, on top of which must be counted his pack, which came in at roughly 14kg. As well as their weaponry, as Josephus writes, legionaries carried 'a saw and a basket, a pickaxe and an axe, a thong of leather and a hook, with provisions for three days'. With the air of a man who has never served in the ranks, he concludes brightly, 'so the legionary has no great need of a mule to carry his burdens'.[10]

By far the most significant number of finds fall into this category. For example, a *dolabra*, was found in 1989. This cross between an axe and a pickaxe, 53cm long, was primarily used in the construction of forts and in clearing routes. Numerous examples have been found in early Roman forts and their use is illustrated on Trajan's Column. Other tools found include an *ascia*, a mason's hammer, 13.4cm long; the iron blade of a sickle, 25.7cm long; and two types of chisel. Surveying equipment has also been uncovered in the form of a number of lead plumb-bobs. These were part of the *groma*, the tool Roman surveyors used to keep their roads straight and to plot right angles in the field. The first professional surveyor mentioned was Decidius Saxa, 'a skilful and experienced surveyor' who had worked for Julius Caesar before deserting him for Mark Antony. Cicero writes that 'he used to be a measurer of ground for camps; now he hopes to measure out and value the city'.[11] The bobs found at Kalkriese are of note, as one boasts the inscription 'CHO1', identifying it as belonging to the first cohort of an unknown legion.

MEDICAL EQUIPMENT

It is perhaps not that surprising that medicine was taken extremely seriously. Under Augustus' reforms to the army, every legion had its own doctors, surgeons and eye doctors. From gravestones we know the names of numerous medical personnel stationed in Germany. Even auxiliary units had their own medical staff, and hospitals are a common feature of forts. Most of the ones excavated in Germany so far – at Xanten, Bonn and Neuss – date to a later period, but that is because they were made of stone, presumably on earlier wooden structures. Certainly the excavation of Haltern has revealed the remains of an 80m by 40m hospital in the centre of the camp, and numerous medical instruments have been found. At Kalkriese, two instruments point to the presence of doctors in Varus' army: a partly silver-plated bone elevator, 14.3cm long, and the bronze handle of a surgical knife, decorated with a bronze rhomboid pattern.

PERSONAL ARTICLES

The personal objects found at Kalkriese have perhaps the greatest resonance. While few people today have direct experience of war, these pieces provide more of a direct link to the ancient world. In 1993, for example, an iron ring was found, its orange-brown carnelian gem (1.5cm by 1.2cm) engraved with two full cornucopiae crossed over a caduceus, the staff of Mercury, and surrounded by ears of corn; it would not look completely out of place if worn today. The same is true of a number of counters made of coloured opaque glass that legionaries used for board games.

Even if the design is unfamiliar or if the object is no longer used in the modern world, they provide a useful touchstone for those who fell at Kalkriese: four 2cm-tall seal-boxes made of bronze, their lead lids decorated with images; unfamiliar looking iron keys, clearly carried by officers; and toiletries, like a pair of iron scissors, 16.4cm long, the handle of a razor; a bronze carrying ring for strigils, and small curved metal tools that were used by bathers to scrape off dirt and oil after bathing.

A significant number of parts of objects that relate to eating and drinking have been found, such as fragments of bronze cooking pots and pottery objects like oil lamps and large jugs. Three pieces in particular stand out: a silver spoon, 11.3cm long; a simply decorated wine sieve of bronze, 12.4cm across; and the beautiful flat handle of a *skyphos* drinking cup, 3.6cm long. The handle, made of silver and decorated with crudely stylised birds, was found in 1996.

Notes

INTRODUCTION

1. While this is obviously a reconstruction, it is hopefully a plausible one. For broad events see Tacitus, *Annals*, 1.61–2, 2.7, 2.45 and *Germania*, 6. See also Susanne Wilbers-Rost, 'Kalkriese und die Varusschlacht – Archäologische Nachweise einer militärischen Auseinandersetzung zwischen Römern und Germanen' in Philip Freeman (ed.) *et al.*, *Limes XVIII: Proceedings of the XVIIIth International Congress of Roman Frontier Studies held in Amman, Jordan, September 2000* (Oxford, 2002), pp. 515–26; Claus von Carnap-Bornheim, 'Archäologisch-historische Überlegungen zum Fundplatz Kalkrieser-Niewedder Senke in den Jahren zwischen 9 n. Chr. und 15 n. Chr.' in Wolfgang Schlüter (ed.), *Rom, Germanien und die Ausgrabungen von Kalkriese* (Osnabrück, 1999), pp. 495–508.
2. Velleius Paterculus, *Roman History*, 2.119.1; Florus, *Epitome of Roman History*, 2.30.
3. Suetonius, *Augustus*, 28.
4. Virgil, *Aeneid*, 6.792–3; *Eclogues*, 4.9; Horace, *Odes*, 1.35.29–30.
5. Tacitus, *Germania*, 37.
6. A.A. Gill, *AA Gill is Away* (London, 2002), p. 179.
7. Deuteronomy, 12.3. See also 7.5 and 16.21.
8. The British view of forests is divided between those, like Rowling and Kenneth Grahame, who preserve the southern European tradition, and others, like A.A. Milne, whose Hundred Acre Wood is a sanctuary.
9. There have been two accounts of the battle specifically since the discoveries of the 1990s. Tony Clunn's *In Quest of the Lost Legions: The Varusschlacht* (Minerva, 1999), updated as *Quest for the Lost Roman Legions* (Spellmount, 2005), and Peter Wells' *The Battle That Stopped Rome: Emperor Augustus, Armenius, and the Slaughter of the Legions in the Teutoburg Forest* (Norton, 2003). The former is a thrilling account of the discovery of the site, much of it

207

based on the author's own diaries, while the latter is particularly strong on the archaeological evidence.

10. Dieter Timpe, *Der Triumph des Germanicus: Untersuchungen zu den Feldzügen der Jahre 14–16 n. Chr. in Germanien* (Bonn, 1968), p. 2.
11. Velleius Paterculus, *Roman History*, tr. Frederick Shipley (London, 1924), p. viii.
12. Velleius Paterculus, *Roman History*, 2.118.1, 2.117.3, 2.120.5.
13. Pliny the Younger, *Letters*, 7.20. For the plausible suggestion that Tacitus commanded a legion in Germany, see Herbert Benario, 'Tacitus, Trier and the Treveri', *Classical Journal* 83 (1987/8), 233–9, specifically 238–9.
14. Herbert Benario, 'Arminius into Hermann: History into Legend', *Greece & Rome* 51 (2004), 84.
15. Cassius Dio, *Roman History*, 56.18.2, 56.22.2a, 78.21.2.
16. Florus, *Epitome of Roman History*, 2.30.
17. Reinhard Wolters, 'Hermeneutik des Hinterhalts: die antiken Berichte zur Varuskatastrophe und der Fundplatz von Kalkriese', *Klio* 85 (2003), 132.
18. Colin Wells, 'What's new along the Lippe: recent work in North Germany', *Britannia* 29 (1998), 458.
19. Tacitus, *Annals*, 1.60.
20. Vincent Goulding, 'Back to the future with asymmetric warfare', *Parameters* (winter 2001/2), 21–30.

CHAPTER ONE

1. Tacitus, *Annals*, 3.48; Velleius Paterculus, *Roman History*, 2.97.1 and 2.102.1; Robin Seager, *Tiberius* (London, 1972), p. 269.
2. Pliny, *Natural History*, 9.58.
3. Cassius Dio, *Roman History*, 54.20.4–6. A date of late summer is assumed, as Lollius was in Rome to celebrate the Ludi Saeculares from 1–3 June. CIL 6.32323 in Kitty Chisholm and John Ferguson (eds), *Rome, the Augustan Age: A Sourcebook* (Oxford, 1981), D2b, p. 150.
4. Suetonius, *Augustus*, 21.
5. Crinagoras, *Greek Anthology*, 7.741; Suetonius, *Augustus*, 23; Tacitus, *Annals*, 1.10.3.
6. Julius Caesar, *The Gallic War*, 6.24.
7. Julius Caesar, *The Gallic War*, 1.31, 4.17–19; Derek Williams, *Romans and Barbarians* (London, 1998), p. 69.
8. Suetonius, *Vitellius*, 8.
9. Propertius, *Elegies*, 4.6.77; Horace, *Odes*, 4.5.25–7.
10. Cassius Dio, *Roman History*, 48.49.3.
11. Julius Caesar, *The Gallic War*, 4.3. For details of the foundation of Cologne, see Michael Gechter, 'Early Roman military installations and Ubian settlements

in the Lower Rhine' in Thomas Blagg and Martin Millett (eds), *The Early Roman Empire in the West* (Oxford, 1990), pp. 97–102.

12. T. Kolnik, 'Q Atilius Primus – Interprex, Centurio et Negotiator', *Acta Archaeologica Academiae Scientarum Hungaricae* 30 (1978), 61–75.
13. Pliny, *Natural History*, 37.11.
14. Arrien, *Périple du Pont-Euxin* (Paris, 1995), pp. 7–8.
15. Josephus, *The Jewish War*, 3.79–84.
16. Velleius Paterculus, *Roman History*, 2.97.2.
17. Horace, *Odes*, 4.4.73–6.
18. Plutarch, *Antony*, 87.3; Valerius Maximus, *Memorable Doings and Sayings*, 4.3.3.
19. Augustus, *Res Gestae*, 26.4; Pliny the Elder, *Natural History*, 2.67.
20. For the Drusus Ditch see Suetonius, *Claudius*, 1; Tacitus, *Annals*, 2.8.1. For Claudius' invasion of Britain, Cassius Dio, 60.19.2. I am extremely grateful to Jona Lendering for suggesting this solution and recommending Kerst Huisman, 'De Drususgrachten: een nieuwe hypothese', *Westerheem* 44 (1995), 188-194.
21. Cassius Dio, *Roman History*, 54.33.1–4.
22. On the archaeological discoveries, see Siegmar von Schnurbein, 'The organization of the fortresses in Augustan Germany' in Richard Brewer (ed.), *Roman Fortresses and their Legions* (London, 2000), p. 30.
23. Heinz Günter Horn (ed.), *Die Römer in Nordrhein-Westfalen* (Stuttgart, 1987), p. 38; Cassius Dio, *Roman History*, 54.36.2.
24. Cassius Dio, *Roman History*, 55.1.2.
25. *Ibid.*, 55.1.3. See similar account in Suetonius, *Claudius*, 1.1.3.
26. For the supposed mutiny, Dieter Timpe, 'Drusus' Umkehr an der Elbe', *Rheinisches Museum für Philologie* 110 (1967), 290.
27. Livy, *Summaries*, 142; Seneca, *Dialogues*, 6.3.1.
28. Valerius Maximus, *Memorable Doings and Sayings*, 5.5.3.
29. Strabo, *Geography*, 5.3.8.
30. Among others, the tomb was eventually also to hold Livia, Tiberius, Germanicus' wife Agrippina and two of her sons, Nero's infamous wife Poppaea, and finally the Emperor Nerva.
31. For a reconstruction, see H.G. Frenz, 'Zum Beginn des repräsentiven Steinbaus in Mogontiacum' in Bendix Trier (ed.), *Die römische Okkupation nördlich der Alpen zur Zeit des Augustus* (Münster, 1991), p. 88.
32. *A poem of consolation*, 271–82. Although the poem is conventionally ascribed to Ovid or Albinovanus Pedo (see chapter five), most now believe that it is by neither. Nonetheless, the full text is to be found in Ovid, *The Art of Love and Other Poems*, tr. J.H. Mozley (London, 1929).
33. Florus, *Epitome of Roman History*, 2.30.
34. Cassius Dio, *Roman History*, 57.10.5; Suetonius, *Tiberius*, 32.
35. Suetonius, *Tiberius*, 21.

36. Velleius Paterculus, *Roman History*, 2.97.4.
37. Josephus, *Jewish War*, 3.90. Gordon Maxwell, *The Romans in Scotland* (Edinburgh, 1989), pp. 100–5.
38. Suetonius and Velleius Paterculus suggest that he wanted a rest from work (Suetonius, *Tiberius*, 10.2; Velleius Paterculus, *Roman History*, 2.99.1–2). Cassius Dio (*Roman History*, 55.9.1–6) says that he wished to avoid a possible confrontation with Gaius and Lucius Caesar, with whom he did not get along. See also Barbara Levick, 'Tiberius' Retirement to Rhodes in 6 BC', *Latomus* 25 (1972), 779–813.
39. Ancient references to him. Suetonius, *Nero*, 4; Velleius Paterculus, *Roman History*, 2.72.3; Tacitus, *Annals*, 4.44.
40. Cassius Dio, *Roman History*, 55.10a.3.
41. Velleius Paterculus, *Roman History*, 2.104.2.
42. *Ibid.*, 2.104.4.
43. von Schnurbein, 'Organization of the Fortress', p. 30.
44. Velleius Paterculus, *Roman History*, 2.108.1.
45. Tacitus, *Annals*, 2.63.
46. Velleius Paterculus, *Roman History*, 2.108.2.
47. Strabo, *Geography*, 7.1.3; Suetonius, *Augustus*, 48.
48. Josef Dobias, 'King Maroboduus as a Politician', *Klio* 38 (1960), 157.
49. Tacitus, *Annals*, 2.46. A possible solution is that not all legions were in action at any one time.
50. Velleius Paterculus, *Roman History*, 2.110.3.
51. *Ibid.*, 2.111.1; Suetonius, *Tiberius*, 16.1.
52. Suetonius, *Tiberius*, 16.2; Cassius Dio, *Roman History*, 55.31.1–2; Velleius Paterculus, *Roman History*, 2.112–13.

CHAPTER TWO

1. B. van Wickevoort Crommelin, 'P. Quinctilius Varus – Das Bild des Verlierers', *Osnasbrücker Online – Beiträge zu den Altertumswissenschaften* (2/1999), 1–10; C.M. Wells, *The German Policy of Augustus* (Oxford, 1972), p. 238; Maureen Carroll, *Romans, Celts & Germans: The German Provinces of Rome* (Stroud, 2001), p. 40. For the cartoon, see www.hermannsdenkmal.de.
2. Velleius Paterculus, *Roman History*, 2.117; Florus, *Epitome of Roman History*, 2.30; Suetonius, *Tiberius*, 18; Cassius Dio, *Roman History*, 56.18–19.
3. Julius Caesar, *The Civil War*, 1.23, 2.28; Velleius Paterculus, *Roman History*, 2.71.2.
4. Horace, *Odes*, 1.18.
5. Horace, *Ars poetica*, 438–44. See also *Odes* 1.18 and 24.
6. Peter Levi, *Horace: A Life* (London, 1997), p. 237.
7. Cassius Dio, *Roman History*, 54.7.

8. Pliny, *Natural History*, 35.46.
9. Plutarch, *Antony*, 84. See also Tacitus, *Annals*, 4.66.
10. On Varus' marriages, see Ronald Syme, *The Augustan Aristocracy* (Oxford, 1986), chapter 23. For the funeral oration, see 'Laudatio funebris des Augustus auf Agrippa', *Kölner Papyri Volume 1* (Opladen, 1976), 10, =33–8.
11. John Pollini, 'Ahenobarbi, Appuleii and some others on the Ara Pacis', *American Journal of Archaeology* 90 (1986), 459–60.
12. Derek Williams, *Romans and Barbarians* (London, 1998), p. 92.
13. Cicero, *Pro lege Manilia*, 34; Plutarch, *Julius Caesar*, 55; Augustus, *Res Gestae*, 5,15.
14. Cassius Dio, *Roman History*, 55.28.3–4.
15. Syme, *Augustan Aristocracy*, p. 322.
16. Josephus, *The Jewish War*, 1.637–40.
17. Josephus, *The Jewish War*, 1.656; J.V. Hirschmann, P. Richardson, R.S. Kraemer and P.A. Mackowiak, 'Death of an Arabian Jew', *Archives of Internal Medicine* 164 (2004), 833–9.
18. Corroborated by St Matthew, 2.19.23. When the Holy Family heard that Herod was dead, they did return to Judaea, but were too scared to return to Bethlehem and instead settled in Galilee.
19. Josephus, *The Jewish War*, 1.648–50.
20. *Ibid.*, 2.13.
21. It is convention rather than ancient sources that names the city Caesarea Maritima. It is a convenient way to distinguish it from Caesarea Philippi.
22. Josephus, *The Jewish War*, 1.410.
23. Mary Smallwood, *The Jews under Roman Rule* (Leiden, 1976), p. 106.
24. Josephus, *The Jewish War*, 2.70.
25. *Ibid.*, 2.72.
26. Herwig Wolfram, *Die Germanen* (Munich, 2001), p. 39.
27. Cassius Dio, *Roman History*, 56.16.3; Velleius Paterculus, *Roman History*, 2.117.2.
28. Velleius Paterculus, *Roman History*, 2.120.3.
29. *Ibid.*, 2.119.4; Horace, *Epistles*, 1.15. For details of epigraphic evidence, see Reinhard Wolters, 'C. Numonius Vala und Drusus. Zur Auflösung zweier Kontermarken augusteischer Zeit', *Germania* 73 (1995), 146.
30. W. Zanler, 'Ein römische Katapultpfeilspitze der 19. Legion aus Oberammergau', *Germania* 72 (1994), 587–96.
31. For the argument that Caelius' gravestone refers to another battle, see Ute Schilling-Häfele, 'Varus und Arminius in der Überlieferung,' *Historia* 32 (1983), 126, footnote 9. For Legion XIX, Tacitus, *Annals*, 1.60.
32. For a full discussion of the evidence, see L. Keppie, 'Legiones XVII, XVIII, XIX: Exercitus omnium fortissimus' in L. Keppie, *Legions and Veterans: Roman Army Papers 1971–2000* (Stuttgart, Franz Steiner, 2000), 161–5.

33. Cassius Dio, *Roman History*, 56.19.1.
34. *Ibid.*, 56.18.3.
35. Florus, *Epitome of Roman History*, 2.30; Velleius Paterculus, *Roman History*, 2.117.4.
36. Tacitus, *Germania*, 5.
37. Cassius Dio, *Roman History*, 56.18.2; Tacitus, *Annals*, 1.59.
38. Discussed by Armin Becker in 'Lahnau-Waldgirmes: eine augusteische Stadtgründung in Hessen', *Historia* 52 (2003), 344–50.
39. Cicero, *De lege manilia*, 28.

CHAPTER THREE

1. Ptolemy, *Geography*, 2.11.10.
2. Julius Caesar, *The Gallic War*, 6.10.
3. *Ibid.*, 4.1; Tacitus, *Germania*, 14.
4. Pliny, *Natural History*, 17.4. For more details see Carroll, *Romans, Celts & Germans*, pp. 16–17 and chapter 4.
5. A. Kreuz, 'Becoming a Roman Farmer. Preliminary Report on the Environmental Evidence from the Romanization Project' in Creighton and Wilson (ed.), *Roman Germany*, 71–98.
6. Athenaeus, *Deipnosophistae*, 4.153.
7. Cassius Dio, *Roman History*, 55.1.2; Suetonius, *Augustus*, 21; Cassius Dio, *Roman History*, 55.6.2.
8. Cassius Dio, *Roman History*, 55.10a.3.
9. Velleius Paterculus, *Roman History*, 2.105.1.
10. Tacitus, *Agricola*, 21.
11. Tacitus, *Germania*, 42. See also Julius Caesar, *The Gallic War*, 1.43, and Livy, *Ab urbe condita*, 27.4.
12. Tacitus, *Annals*, 13.55.
13. Malcolm Todd, *The Early Germans* (Oxford, 1992), p. 102.
14. Tacitus, *Germania*, 5; Tacitus, *Annals*, 2.62.
15. Tacitus, *Germania*, 41.
16. Dieter Timpe, *Arminius-Studien* (Heidelberg, 1970), p. 13.
17. See Harald von Petrikovits, 'Arminius', *Bonner Jahrbücher* 166 (1966), 175–93 and Timpe, *Arminius-Studien*, pp. 14–19. It is discussed in detail by D.H. Green in *Language and History in the Early Germanic World* (Cambridge, 1998), pp. 114ff. On 'her-', see also Chris Wells, 'hin und he(h)r?' in *Blütezeit: Festschrift für L.P. Johnson* (Berlin, 2000), pp. 447–79.
18. Tacitus, *Annals*, 2.88. It is sometimes suggested that Arminius' twelve years in power should be dated from AD 9 and that he in fact died around AD 21. Tacitus' motivation for having the death recorded two years early would be

to make it simultaneous with that of Germanicus and at the end of a book. I remain convinced, however, that Arminius' leadeship should be dated to AD 7.

19. *Ibid.*, 2.10.
20. Timpe, *Arminius-Studien*, p. 56; Tacitus, *Annals*, 2.10.
21. Cassius Dio, *Roman History*, 54.21.4.
22. Georgia Franzius, 'Die römischen Funde aus Kalkriese' in Wolfgang Schlüter (ed.), *Kalkriese – Römer in Osnabrücker Land* (Bramsche, 1993), p. 125.
23. Velleius Paterculus, *Roman History*, 2.118.2; Strabo, *Geography*, 7.1.4.
24. Tacitus, *Annals*, 2.10.
25. Tacitus, *Germania*, 6.
26. J.B. Rives, *Tacitus: Germania* (Oxford, 1999), p. 137.
27. M. Orsnes, 'The Weapon-Find in Ejsbøl Mose at Haderslev', *Acta Archaeologica* 34 (1963), 232–47.
28. Tacitus, *Germania*, 6.
29. *Ibid.*, 6.
30. Herwig Wolfram, *Die Germanen* (Munich, 2001), p. 43 makes a convincing case for Arminius' marriage to Thusnelda taking place after the Battle of Teutoburg Forest. As their son was 3 in AD 16, a marriage in AD 12/13 can be suggested.
31. Tacitus, *Annals*, 11.16.
32. Tacitus, *Germania*, 14.
33. Cassius Dio, *Roman History*, 56.18.3.
34. Tacitus, *Annals*, 4.72.
35. Dio Chrysostom, *Discourses*, 1.28; Juvenal, *Satires*, 16.
36. Brian Campbell, *The Roman Army, 31 BC – AD 337* (London, 1994), p. 178.
37. For more detailed discussion and further examples see Stephen Dyson, 'Native revolts in the Roman empire', *Historia* 20 (1971), 239–74.
38. Tacitus, *Annals*, 2.88.
39. Von Petrikovits, 'Arminius', p. 187.
40. Cassius Dio, *Roman History*, 56.19.2.

CHAPTER FOUR

1. Velleius Paterculus, *Roman History*, 2.119.1.
2. For the current arguments, see Reinhard Wolters, 'Hermeneutik des Hinterhalts: die antiken Berichte zur Varuskatastrophe und der Fundplatz von Kalkriese', *Klio* 85 (2003), 131–70. The most vocal of those who disagree with Kalkriese as the site of the Teutoburg massacre is www.varusschlacht-am-harz.de, who prefer to see it at Halberstadt.
3. Velleius Paterculus, *Roman History*, 2.118.4.
4. Mary Sheldon, 'Slaughter in the Forest: Roman intelligence mistakes in Germany', *Small Wars and Insurgencies* 12/3 (autumn 2001), 25.

5. Tacitus, *Annals*, 13.55 for the Ampsivarii, 1.60 for the Chauci.
6. Pliny the Younger, *Letters*, 2.7.
7. Klaus Tausend, 'Wohin wollte Varus?', *Klio* 79 (1997), 375–80.
8. Josephus, *The Jewish War*, 3.115–26.
9. Velleius Paterculus, *Roman History*, 2.117.1.
10. Vindolanda Tablet 154, inventory number 88.841. See Vindolanda Tablets Online, vindolanda.csad.ox.ac.uk. For the ostracon, see Campbell, *The Roman Army*, p. 112. The Vindolanda Tablet is also reproduced on p. 113 of that book.
11. Tacitus, *Annals*, 1.61.
12. Julius Caesar, *The Gallic War*, 1.48; Probus, *Historiae Augustae*, 15.1; Ammianus Marcellinus, *Roman History*, 16.12.1ff. See, especially, Michael Hoeper and Heiko Steuer, 'Zu germanischen "Heeresverbänden" bzw "Heerlagern" im Spiegel der Archäologie' in Wolfgang Schlüter (ed.), *Rom, Germanien und die Ausgrabungen von Kalkriese* (Osnabrück, 1999), pp. 467–93.
13. Julius Caesar, *The Gallic War*, 4.2.4.
14. Cassius Dio, *Roman History*, 56.20.5.
15. Tacitus, *Annals*, 1.60.
16. *Ibid.*, 1.64.
17. Some have suggested that these were the fallen ramparts mistaken by Germanicus for where the shattered remnants of Varus' army had taken their final position. This is unlikely, as of course Germanicus had survivors with him.
18. Ammianus Marcellinus, *Roman History*, 16.12.
19. Susanne Wilbers-Rost, 'Kalkriese und die Varusschlacht – Archäologische Nachweise einer militärischen auseinandersetzung zwischen Römern und Germanen' in Philip Freeman (ed.) *et al.*, *Limes XVIII: proceedings of the XVIIIth International Congress of Roman Frontier Studies held in Amman, Jordan, September 2000* (Oxford, 2002), p. 517.
20. Velleius Paterculus, *Roman History*, 2.119.4.
21. Strabo, *Geography*, 7.2.3.
22. Velleius Paterculus, *Roman History*, 2.119.3.
23. Cassius Dio, *Roman History*, 56.21.5; Florus, *Epitome of Roman History*, 2.30.
24. Cassius Dio, *Roman History*, 56.22.1–2.
25. Orosius, *Historiae adversum Paganos*, 5.16 in Orose, *Histoires: contre les païens*, ed. Marie-Pierre Arnaud-Lindet (Paris, 1991); Tacitus, *Annals*, 13.57.
26. Florus, *Epitome of Roman History*, 2.30.
27. Ammianus Marcellinus, *Roman History*, 16.2.
28. Cassius Dio, *Roman History*, 56.22.2b.

29. C.M. Wells, *The German Policy of Augustus* (Oxford, 1972), p. 152. The identification of Aliso with Haltern was first made by Carl Schuchhardt, 'Das Römercastell bei Haltern an der Lippe', *Sitzungsberichte der königlich preussischen Akademie der Wissenschaften* (1900), 303–16.
30. Cassius Dio, *Roman History*, 56.22.2b.
31. Frontinus, *Stratagems*, 2.9.4.
32. For literary accounts, see Cassius Dio, *Roman History*, 56.22.2–4; Velleius Paterculus, *Roman History*, 2.120.4; Frontinus, *Stratagems*, 3.15.4, 4.7.8.
33. For more details see A.P. Fitzpatrick, 'Ex Radice Britanica', *Britannia* 22 (1991), 143–6.
34. For what is admittedly only a theory, albeit a particularly attractive one, see B. Galsterer, *Die Graffiti auf der römischen Gefässkeramik aus Haltern* (Münster, 1983), p. 30.

CHAPTER FIVE

1. Cassius Dio, *Roman History*, 56.23; Suetonius, *Augustus*, 23; *Tiberius*, 17.
2. Velleius Paterculus, *Roman History*, 2.120.3.
3. Cassius Dio, *Roman History*, 56.24.3–5.
4. Ovid, *Tristia*, 3.12.45, 4.2.33–4; Marcus Manilius, *Astronomica*, 1.896–905.
5. Cassius Dio, *Roman History*, 56.23.2–3; Tacitus, *Annals*, 2.5.
6. For the rescue of captives in AD 50, Tacitus, *Annals*, 12.27. For the ransoming of captives, Cassius Dio, *Roman History*, 56.22.4. Vasile Lica examines their legal status in convincing detail in 'Clades Variana and Postliminium', *Historia* 50 (2001), 496–501.
7. Velleius Paterculus, *Roman History*, 2.119.5.
8. Suetonius, *Tiberius*, 19; Velleius Paterculus, *Roman History*, 2.120–1.
9. Suetonius, *Caligula*, 3; Tacitus, *Annals*, 2.73.
10. Anthony Barrett, *Caligula: The Corruption of Power* (London, 1989), p. 5.
11. Cassius Dio, *Roman History*, 56.33.5. See also Tacitus, *Annals*, 1.11.
12. Tacitus, *Annals*, 1.31.
13. Jürgen Kunow, 'Die Militärgeschichte Niedergermaniens' in Heinz Günter Horn (ed.), *Die Römer in Nordrhein-Westfalen* (Stuttgart, 1987), pp. 47–9.
14. Tacitus, *Annals*, 1.23, 1.32.
15. Campbell, *The Roman Army*, p. 24.
16. Tacitus, *Annals*, 1.32.
17. It is a confused episode. S.J.V. Malloch, 'The end of the Rhine mutiny in Tacitus, Suetonius, and Dio', *Classical Quarterly* 54 (2004), 198–210 untangles the various traditions.
18. Dieter Timpe, *Der Triumph des Germanicus: Untersuchungen zu den Feldzugen der Jahre 14–16 n. Chr. in Germanien* (Bonn, 1968), p. 29. Tacitus, *Annals*, 1.43; Cassius Dio, *Roman History*, 57.6.1.

19. Tacitus, *Annals*, 1.56.
20. *Ibid.*, 1.57.
21. Strabo, *Geography*, 7.1.4.
22. Tacitus, *Annals*, 1.70.
23. *Ibid.*, 1.63.
24. *Ibid.*, 1.65.
25. *Ibid.*, 1.66.
26. *Ibid.*, 3.33.
27. *Ibid.*, 2.6.
28. *Ibid.*, 2.10.
29. *Ibid.*, 2.15, 2.16.
30. *Ibid.*, 2.17.
31. *Ibid.*, 2.17.
32. *Ibid.*, 2.21.
33. Seneca the Elder, *Suasoriae*, 1.15. A more comprehensive text, with useful critical commentary, is Edward Courtney (ed.), *The Fragmentary Latin Poets* (Oxford, 1993), pp. 315–19.
34. Erich Koestermann, 'Die Feldzüge des Germanicus 14–16 n. Chr', *Historia* 6 (1957), 468.
35. Tacitus, *Annals*, 2.22; Timpe, *Der Triumph des Germanicus*, p. 35.
36. Strabo, *Geography*, 7.1.4. Cf. Tacitus, *Annals*, 2.41.
37. Kunow, 'Die Militärgeschichte Niedergermaniens', p. 50. The final eagle was not recovered until AD 42, in the second year of Claudius' reign. Publius Gabinus Secundus, commander of Lower Germany, retrieved it from the Chauci. Cassius Dio, *Roman History*, 60.8.7.
38. Nikos Kokkinos, *Antonia Augusta: Portrait of a Great Roman Lady* (London, 1992), p. 23, fragment 1, lines 26–32. The fullest edition and discussion of the text is Alvaro Sánchez-Ostiz, *Tabula Siarensis: Edición, Traducción y Comentario* (Navarra, 1999). See also W.D. Lebek, 'Die drei Ehrenbögen für Germanicus', *ZPE* 67 (1987), 129–48. For the arch itself, see H.G. Frenz, 'Zum Beginn des repräsentiven Steinbaus in Mogontiacum' in Bendix Trier (ed.), *Die römische Okkupation nördlich der Alpen zur Zeit des Augustus* (Münster, 1991), pp. 91–5.
39. Tacitus, *Annals*, 2.45.
40. Velleius Paterculus, *Roman History*, 2.129; Tacitus, *Annals*, 2.63.
41. Tacitus, *Annals*, 2.88.
42. Tacitus, *Germania*, 36.
43. Tacitus, *Annals*, 2.88.

CHAPTER SIX

1. Richard Kuehnemund, *Arminius or the Rise of National Symbol in Literature* (Chapel Hill, 1953), p. xiii.

2. Kuehnemund, *Arminius*, p. 1.
3. Conrad Celtis, *Oratio in gymnasio in Ingelstadio*, 3.1, 6.1, tr. Leonard Forster, *Selections from Conrad Celtis* (Cambridge, 1948).
4. Velleius Paterculus, *Compendium of Roman History*, p. xviii.
5. Kuehnemund, *Arminius*, p. xi.
6. *Ibid.*, p. 18.
7. Cited in Herbert Benario, 'Arminius into Hermann: History into Legend', *Greece & Rome* 51 (2004), 87.
8. Peter Wells, *The Battle that Stopped Rome: Emperor Augustus, Arminius and the Slaughter of the Legions in the Teutoburg Forest* (New York, 2003), p. 107.
9. Johann Gottlieb Fichte, 'Hauptverschiedenheit zwischen den deutschen und den übrigen Völkern germanischer Abkunft' in Rudolf Eucken (ed.), *Fichtes Reden an die deutsche Nation Roman History* (Leipzig, 1922).
10. Heinrich von Kleist, *Die Hermannsschlacht*, Act IV, Scene ix:
    > Solange sie in Germanien trotzt,
    > Ist Haß mein Amt und meine Tugend Rache!
11. Cited in G. Smolla, 'Gustaf Kossinna nach 50 Jahren', *Acta Praehistorica et Archaeologica* 16/17 (1984/5), 12.
12. Myron Sandford, 'Germany's tribute to Arminius', *New England Magazine* (April 1895), 164ff.
13. In 1897, the US town of New Ulm in Minnesota built its own Hermann Monument, designed by Julius Berndt, 31m smaller than the original. It was rededicated in November 2004 after a year-long and £900,000 facelift. The inscription on the statue's copper heart reads: 'Hermann, 9 AD, A Freedom Fighter, Born Again in New Ulm, Minnesota USA, 2004'.
14. Heinrich Heine, *Deutschland: Ein Wintermärchen*, Caput 11.
15. Torsten Kaufmann, 'Edler Wilder, grausiger Heide, Fürstenknecht und Kämpfer für die Nation', in Mamoun Hansa (ed.), *Varusschlacht und Germanenmythos* (Oldenburg, 2001), p. 56.
16. Despite numerous attempts to do so, Dieter Timpe is surely right that: 'Nobody would suspect that the Varusschlacht lay behind the myth of the hero and dragon-slayer, if the battle were not known from Roman representations.' (*Arminius-Studien*, p. 12). See also Herwig Wolfram, 'It is, to put it mildly, Germanistic exuberance to make a, or the song of Siegfried out of that.', *Die Germanen* (Munich, 2001), p. 46.
17. Herbert Benario, 'Arminius into Hermann', 89.
18. For an overview of operatic attempts on Arminius' life, see Paola Barbon and Bodo Plachta, 'Che la dura la vince – Wer ausharrt, siegt. Arminius auf der Opernbühne des 18. Jahrhunderts' in Rainer Wiegels and Winfried Woesler (eds), *Arminius und die Varusschlacht: Geschichte, Mythos, Literatur* (Paderborn, 2003), pp. 265–90. Note, however, that the Max Bruch oratorio that Barbon

and Plachta refer to (p. 290) is in fact about Jacobus Arminius the theologian, not Arminius the Cheruscan. The two recordings are Biber B000001RX in 1998 by cpo, and Handel Virgin Clas (EMI) B00005A9NG in 2001.

19.

Was this why Hermann won the day,
or why the Turks were routed –
so foreign powers might hold sway,
and Germania be flouted?
Was the Battle of the Nations fought
on Leipzig's field of old,
Chorus: so we might wear chains that are wrought
out of some foreign gold?

Gab's darum eine Hermannschlacht
Und all' die Türkenkriege,
Daß heute gegen welsche Macht
Das Deutschtum unterliege?
Und deshalb auf dem Leipz'ger Feld
Die Völkerschlacht geschlagen,
Chorus: Daß wir nun doch aus Welschengeld
Geschweißte Ketten tragen?

Some Romans once got uppity
Rum tum tiddle um tum
And marched to Northern Germany
Rum tum tiddle um tum.
Trumpets sounding at the head
Taran-tara taran-tara
They were by their General led
Taran-tara taran-tara
Mister Quintilius Varus.

Als die Römer frech geworden,
Sim serim sim sim sim sim,
Zogen sie nach Deutschlands Norden,
Sim serim sim sim sim sim.
Vorne mit Trompetenschall,
Te rä tä tä tä te rä,
Ritt der Generalfeldmarschall,
Te rä tä tä tä te rä,
Herr Quintilius Varus.

20. Manuela Struck, 'The *Heilige Römische Reich Deutscher Nation* and Hermann the German' in Richard Hingley (ed.), *Images of Rome: Perceptions*

of *Ancient Rome in Europe and the United States in the Modern Age* (Portsmouth, 2001), p. 100.

21. Simon Schama, *Landscape and Memory* (London, 1996), p. 118.

22. Cited in Volker Losemann, 'Varuskatastrophe und Befreiungstat des Arminius' in Hansa, *Varusschlacht und Germanenmythos*, p. 35.

23. Rosenburg cited in Frank Fetten, 'Archaeology and anthropology' in Heinrich Härke (ed.), *Archaeology, Ideology and Society: The German Experience* (Frankfurt am Main, 2000), p. 147; Wolfgang Sydow, *Deutung und Darstellung des Arminiusschicksals in seinen wesentlichen Ausprägung* (Diss. Greifswald, 1937); Otto Riedrich, 'Die Germanische Seele im Zeitalter der Gotik', *Odal: Monatsschrift für Blut und Boden* (1936), 468.

24. Hans Reinerth, 'Die politische Waffe der Vorgeschichtsforschung', *Volk und Heimat* 4 (1937), 90.

25. Gustaf Kossinna, 'Über die vorgeschichtliche Ausbreitung der Germanen in Deutschland', *Correspondenz-Blatt der deutschen Gesellschaft für Anthropologie, Ethnographie und Urgeschichte* 26, 1–14.

26. Tacitus, *Germania*, 4. The speech of 13 October 1934 was published and widely distributed. Walter Groß, *Nationalsozialistische Rassenpolitik. Eine Rede an die deutschen Frauen* (Dessau, 1934). Julius Streicher, 'Das Grauen im Osten', *Der Stürmer*, #8/1945.

27. Hugh Trevor Roper, *Hitler's Table Talk 1941–1944* (London, 1953), p. 78. See also: 'Our history goes back to the days of Arminius and King Theoderic, and among the German Kaisers there have been men of the most outstanding quality; in them they bore the germ of German unity', p. 436; and: 'If the Romans had not recruited Germans in their armies, the latter would never have had the opportunity of becoming soldiers and, eventually, of annihilating their former instructors. The most striking example is that of Arminius who became Commander of the Third Roman Legion [*sic*]. The Romans instructed the Third in the arts of war, and Arminius afterwards used it to defeat his instructors', p. 486.

28. Cited in Henning Haßmann, 'Archaeology and the Third Reich' in Härke, *Archaeology, Ideology and Society*, p. 71.

29. Stefan Cramme maintains a constantly updated (at the time of writing) database of fiction about the Roman world. See www.hist-rom.de/index.html.

CHAPTER SEVEN

1. Figure provided by the German Tourist Office.

2. C.W. Ceram, *Götter, Gräber und Gelehrte* (Rowalt, 2000) is the current edition.

3. Kuno Kruse, 'Terrain der Konservativen', *Stern*, 5 December 2004.

Notes

4. Interview, 'Der Mensch ist böse', *Die Zeit*, 3 March 2005.
5. Bruce Nelan, 'Anything to fear', *Time*, 26 March 1990; Roberto Pazzi, 'Germans are from Mars, Italians are from Venus: European tensions, ancient and postmodern', *International Herald Tribune*, 14 July 2003.
6. Theodor Mommsen, 'Die Örtlichkeit der Varusschlacht', *Sitzungsberichte der königlich preussischen Akademie der Wissenschaften* (1885), 63–92.
7. Tony Clunn, *Quest for the Lost Roman Legions* (Spellmount, 2005), p. 4.
8. Kirsten Heuer, 'Wo sich Römer blutige Köpfe holten', *Die Welt*, 7 April 2002.
9. 'Ausgrabungen in Kalkriese ein zweites Troja', *Neue Osnabrücker Zeitung*, 9 February 2002; anonymous, *Prisma*, 1–7 August 1998, 4–5, 8.
10. Max Hastings, 'Two years on, the echoes of Vietnam are getting louder', *Guardian*, 24 June 2005.

APPENDIX

1. Tacitus, *Annals*, 1.61.
2. *Ibid.*, 1.68, 2.45.
3. Virgil, *Aeneid*, 9.698–9.
4. Plutarch, *Marius*, 25.
5. Julius Caesar, *The Gallic War*, 1.25.
6. Virgil, *Georgics*, 1.309.
7. Juvenal, *Satires*, 16.48.
8. Carol van Driel-Murray, 'Dead Men's Shoes' in Schlüter, *Rom, Germanien und die Ausgrabungen von Kalkriese*, p. 172.
9. Franzius, 'Die römischen Funde aus Kalkriese', p. 143.
10. Josephus, *The Jewish War*, 3.93.
11. Cicero, *Philippics*, 14.10, 11.12.

Select Bibliography

INTRODUCTION

Goulding, Vincent. 'Back to the future with asymmetric warfare', *Parameters* (winter 2001/2), 21–30

Harrison, Robert Pogue. *Forests: The Shadow of Civilisation*, Chicago, 1993

Millar, Fergus. *A Study of Cassius Dio*, Oxford, 1964

Starr, R.J. 'The Scope and Genre of Velleius' History', *Classical Quarterly* 31 (1981), 162–74

Sumner, G.V. 'The truth about Velleius Paterculus: Prolegomena', *Harvard Studies in Classical Philology* 74 (1970), 257–97

Syme, Ronald. *Tacitus*, Oxford, 1958

Wells, Colin. 'What's new along the Lippe: recent work in North Germany', *Britannia* 29 (1998), 457–64

Woodman, A.J. *Velleius Paterculus: The Tiberian Narrative (2.94–131)*, Cambridge, 1977

CHAPTER ONE

Carroll, Maureen. *Romans, Celts & Germans: The German Provinces of Rome*, Stroud, 2001

Christ, Karl. 'Velleius und Tiberius', *Historia* 50 (2001), 180–92

Dixon, Karen and Southern, Pat. *The Roman Cavalry: From the First to the Third Century AD*, London, 1992

Dobias, Josef. 'King Maroboduus as a Politician', *Klio* 38 (1960), 155–66

Gechter, Michael. 'Early Roman military installations and Ubian settlements in the Lower Rhine' in Thomas Blagg and Martin Millett (eds), *The Early Roman Empire in the West*, Oxford, 1990, pp. 97–102

Gruen, E.S. 'The Imperial Policy of Augustus' in Kurt Raaflaub and Mark Toher (eds), *Between Republic and Empire: Interpretations of Augustus and his Principate*, Berkeley, 1990, pp. 395–416

Holland, Tom. *Rubicon: The Triumph and Tragedy of the Roman Republic*, London, 2003

Horn, Heinz Günter (ed.). *Die Römer in Nordrhein-Westfalen*, Stuttgart, 1987

Hyland, Ann. *Equus: The Horse in the Roman World*, London, 1990

Kokkinos, Nikos. *Antonia Augusta: Portrait of a Great Roman Lady*, London, 1992

——. 'The honorand of the Titulus Tiburtinus: C Sentius Saturninus?', *Zeitschrift für Papyrologie und Epigraphik* 105 (1995), 21–36

Kolnik, T. 'Q Atilius Primus – Interprex, Centurio et Negotiator', *Acta Archaeologica Academiae Scientarum Hungaricae* 30 (1978), 61–75

von Schnurbein, Siegmar. 'The organization of the fortresses in Augustan Germany' in Richard Brewer (ed.), *Roman Fortresses and their Legions*, London, 2000, pp. 29–39

Syme, Ronald. 'Some notes on the legions under Augustus', *Journal of Roman Studies* 23 (1933), 14–33

Timpe, Dieter. 'Drusus' Umkehr an der Elbe', *Rheinisches Museum für Philologie* 110 (1967), 289–306

Trier, Bendix (ed.). *Die römische Okkupation nördlich der Alpen zur Zeit des Augustus*, Münster, 1991

Wells, C.M. *The German Policy of Augustus*, Oxford, 1972

Williams, Derek. *Romans and Barbarians*, London, 1998

Wolters, Reinhard. *Die Römer in Germanien*, Munich, 2004

CHAPTER TWO

Becker, Armin. 'Lahnau-Waldgirmes: eine augusteische Stadtgründung in Hessen', *Historia* 52 (2003), 337–50

Keppie, Lawrence. 'Legions in the East from Augustus to Trajan' in Philip Freeman (ed.), *The Defence of the Roman and Byzantine East: proceedings of a colloquium held at the University of Sheffield in April 1986*, Oxford, 1986, pp. 411–29

Kramer, Bärbel (ed.). *Kölner Papyri Volume 1*, Opladen, 1976, 10, 33–8

Pollini, John. 'Ahenobarbi, Appuleii and some others on the Ara Pacis', *American Journal of Archaeology* 90 (1986), 453–60

Reinhold, Meyer. 'Marcus Agrippa's son-in-law P. Quinctilius Varus', *Classical Philology* 67 (1972), 119–21

Richardson, Peter. *Herod: King of the Jews and Friend of the Romans*, Columbia, 1996

von Schnurbein, Siegmar. 'Augustus in *Germania* and his new "town" at Waldgirmes east of the Rhine', *Journal of Roman Archaeology* 16 (2003), 93–108

Smallwood, Mary. *The Jews under Roman Rule*, Leiden, 1976

Syme, Ronald. 'Die Zahl der praefecti castrorum im Herre des Varus', *Germania* 16 (1932), 109–11

——. *The Augustan Aristocracy*, Oxford, 1986

Thomasson, Bengt. 'Verschiedenes zu den *Proconsules Africae*', *Eranos* 67 (1969), 175–91

van Wickevoort Crommelin, B. 'P. Quinctilius Varus – Das Bild des Verlierers', *Osnasbrücker Online – Beiträge zu den Altertumswissenschaften* 2/1999, 1–10

Wiegels, Rainer. 'Schuld – Verantwortung – Verhängnis', *Varus-Kurier* 4 (December 2003), 1–3

Wolters, Reinhard. 'C. Numonius Vala und Drusus. Zur Auflösung zweier Kontermarken augusteischer Zeit', *Germania* 73 (1995), 145–50

Zedelius, Volker. 'P Quinctilius Varus in Achulla', *Bonner Jahrbücher* 183 (1983), 469–74

CHAPTER THREE

Dyson, Stephen. 'Native revolts in the Roman empire', *Historia* 20 (1971), 239–74

Ilkjaer, Jørgen and Jørn Lønstrup, 'Der Moorfund im Tal der Illerup-Å bei Skanderborg in Ostjütland (Dänemark)', *Germania* 61 (1983), 95–116

Murdoch, Adrian. 'Germania Romana' in Brian Murdoch and Malcolm Read (eds), *Early Germanic Literature and Culture*, Rochester, 2004, pp. 55–71

Orsnes, M. 'The Weapon-Find in Ejsbøl Mose at Haderslev', *Acta Archaeologica* 34 (1963), 232–47

von Petrikovits, Harald. 'Arminius', *Bonner Jahrbücher* 166 (1966), 175–93

Rives, J.B. *Tacitus: Germania*, Oxford, 1999

Schmidt, Susanne. 'Die Siedlungen der älteren römischen Kaiserzeit in Südniedersachsen – ein Überblick' in Wolfgang Schlüter (ed.), *Rom, Germanien und die Ausgrabungen von Kalkriese*, Osnabrück, 1999, pp. 583–9

Thompson, E.A. *The Early Germans*, Oxford, 1965

Timpe, Dieter. *Arminius-Studien*, Heidelberg, 1970

Todd, Malcolm. *The Early Germans*, Oxford, 1992

Wells, Peter. *The Barbarians Speak*, Princeton, 1999

Will, Wolfgang. 'Römische 'Klientel-Raandstaaten' am Rhein?', *Bonner Jahrbücher* 187 (1987), 1–61, specifically 44–55

Wolfram, Herwig. *Die Germanen*, Munich, 2001

CHAPTER FOUR

Aßkamp, Rudolf and Renate Wiechers. *Westfälisches Römermuseum Haltern*, Münster, 1996

Benario, Herbert. 'Teutoburg', *Classical World* 96 (2003), 397–406

Brunaux, Jean-Louis. *Les Gaulois, sanctuaries et rites*, Paris, 1986

——. 'Gallic rites', *Archaeology* 54/2 (March/April 2001), 54–7

Harnecker, Joachim. *Arminius, Varus und das Schlachtfeld von Kalkriese*, Bramsche, 2002

Keppie, L. 'Legiones XVII, XVIII, XIX: Exercitus omnium fortissimus' in L. Keppie, *Legions and Veterans: Roman Army Papers 1971–2000*, Stuttgart, Franz Steiner, 2000, pp. 161–5

Schilling-Häfele, Ute. 'Varus und Arminius in der Überlieferung', *Historia* 32 (1983), 123–8

Schlüter, Wolfgang (ed.). *Kalkriese – Römer in Osnabrücker Land*, Bramsche, 1993

—— (ed.). *Rom, Germanien und die Ausgrabungen von Kalkriese*, Osnabrück, 1999

Sheldon, Mary. 'Slaughter in the Forest: Roman Intelligence Mistakes in Germany', *Small Wars and Insurgencies* 12/3 (autumn 2001), 1–38

Tausend, Klaus. 'Wohin wollte Varus?', *Klio* 79 (1997), 372–82

Tönnies, Bernhard. 'Die Ausgrabungen in Kalkriese und Tac. Ann. 1,60,3. Eine Lösung für die Varusschlachtfrage in Sicht?', *Hermes* 120 (1992), 461–3

Wilbers-Rost, Susanne. 'Kalkriese und die Varusschlacht – Archäologische Nachweise einer militärischen Auseinandersetzung zwischen Römern und Germanen' in Philip Freeman (ed.) *et al.*, *Limes XVIII: Proceedings of the XVIIIth International Congress of Roman Frontier Studies held in Amman, Jordan, September 2000*, Oxford, 2002, pp. 515–26

Wolters, Reinhard. 'Hermeneutik des Hinterhalts: die antiken Berichte zur Varuskatastrophe und der Fundplatz von Kalkriese', *Klio* 85 (2003), 131–70

CHAPTER FIVE

Barrett, Anthony. *Caligula: The Corruption of Power*, London, 1989

——. *Agrippina: Sex, Power and Politics in the Early Empire*, London, 1996

Goldsworthy, Adrian. *In the Name of Rome: The Men who Won the Roman Empire*, London, 2003

Koestermann, Erich. 'Die Feldzüge des Germanicus 14–16 n. Chr', *Historia* 6 (1957), 429–79

Levick, Barbara. *Tiberius the Politician*, London, 1976

Lica, Vasile. 'Clades Variana and Postliminium', *Historia* 50 (2001), 496–501

Malloch, S.J.V. 'The end of the Rhine mutiny in Tacitus, Suetonius, and Dio', *Classical Quarterly* 54 (2004), 198–210

Murdoch, Adrian. *The Last Pagan*, Stroud, 2004

Seager, Robin. *Tiberius*, London, 1972

Shotter, David. *Tiberius Caesar*, London, 1992

Timpe, Dieter. *Der Triumph des Germanicus: Untersuchungen zu den Feldzügen der Jahre 14–16 n. Chr. in Germanien*, Bonn, 1968

Select Bibliography

CHAPTER SIX

Benario, Herbert. 'Arminius into Hermann: History into Legend', *Greece & Rome* 51 (2004), 83–94

Buck, Henning. 'Der Literarische Arminius – Inszenierungen einer sagenhaften Gestalt' in Wolfgang Schlüter (ed.), *Kalkriese – Römer im Osnabrücker Land*, Bramsche, 1993, pp. 267–81

Fansa, Mamoun (ed.). *Varusschlacht und Germanenmythos*, Oldenburg, 2001

Fetten, Frank. 'Archaeology and anthropology' in Heinrich Härke (ed.), *Archaeology, Ideology and Society: The German Experience*, Frankfurt am Main, 2000, pp. 140–79

Giesen, Rolf. *Nazi Propaganda Films: A History and Filmography*, London, 2003

Haßmann, Henning. 'Archaeology and the Third Reich' in Heinrich Härke (ed.), *Archaeology, Ideology and Society: The German Experience*, Frankfurt am Main, 2000, pp. 65–139

Kuehnemund, Richard. *Arminius or the Rise of National Symbol in Literature*, Chapel Hill, 1953

Sandford, Myron. 'Germany's tribute to Arminius', *The New England Magazine* (April 1895), 160–9

Schama, Simon. *Landscape and Memory*, London, 1996

Stahl, E.L. *Heinrich von Kleist's Dramas*, Oxford, 1948

Struck, Manuela. '*The Heilige Römische Reich Deutscher Nation* and Hermann the German' in Richard Hingley (ed.), *Images of Rome: Perceptions of Ancient Rome in Europe and the United States in the Modern Age*, Portsmouth, 2001, pp. 93–112

Wiegels, Rainer and Winfried Woesler (eds), *Arminius und die Varusschlacht: Geschichte, Mythos, Literatur*, Paderborn, 2003

CHAPTER SEVEN

Birch, Amanda. 'Field studies', *Architecture* (September 2002), 78–84

Clunn, Tony. *In Quest of the Lost Legions: The Varusschlacht*, London, 1999

Mommsen, Theodor. 'Die Örtlichkeit der Varusschlacht', *Sitzungsberichte der königlich preussischen Akademie der Wissenschaften* (1885), 63–92

Wells, Peter. *The Battle that Stopped Rome: Emperor Augustus, Arminius and the Slaughter of the Legions in the Teutoburg Forest*, New York, 2003

APPENDIX

Bishop, M.C. and Coulston, J.C. *Roman Military Equipment*, Aylesbury, 1989

Cowan, Ross. *Roman Legionary, 58 BC–AD 69*, Oxford, 2003

Franzius, Georgia. 'Die römischen Funde aus Kalkriese' in Wolfgang Schlüter (ed.), *Kalkriese – Römer in Osnabrücker Land*, Bramsche, 1993, pp. 107–82

——. '1987–1997. Zehn Jahre Kalkriese. Eine Fundchronik mit Variationen', *Osnasbrücker Online – Beiträge zu den Altertumswissenschaften* (1/1999)

Goldsworthy, Adrian. *The Complete Roman Army*, London, 2003

Schlüter, Wolfgang. 'The Battle of the Teutoburg Forest: Archaeological Research at Kalkriese near Osnabrück' in J.D. Creighton and R.J.A. Wilson (eds), *Roman Germany: Studies in Cultural Interaction*, Portsmouth, 1999

Webster, Graham. *The Roman Imperial Army of the First and Second Centuries AD*, London, 1985

Index

Index

The Last Roman –
Romulus Augustus and the
Decline of the West

Adrian Murdoch

£18.99
Hardback
978 0 7509 4474 8
224pp

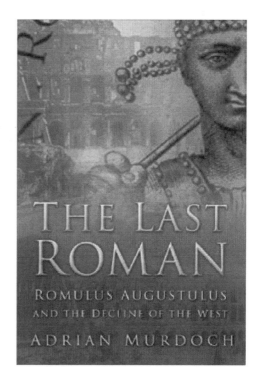

The Last Roman is the first biography about Romulus Augustulus. It focuses on the personalities behind this powerful story and reveals the world into which Romulus was born – an empire that was about to die. Author Adrian Murdoch explores how Romulus's father Orestes, secretary to Attila the Hun, rose through the ranks to become kingmaker; how all was lost to another usurper in an Italy wracked with civil war; and how Romulus found peace at last, founding a monastery. This dramatic and poignant story of politics, decline and loss has inspired writers as diverse as Valerio Massimo Manfredi, Edward Gibbon and W.H. Auden. Drawing on extensive new archaeological and historical research, and using numerous contemporary sources, many translated for the first time since the nineteenth century, *The Last Roman* is the vivid story of an empire breathing its last.

www.thehistorypress.co.uk

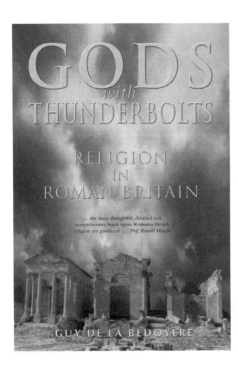

Gods with Thunderbolts

Guy de la Bédoyère

£19.99
Paperback
978 0 7524 4291 4
288pp (+16 colour pages)

One of the Roman Empire's greatest achievements was religious tolerance, at least by modern standards. It was a world in which Fortuna and Fate ruled the minds of men and women. That world left behind a marvellous legacy of literary and archaeological records – temples and shrines, altars and votive gifts, curse tablets and inscriptions.

In addition to the gods of Rome, Roman Britain had native cults, like that of Cocidius from the Northern Frontier, and exotic imports from Persia and Egypt, such as Mithras and Isis. Finally, there were the tensions created by the legitimisation of Christianity in the fourth century.

This is the first book that attempts, systematically, to unravel the wide-ranging evidence that we have for the multifarious beliefs and practices of those living in Roman Britain.

'Tempus books have authority, clarity and superb illustrations …
The mélange of divinities and practices de la Bédoyère brings
readably and authoritatively to light makes for a fascinating story.'
– BBC History

www.thehistorypress.co.uk

Defying Rome –
The Rebels of Roman Britain

Guy de la Bédoyère

£17.99
Paperback
978 0 7524 4440 6
224pp (+16 colour pages)

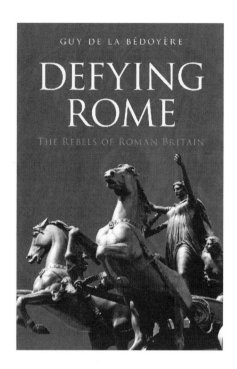

The power of the Roman Empire was under constant challenge. Nowhere was this truer than in Britain, Rome's remotest and most recalcitrant province.

A succession of idealists, chancers and reactionaries fomented dissent and rebellion. Some, like Caratacus and Boudica, were tribal chiefs wanting to expel Rome and recover lost power. Others were military opportunists such as Carausius and Allectus, who wanted to become emperor and were prepared to exploit everything Britain had to offer to support their bids for power.

Each of these rebellions reads like a story in itself, combining archaeology with the dramatic testimony of the historical and epigraphic sources, and explains why Britain was such a hot-bed of dissent.

Historian and archaeologist Guy de la Bédoyère has presented series on Roman Britain for both BBC2 and Radio 4. He is also the regular Roman expert on Channel 4's *Time Team*.

www.thehistorypress.co.uk

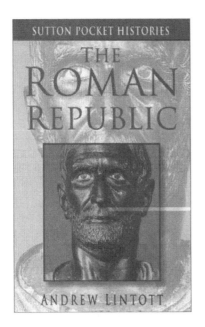

The Roman Republic

Andew Lintott

£5.99
Paperback
978 0 7509 2223 4
128pp

This text offers an account of ancient Rome over five centuries of expansion and shows how, ultimately, it was the empire which brought the Republic to an end.

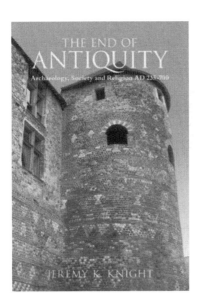

The End of Antiquity – Archaeology, Society and Religion AD 235-700

Jeremy K. Knight

£17.99
Paperback
978 0 7524 4082 8
224pp

This masterly study provides a fresh analysis of the transition from the classical world to medieval Europe – a theme that has exercised historians since Edward Gibbon. It is the first book to make available in English much of the new data from recent excavations in France, Spain and elsewhere in western Europe. Drawing on material from Ireland to the eastern Mediterranean, the author uses new evidence from coins and inscriptions and provides re-assessments of the rich literary sources.

www.thehistorypress.co.uk

Britannia Prima
Britain's Last Roman Province

Roger White

£19.99
Paperback
978 0 7524 1967 1
256pp (+16 colour pages)

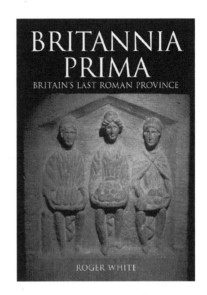

This important work counters the widely held view that the creation of the four provinces of later Roman Britain was an irrelevance – a short-lived hiccup on the way to the demise of the whole country as part of the Roman Empire. In fact Britannia Prima – broadly the West of Britain – had, from the fourth to the late sixth century, a distinctive Romano-British character and cohesiveness that the other provinces did not have or rapidly lost in the face of the Germanic conquest.

Garrison Life at Vindolanda
A Band of Brothers

Anthony Birley

£15.99
Paperback
978 07524 1950 3
192pp (+16 colour pages)

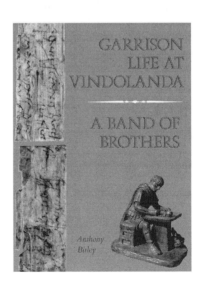

Anthony Birley, Professor of Ancient History at Manchester 1974-90 and at Dusseldorf 1990-2002, is one of Britain's best known ancient historians. The author of many major works, Professor Birley was born and brought up in the house next to Vindolanda, and has taken part in many of the excavations there.

www.thehistorypress.co.uk

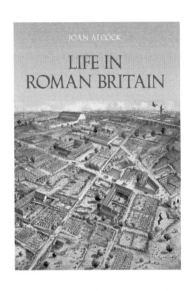

Life in Roman Britain

Joan Alcock

£16.99
Paperback
978 0 7524 3593 0
192pp (+16 colour pages)

This accessible reconstruction of life in Roman Britain begins by placing Britain firmly in an historical context, drawing parallels with other provinces of the Roman Empire and linking the indigenous Celtic people with the Roman invaders. Hereafter individual chapters cover administration and society; religion, belief and death; recreation and leisure; the domestic economy; food and drink; art and decoration; and personal lifestyle.

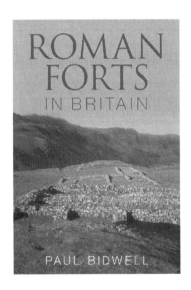

Roman Forts in Britain

Paul Bidwell

£17.99
Paperback
978 0 7524 4107 8
160pp (+16 colour pages)

Focusing on the auxiliary forts that were occupied from the second century onwards, Paul Bidwell looks at the plans and functions of forts, the everyday life of officers and men, what the study of finds tells us about supply systems, and how forts were adapted during the decline of the empire. This book is a must for anyone with an interest in Roman Britain.

www.thehistorypress.co.uk